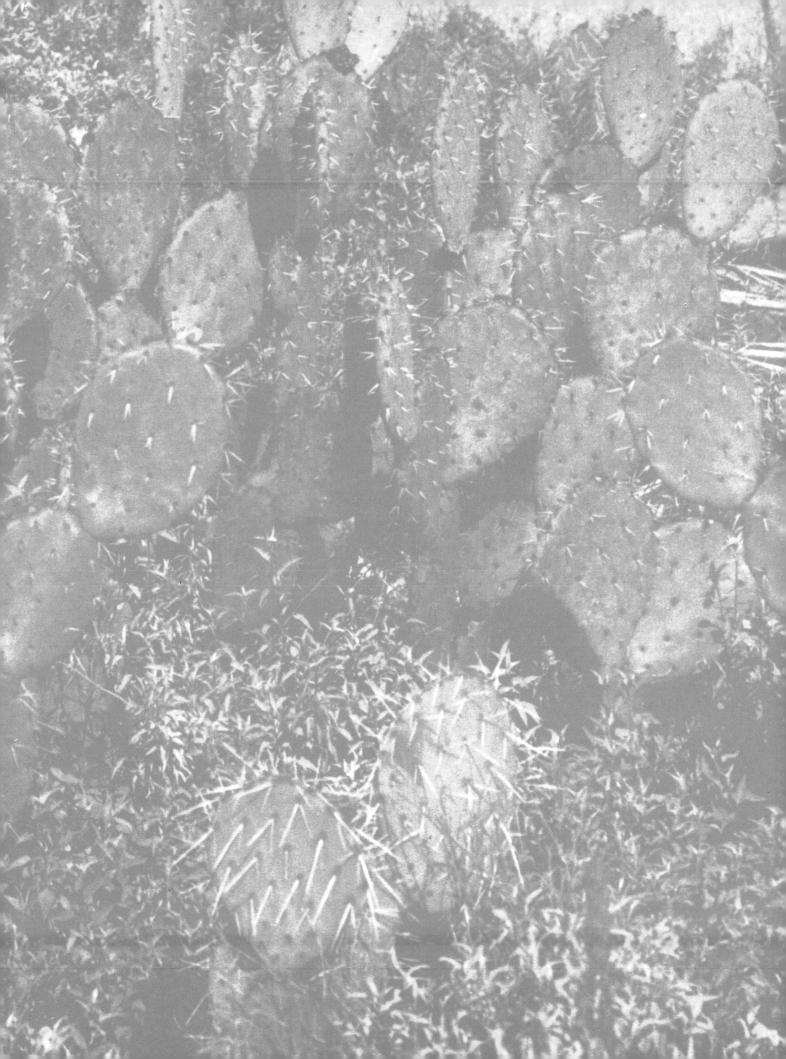

Native Landscaping
FROM EL PASO TO L.A.

Native Landscaping
FROM EL PASO TO L.A.

Sally Wasowski with Andy Wasowski

PHOTOGRAPHS BY ANDY WASOWSKI

THE CONTEMPORARY GARDENER

CONTEMPORARY BOOKS

Library of Congress Cataloging-in-Publication Data

Wasowski, Sally, 1946–
    Native landscaping from El Paso to L.A. / Sally Wasowski with Andy Wasowski ;
photographs by Andy Wasowski ; foreword by Robert Breunig.
        p.   cm. — (The contemporary gardener)
    Originally published: Native gardens for dry climates. 1st ed. New York : C. Potter,
1995. With new foreword.
    Includes bibliographical references.
    ISBN 0-8092-2511-5
    1. Desert gardening—Southwest, New.   2. Native plant gardening—Southwest, New.
3. Desert plants—Southwest, New.   4. Native plants for cultivation—Southwest, New.
5. Desert gardening—Southwest, New—Pictorial works.   6. Native plant gardening—
Southwest, New—Pictorial works.   7. Desert plants—Southwest, New—Pictorial works.
8. Native plants for cultivation—Southwest, New—Pictorial works.   I. Wasowski, Andy,
1939–   II. Wasowski, Sally, 1946– Native gardens for dry climates.   III. Title.   IV. Series.

SB427.5 .W38 2000
635.9′525—dc21   99-53374

Interior design by Lisa Goldenberg
Cover photograph by Andy Wasowski
Plans illustrated by Guy Greene

First published by Contemporary Books in 2000
Originally published as *Native Gardens for Dry Climates*
Published by Contemporary Books
A division of NTC/Contemporary Publishing Group, Inc.
4255 West Touhy Avenue, Lincolnwood (Chicago), Illinois 60712-1975 U.S.A.
Printed and bound in Hong Kong
International Standard Book Number: 0-8092-2511-5
18 17 16 15 14 13 12 11 10 9 8 7 6 5 4 3 2

For Ron and Maureen Gass.
You guys inspire us in many ways.

CONTENTS

FOREWORD

Sally and Andy Wasowski begin *Native Landscaping from El Paso to L.A.* by introducing their readers to the delights of a most amazing garden; a garden that rises from below sea level to an elevation of 6,000 feet; a glorious garden that endures temperatures as cold as near zero and as hot as 120 degrees F; a garden that displays such diversity in form, color, and texture as to be almost unfathomable. This garden is the wondrous garden of nature–nature as defined by the very driest climates of the lower Southwest.

An inspired landscape designer, Sally Wasowski approaches gardening in concert with this nature; with, it could be said, the *ecology* of a region. To illustrate her approach, writer/photographer Andy Wasowski, in Part One of this book, captures views of the unaltered, wild landscapes of the lower Southwest; followed by scenes from some of the best naturalistic gardens tended within each region, and, in Part Two, close-ups of 146 of the many landscaping species that are indigenous to these regions.

The Wasowskis divide the Southwest's driest regions into seven bio-geographic zones, taking into consideration not only temperature, but also rainfall and soil type, as shown by the vegetation map on page 7. Within these zones of desert and chaparral lie the metropolitan expanses of San Diego, Los Angeles, Phoenix, Las Vegas, El Paso, and other fast-growing cities. Populating these sunbelt zones are large numbers of migrants from cooler, moister climates, particularly eastern and midwestern states. These newcomers often need time and experience with the land to become comfortable with the natural characteristics of their new, xeric environments–dry, desert-like places where water and rain are precious, where sunlight is intense, and where plants indigenous to the region may seem so unfamiliar as to appear forbidding.

I was just such a newcomer when I first moved from Flagstaff, Arizona to Phoenix in 1982. None of the plants around me looked anything like those of my boyhood home in Indiana or my adopted mountain home in Flagstaff. In Flagstaff, I had been living under ponderosa pines that towered 120 feet over my head. Now I was standing on a desert floor where trees seemed to reach, on average, little more than two to three times my height. These were leafy trees, not pines. And, unlike the hand-sized leaves of Indiana's maples, bass-

woods, and tuliptrees, the leaves of these desert trees were smaller than a fingernail. Shrubs, too, seemed strange–and spiny. And the lush green associated with the "American home landscape" seemed mostly absent, except on water-guzzling golf courses. I felt astounded, perhaps even dismayed, by these differences in the landscape.

Fortunately, it took but a short while for my spouse, Karen Enyedy, and me to develop a deep feeling for this landscape–one that soon included a passion for desert plants. I suspect this had much to do with the fact that stretches of unaltered desert still remained intact in many places around our new home. Here, in the natural environment of the desert, I learned again a lesson that has become clear to me in every place I have lived or visited–that every place, when it is natural, is inherently beautiful.

But I would be remiss not to mention that our emerging love for the native landscape was further inspired by the displays and programs at the Desert Botanical Garden in Phoenix, an institution I would later come to direct. After taking a landscaping class offered at the DBG, we redesigned our own urban yard, replacing hedges of yew and a Bermuda grass lawn with flowering trees, shrubs and ground covers indigenous to the Sonoran Desert, replacing a water-wasting sprinkler system with drip irrigation tubing, and withdrawing all use of pesticides and herbicides.

Geckos soon made a reappearance, and where the yards of our neighbors attracted pigeons and starlings ours was frequented by mourning doves, curve-billed thrashers, verdins, finches, and–at almost any hour of the day–the splendor of hummingbirds. Not only wildlife, but people, came to visit. One neighbor wanted to know where on earth such beautiful plants had come from! Parents with babies in strollers would often linger in front of our yard, and older children were fascinated by the interaction of so many insects and birds with these plants. We found we could feel "close to nature" even though we lived in the heart of urban Phoenix.

The lessons learned in Phoenix came home to me again after I moved to Santa Barbara, California, in 1994. There, in highly altered landscapes, often so dominated by exotic plants that it is hard to discern what the natural landscape looks like, I found the Santa Barbara Botanical Garden–a place that celebrates the native flora of Southern California. There I discovered an incredible array of native plants, perfectly adapted to the demands of the climate, and displayed in naturalistic exhibits in the garden. How unfortunate, I said to myself, that these plants seem so unappreciated and underutilized in their own home country. The Wasowskis address this same observation, noting that, especially in southern coastal California, gardeners may have to search out increasingly rare remnants of unaltered land upon which to model their naturalistic garden designs.

It is important, the Wasowskis advise the reader, before planning a dry climate garden, to first observe the unaltered landscapes of nature, where ". . . instead of straight lines and rows, there is a harmony of textures and colors and a relaxed mingling of elements . . . far more complex and satisfying than in a formal landscape design." Each of the seven regions in this book offers gardeners a "wonderfully beautiful habitat worthy of emulation in the garden."

While stressing the inclusion of plant material that is indigenous to a region, the Wasowskis remain open to the incorporation of *non-native* plants in naturalistic gardens. In selecting nonnatives, however, they advise choosing ones with horticultural requirements that match what a site naturally provides in the way of light, soil, and rainfall. They also advise against selecting any nonnatives which might be invasive or threatening to the native flora of the region.

Visual compatibility is yet another concept for gardeners to consider. For example, it is an assault to a region's natural appearance to plant exotic trees that will protrude above the canopy of a region's native trees. Any nonnative trees and shrubs selected should resemble in form and texture those of the natural habitat. In the category of accent plants, one example of an acceptable nonnative for some deserts might be the use of non-invasive fast-growing African aloes to mimic the forms of slower growing agaves that are native to America.

By beginning their book with a discussion of ecological as well as climatic aspects of the regions, the Wasowskis distinguish their approach to landscaping from that of many others. Only after this foundation is laid do the authors address the pragmatic aspects of gardening in dry regions. Their enlightened presentation includes a thorough discussion of the importance of working within a "building envelope" where land is under development. A site plan for an "Envelope Garden" shows the reader how to set a home within an existing landscape to preserve as much of the natural flora of the site as possible. Accompanying this are ideas for revegetating areas disturbed

during construction, as well as plans for enhancing private areas around the house with thematic courtyard gardens such as a "Moonlight Garden," a "*Curandera* Garden," and a "Hummingbird Garden." The plans are keyed to indigenous charts found at the back of the book, making each plan adjustable to the regional character of any one of the seven zones addressed.

From beginning to end, *Native Landscaping from El Paso to L.A.* celebrates the respect for regionalism that Lady Bird Johnson aspired to resurrect in Americans during her travels across the United States as First Lady. Wherever she went, she encouraged communities to appreciate and conserve the natural character of their own regions. Asking the now celebrated question, "Why can't Texas look like Texas?" she fought a landscaping trend that had been in place since Europeans first settled in America—the trend to replace native flora with exotic plants from other regions and continents. Mrs. Johnson was among the first to point out that such severe manipulation of native landscapes not only destroyed the natural character of each region, it was water-consumptive, maintenance-intensive, and incapable of providing birds and other wildlife with the food and shelter to which they were adapted.

Particularly in the southwestern regions of North America, this destructive approach to landscaping seems at last to be giving way to a more naturalistic, regionally appropriate trend. The Wasowskis deserve much credit for their role in advancing this emerging enthusiasm for regional integrity and sustainability in landscape design. "The best designed native plant gardens," they write, "are a balance between raw nature and human control." Through their admirably well-structured presentation of text, drawings, photographs, and charts, this new edition of *Native Gardens for Dry Climates* will go far in enabling gardeners of the Southwest's driest regions to achieve this balance.

Robert Breunig, Ph.D.
Executive Director of the
Lady Bird Johnson Wildlife Center

Horizons in the desert stretch off forever, and storms, such as this one over Altar Valley near the Sonoran Desert Museum in Tucson, can often be seen many miles away. The scent of creosote makes the air spicy and alive.

PREFACE

It was one of the most gorgeous lawns we'd ever seen. The color was rich and dark, and every blade had been mowed to putting-green perfection. Abutting the house was a crisply trimmed box hedge, flanked by rows of shrubs pruned into little mushroom caps. As we drove by–it was midafternoon in July and the temperature was crowding 100 degrees–the sprinkler system was on, and a steady stream of water was flowing down the driveway and into the street.

This lush, verdant landscape wasn't in Virginia or Connecticut. It was in a southwestern state where the annual rainfall is a small fraction of what those eastern states get. It was in a city where the water department promotes *xeriscaping*, that is, using native and adapted plants that can exist on only the water that nature provides. The plant materials in this landscape were mostly imported varieties, ill suited to this part of the country, and by and large water-guzzlers.

All the areas covered in this book–from deserts to coastal chaparral–have two things in common above all else: 1) a high percentage of residents who came from somewhere else–usually the Midwest or Northeast–and continue to garden much as they did back home, and 2) low annual rainfalls ranging from a pathetic 2 inches per year around Mexicali to 16 inches in Los Angeles. These areas have periodic droughts and even, from time to time, water rationing. In some places water problems include salinity and pollution.

To meet the needs of a growing population–Las Vegas, for example, adds 4,000 people every month–water must be imported from other regions, even other states. As one water department employee told us, "It's a constant scramble to find new and affordable sources."

Interestingly, many Southwest communities pay less for their water than does the rest of the country. While the national average is $1.67 per 1,000 gallons, Los Angeles residents pay a little over $1.50 and Las Vegas and Phoenix residents pay about $1.00. Traditionally, water rates are kept artificially low to encourage people and businesses to move to the Southwest; this also helps foster the illusion that water is not a problem.

But one thing is certain: Rates will rise. The Federal Safe Drinking Water Act means that communities are having to install additional and costly treatment facilities to meet the new purity standards for potable water. Those costs will, of course, be passed on. While

Lush, green lawns—like this one—are ill suited to the dry climate of the Southwest and require wasteful amounds of water.

nationally 40 to 60 percent of household water is poured on landscapes, in the arid Southwest the figure jumps to as high as 80 percent! As the cost of water rises, many residents are rethinking the idea of maintaining lawns and are looking at alternatives.

It's not merely the rising cost of water that should dissuade homeowners from using it so extravagantly on landscapes, however. Consider, too, what all that water actually accomplishes. The overly watered ground becomes a hospitable breeding ground for alien pollen and mold-producing weeds, which of course cause hay fever. Remember that TV commercial years ago that told us to "send your sinuses to Arizona"? That may have been true back in the 1950s, but not today.

THE GRAVEL NIGHTMARE

While back-East-style landscapes are all too common in these parts, there is another style that one sees just as often: a barren caricature of the desert, with a few cacti here and there and lots of gravel. Although it is certainly not extravagant with water, this landscape style goes too far in the opposite direction. When you consider the amount of reflected heat that comes bouncing off that gravel in the summer, you have to wonder if higher air-conditioning costs aren't canceling out the water savings.

Cities like Las Vegas must import water from other regions to meet the needs of growing populations.

THE NATIVE ALTERNATIVE

Scattered throughout Southern California and the Southwest, you *can* find alternative landscapes that use native plant materials superbly suited to their environments. These are not boring rock-and-cacti layouts; they are soft and colorful. Since native plants have been coping with the region's extremes for millennia, they have exactly calibrated themselves to the locale. Once established, they exist quite well on whatever meager sprinkles nature provides. Native landscapes, in addition to being drought-tolerant, are extremely low-maintenance, and environmentally friendly; healthy natives thrive without pesticides. They also provide habitats for many species of wildlife–birds, insects, and mammals–that are a vital part of a well-balanced ecosystem. Yet these creatures are becoming endangered as new roads, housing developments, shopping malls, and business parks are interrupting migratory routes and destroying age-old nesting and feeding sites. Native landscapes are also a feast for the eyes–sometimes delicately pretty, sometimes magnificently beautiful.

They are also, for the time being, rare. But if we succeed in whetting your appetite for native plants with this book, the time may well come when native and natural landscapes will be commonplace.

OLD IDEAS, NEW IDEAS

Recently we were looking at old family slides. One slide, from 1965, shows Andy as a tourist in Europe, wearing a suit and tie as if he were going to a business meeting. A vacation slide of me around that same time shows me in white gloves and heels. Today we go on vacation in sneakers, jeans, and T-shirts.

American attitudes have changed about many things: our way of eating now tends toward low-fat, low-cholesterol, more natural foods; we are smoking a good deal less; even our attitudes about the opposite sex are becoming more enlightened. Attitudes about our environment are also changing, and while the majority of us will admit to being overwhelmed by some of the arcane arguments being used by people on both sides of any environmental issue, most of us seem to sense that things are not as good as they used to be, and something must be done.

One thing we can all do is look at our own front and back yards. We may not feel able or qualified to tackle concerns such as acid rain and ozone depletion, but we can certainly tackle concerns close to home. Consider for a second the matter of pesticides. According to the National Coalition Against the Misuse of Pesticides, in Wash-

This gravel landscape requires little water, but does not add much charm to its surroundings.

Native species, like this hawk, at left, and horned lizard, above, thrive in a well-balanced ecosystem.

Australian eucalyptus thrives in California, but creates a fire hazard.

would not only be too expensive to buy but also too heavy to lift.

For most readers, this book will be a basic primer—an introduction to a brand-new palette of plant materials, as well as a brand-new way of thinking about gardening. For those who are already somewhat familiar with native plants, we hope to offer exciting new possibilities for designers as well as growers.

The native plants in this book were selected only after much research and countless conversations with designers, botanists, growers, and lay gardeners. These natives are the showiest and easiest to buy and/or grow or are so important to the basic regional habitats that it would be quite difficult to garden without them. Many of the plants we omitted are for sale in nurseries and are covered in other identification books, along with photos and descriptions.

Using natives doesn't mean that you have to reject nonnatives out of hand; many naturalized plants and some cultivars are well adapted and will work for you. But a word of caution: Many naturalized plants work too well. Australian eucalyptus, for example, thrives in California, so well that it is taking over and destroying native habitats. Eucalyptus is also trashy, dropping shreds of bark and dead wood around the base of its trunk and creating a very real fire hazard. The rule to follow is: Use what works without endangering the environment. What works best, I believe, is native plants.

I hope this book guides you to the same thrill of discovery I found when I first started using natives.

Sally Wasowski
Taos, New Mexico

ington, D.C., American homeowners apply four times more pesticides on their landscapes than all the farmers in the country use on their treated acreage. Consider, too, all that household water we use just to keep those conventional landscapes alive.

And lastly, consider just how much time and money is spent each year to maintain those conventional landscapes. Isn't it time we rethought our traditional notions of landscaping? Isn't it time to shed those horticultural three-piece suits and white gloves?

WHAT TO EXPECT

This book is not intended to be the definitive work on the subject; there are thousands of native plants throughout Southern California and the Southwest, and any book that attempted to cover all of them

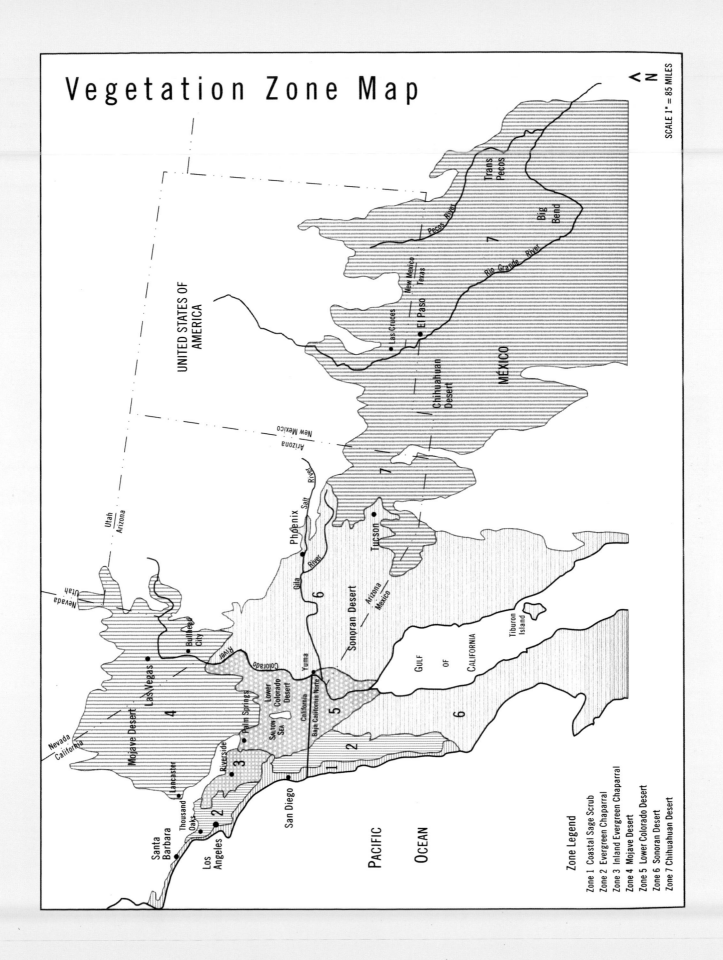

Vegetation Zone Map

SCALE 1" = 85 MILES

Zone Legend

Zone 1 Coastal Sage Scrub
Zone 2 Evergreen Chaparral
Zone 3 Inland Evergreen Chaparral
Zone 4 Mojave Desert
Zone 5 Lower Colorado Desert
Zone 6 Sonoran Desert
Zone 7 Chihuahuan Desert

7

INTRODUC

GARDENING WITH NATIVE PLANTS DOES NOT MEAN ADHERING TO A SINGLE, RIGID WAY

of landscaping. In a formal, traditional garden, one can substitute native plants for more

conventional nursery stock. There is also a naturalistic approach, in

which the gardener may opt for a less controlled, more free-flowing

look. Thirdly, there is the natural habitat garden that relies totally on

indigenous plants and becomes a self-sustaining ecosystem.

FORMAL GARDENS

Most people get into native plants the way they get into cold swimming

pools—very carefully. A gardener goes out and buys a pretty native

plant—but only one—and introduces it into the existing landscape. If that landscape

requires lots of water, the native drowns and the gardener concludes that the native plant

failed. If overwatering isn't a problem, chances are the native will out-thrive the exotics

in the garden. The gardener will be impressed and encouraged, and will buy another one.

It usually takes about three successes such as this to make a true native-plant lover.

In September the focus of color is close to the front door. In pots and in the ground are red-flowered zauschneria, pale lavender seaside daisy, and silver-leaved saffron buckwheat (*Eriogonum crocatum*). On either side of the entrance, two Channel Island tree poppies are in flower, though not as lushly as in the spring. And in the far corner, Catalina silverlace raises its yellow heads above lacy silver foliage.

8

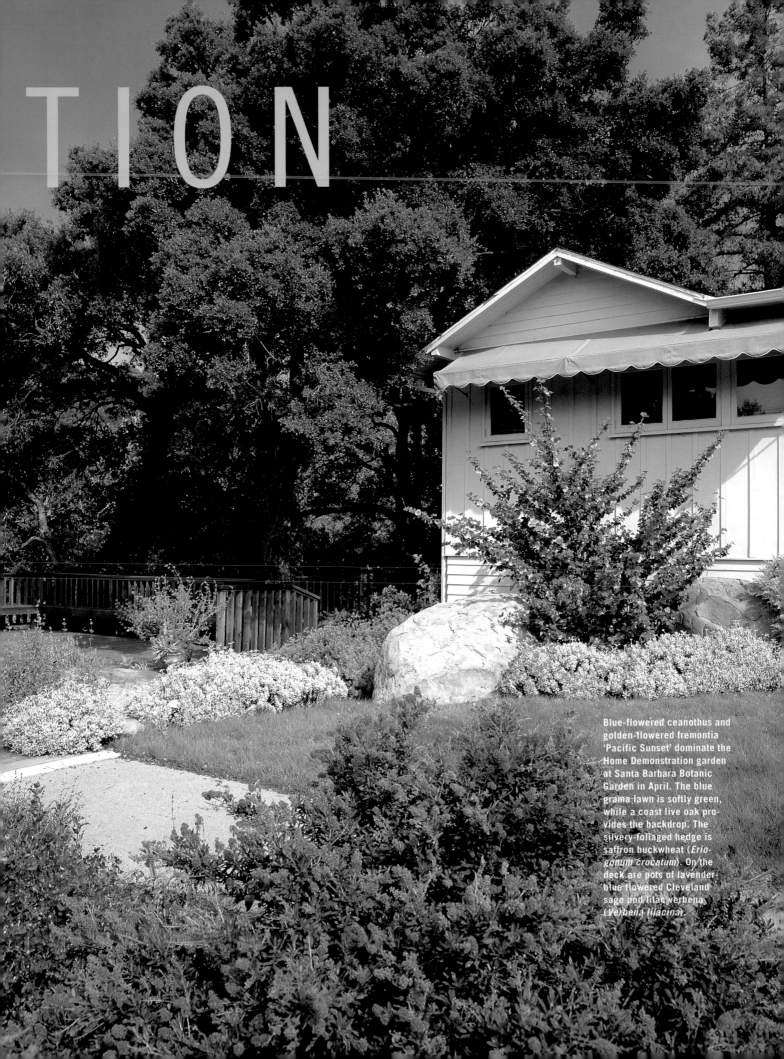

Blue-flowered ceanothus and golden-flowered fremontia 'Pacific Sunset' dominate the Home Demonstration garden at Santa Barbara Botanic Garden in April. The blue grama lawn is softly green, while a coast live oak provides the backdrop. The silvery-foliaged hedge is saffron buckwheat (*Eriogonum crocatum*). On the deck are pots of lavender-blue flowered Cleveland sage and lilac verbena, (*Verbena lilacina*).

Once converted, the gardener may decide to replace the lawn with a native turf grass and replace the evergreen shrubs with native leafy evergreen shrubs. In terms of design, the landscape is still structured and conventional. The difference is that natives have replaced the traditional nursery plants, and the gardener is now able to dramatically reduce watering and maintenance. The natives also feed songbirds, attract butterflies, and provide important habitat for other small native creatures.

Some people think that by using native plants, their gardens will be messy and unkempt. This is probably because, when seen in the wild, natives do not look their neatest. These skeptics are missing the obvious point that the same plant can look very different in a garden setting with minimal care. If you'd spent a week on a camping trip, would you look as neat as you normally do at home?

The average homeowner's first landscape consideration is an aesthetic one. Maintenance, the gardener's secondary concern, is another benefit of the native garden, and wildlife protection is a third. Only the native garden can provide all three. Even if the setting is formal, as it is at a residence at Desert Highlands in Scottsdale, the natives provide nesting for birds, nectar for butterflies, and rocky hideouts for lizards.

ABOVE: While the saguaro was left in place during construction of this residence at Desert Highlands in Scottsdale, Arizona, designed by Phil Hebets, the foothill paloverde was boxed up, set aside, and then replanted after work was completed. The color from left to right is claret-cup cactus, Mexican evening primrose, Parry's penstemon, mountain marigold, calylophus (*Calylophus* spp.), and a nonnative white-flowered acacia (*Acacia aneura*). LEFT: There are two flowery courtyards within the wall of Dan MacBeth's garden in Phoenix. Next to the front entrance shown here are an existing honey mesquite, desert Canterbury-bells, and brittlebush. RIGHT: This wonderful outcropping of rock occurs on landscape architect Jeff Powers's Laguna Beach, California, hillside property halfway between his house and the street below. In its crevices four kinds of indigenous ferns grow, while above it and out of the shade are chaparral plants such as lemonadeberry.

NATURALISTIC GARDENS

As people get more enthusiastic about native plants, an interesting and almost predictable thing happens: They start looking at their conventional landscape and sense a stirring of dissatisfaction. It's all so controlled. Then they see a natural landscape–perhaps in the wild, perhaps in a botanic garden, perhaps even around a neighbor's home–and they are struck with a sudden realization. Instead of straight lines and rows, there is a harmony of textures and colors and a relaxed mingling of elements. It's clear that the way plants fit together in nature is also orderly, but in ways that are far more complex and satisfying than in a formal landscape design. The result is both more exciting and more restful than our

contrived plans. Like nature itself, the naturalistic garden has the power to make us feel good.

But, unlike nature, the naturalistic landscape also artfully accentuates all that is most colorful and eye-catching. It is not meant to be a re-creation of nature, and therefore the plant materials do not all have to be indigenous. Some plants may be native to other areas of the state. Some may even come from other continents. What they all have in common is that they are relatively self-sufficient in and well adapted to the site. For example, a gardener who is passionate about blue and yellow flowers and silver foliage might use all indigenous chaparral plants in those colors for a native landscape. In a naturalistic landscape, native plants would be mixed with plants from other regions that have the same colors, textures, and water requirements.

It is not necessary to have a large property or an unusual plot of land to make a naturalistic garden or to imitate a native habitat. Even the most ordinary yard imaginable can still be converted to a naturalistic landscape. Many homeowners have naturalistic or native landscapes in their front yards as well as the back and reap compliments from their neighbors.

In case this sounds like a plan that requires professional help, let me make clear that excellent results can be achieved by amateurs. Dan MacBeth is a good example. A talented home builder, MacBeth created his garden after a six-week course in landscaping at the Desert Botanical Garden in Phoenix.

NATURAL HABITAT GARDENS

For gardeners who become passionate about native plants and their benefits to the Earth, there comes a time—usually about 10 years after the initial purchase of a native plant—when the distinction between "native" and "indigenous" becomes supremely important.

In the dictionary, the two terms are essentially synonymous. But in the world of nurseries and home gardening, they have come to mean different things. Many plants are sold as "natives," meaning that they originated in the general region. A northern California "native" or a "native" plant from the Chihuahuan Desert might blend beautifully into a southern Cali-

fornia chaparral landscape, but neither is "indigenous"–that is, *truly* native to that specific site. The dwarf artemisia that is native in the San Francisco area may be related to the artemisia of San Diego, but it is not really the same. Sometimes the non-indigenous plant succumbs to a quirk of weather, underlining the point. The more you learn about natives–from books or lectures or field trips–the more you'll appreciate the distinction.

The principal way to make use of this distinction is in reconstructing a truly indigenous habitat through *revegetation,* either by hiring an expert in this area of landscape design or by doing it yourself. Doing it yourself is challenging, but it is also endlessly fascinating. There are always more plants to discover and new combinations. Revegetation allows you to be both detective and artist, leading to investigations in geology, botany, hydrology, soil chemistry, pollinators, and weather patterns, as well as to creative experiments with fire and grazing regimens.

As challenging as creating a natural habitat can be, it can also be the easiest of all kinds of gardening, and it's not necessary to know the name of a single plant to do it. All the native gardener needs to do is preserve what's there, as in the "building envelope" method of landscaping discussed on pages 24 to 33.

LEFT: Robert Breunig, director of Phoenix Botanical Garden, loves native plants and wanted to express that in his home landscape. Into his very typical suburban front yard he brought together an assortment of drought-tolerant flowering shrubs, perennials, and small trees that feed hummingbirds most of the year. In mid-March, most of them bloom together for a spectacular show. Chuparosa, Parry's penstemon, globe mallow, California gold poppy, lupine, and brittle-bush are visible in this view. ABOVE: A few housing developments around Phoenix have purchase agreements enforcing the "building envelope" method of landscaping. The foreground and background of this private home in Carefree, Arizona, designed by Steve Martino, show undisturbed Sonoran Desert, while next to the house a few nonnative plants have been allowed. In between, where the desert was disturbed during construction, the land has been revegetated. RIGHT: This chaparral garden was planted at the Santa Barbara Botanic Garden, not preserved. Drought-tolerant shrubs and flowers are grouped together to illustrate how colorful a native garden can be.

A SENSE OF PLACE

One evening in Santa Barbara, Andy and I stood on the beach. "What if you'd been blindfolded," Andy asked, "whisked magically around the world, and then set down here by a genie? Would you know where you were just by looking at the vegetation?" I looked around and spotted fig marigold and iceplant from southern Africa, palm trees from northern Africa, oleander from the Near East, eucalyptus from Australia, pampas grass from South America, and a camellia from China or Japan. "I can't even tell what continent I'm on!" I exclaimed.

The people most responsible for southern California landscapes, according to a landscape architect friend, are not other landscape architects but land developers and real estate brokers. For many decades, they have been promoting this part of the country as a "tropical paradise," and they have been so successful that today's residents boast of having gardens of lush—and thirsty—roses, azaleas, camellias, hydrangeas, and Indian hawthorn. Even the "drought-tolerant" plants so popular with well-intentioned landscapers such as Hall's honeysuckle, cape plumbago, pyracantha, and gazania cannot survive in southern California without supplemental irrigation.

In Roman Polanski's film *Chinatown,* a Los Angeles city councilman makes the following speech: "Now, remember," he says, "we live next door to the ocean. But we also live on the edge of a desert. Los Angeles is a desert community. Beneath the buildings, beneath our streets, is desert!" While that is not completely accurate—deserts average less than 10 inches of annual rainfall—Los Angeles does receive only 16 inches of rainfall a year. Even thornscrub requires over 20 inches a year. Italy, the south of France, and Greece—the Mediterranean countries whose climates are so often compared to that of southern California—average 20 to 60 inches a year.

Creating a landscape with a true sense of place simply means that El Paso should look like El Paso and not Hartford, Connecticut, and Los Angeles ought to look like Los Angeles and a lot less like Managua. Desert and chaparral are distinctly different in texture and feeling, and each of the deserts has its own character. In contrast to desert vegetation, which might cover only 10 percent of the ground, chaparral vegetation usually covers at least 90 percent, because it has the benefit of cooler temperatures or rainfall as high as 20 inches a year. To develop that most basic sense of place, it is important to preserve the proper amount of bare ground.

I have divided southern California and the Southwest into seven regions. Regions 1, 2, and 3 are varying versions of southern California chaparral. Regions 4, 5, 6, and 7 designate the four warm deserts. Each is a distinct and wonderfully beautiful habitat worthy of emulation in the garden. Yet so much native landscape has been obliterated that discovering the original flavor of a particular landscape is sometimes difficult if not impossible. This chapter is designed to help you create that vision. First look at the map on page 168 to find which region is yours. Then read the pertinent description, making sure that elevation, temperature, and rainfall match the conditions of your land. (In southern California, the regions are really more complex than a map can indicate.) A photograph of a regional garden and the wild land that it imitates should stimulate your imagination and open the door to new gardening possibilities.

Deep blue-flowered ceanothus, yellow-flowered mountain marigold, and silver-leaved St. Catherine's lace create the colors and scents of the native coastal chaparral found near Jana Ruzicka's home in Laguna Beach. Other plants in this scene, or just out of the picture, are artemisia, cenizo, western sycamore, hollyleaf cherry, purple needlegrass, a pine, and native rocks. This is not a re-creation of an indigenous habitat, but it definitely captures the essence of coastal southern California.

SOUTHERN CALIFORNIA CHAPARRAL (REGIONS 1, 2, 3)

Chaparral, the dominant vegetation of the most populated parts of southern California, is a continuous leafy mass of intertwining shrubs 3 to 12 feet tall, broken by intervals of bare rocky slope or tree-filled crevices. It is found where temperatures are moderate and rainfall averages 10 to 20 inches a year, which puts it in a band between the Pacific Ocean and the pine forests of the mountains or between those mountains and the deserts to the east. There are basically two types: coastal sagescrub (soft chaparral) and evergreen chaparral (hard chaparral). Coastal sagescrub is often seen mixed with evergreen chaparral. That's because when evergreen chaparral has been burned and the soil is exposed to sun and drought, the coastal sagescrub plants, along with bulbs, perennials, and annuals, are the first to rush in and fill the gaps left by the fire. Evergreen chaparral is supposed to burn in late summer or fall every 15 to 50 years, and it takes about 15 years to recover. If evergreen chaparral is burned every 5 to 10 years, it is replaced by coastal sagescrub. If coastal sagescrub is burned at intervals of less than 5 years, the sages are killed, and nonnative annual grasses seem to become dominant.

Region 1	*Coastal sagescrub*
Elevation	*Sea level to 3,000 feet, usually below evergreen chaparral*
Area	*Coastal southern California, from Santa Barbara to San Diego*
Temperature	*Rarely below freezing, generally 40 to 80 degrees F*
Rainfall	*Averages 8 to 12 inches a year, mostly in winter*

Coastal sagescrub is short—about 5 feet tall or less—and is flowery in the spring but almost bare of leaves in the summer. Some of the leaves actually drop, and others curl up; some stems die back to the roots. This is how coastal sagescrub tolerates drier, more desertlike conditions than evergreen chaparral. It occurs along the coast as you would expect, but it is also found inland on low, dry, east-facing slopes of the Coast Ranges and around Riverside. What is most striking about coastal sagescrub is its scent—a marvelous combination arising from the aromatic leaves of coastal sagebrush, white sage, black sage, and purple sage. Other important coastal sagescrub plants are coast sunflower, California buckwheat, dudleya, and coyote brush. In swales or along the borders of coastal sagescrub are taller evergreens such as laurel-leaf sumac and lemonadeberry. Farther south, succulent evergreens such as prickly pear and agave, along with jojoba and other leafy desert shrubs, are added to the mix to form a habitat called succulent coastal sagescrub.

RIGHT: This patch of coastal sagescrub, attached to the Hortense Miller garden in Laguna Beach, California, burned 13 years ago. Chaparral mallow (*Malacothamnus fasciculatus*) appeared as if by magic to lay a green bandage over the scorched earth. Now that its job is over, it is slowly dying back as the more permanent chaparral plants return. Most prevalent here is lemonadeberry. With it are dark green toyon, gray-leaved coastal sagebrush, yellow-green California buckwheat, ceanothus (*Ceanothus cyaneus*), black sage, coast sunflower, and chalk dudleya. The scents are spicy and mingled and fresh, but not overwhelming. Our guide, landscape architect Jana Ruzicka, speculated that there were originally coast live oaks in the crevices, but they were cut down and taken out by sailors needing wood for shipboard repairs.

Region 2	*Evergreen chaparral*
Elevation	*50 to 6,000 feet, above coastal sagescrub and below woodland*
Area	*Los Angeles, Thousand Oaks, Escondido, north- or east-facing slopes*
Temperature	*Rarely below freezing, generally 40 to 90 degrees F*
Rainfall	*Averages 16 inches a year, mostly in winter*

Evergreen chaparral is green all year long. In Region 2, 100 percent of the ground is covered, and the dominant shrubs are likely to be chamise, toyon, California scrub oak, hollyleaf cherry, coffeeberry, birchleaf mountain mahogany (*Cercocarpus betuloides*), Santa Barbara ceanothus, white lilac, greenbark ceanothus, tree poppy, lemonadeberry, and laurel-leaf sumac. Chamise has yellow-green needles, but the other shrubs have larger, broader leaves that tend to be dark green, firm, and glossy. Height might be as low as 3 feet, but the canopy is generally over one's head. Mature stands average about 12 feet tall. Chaparral is naturally impenetrable, but it can be made to feel like short woodland if the undergrowth is cut way back and old shrubs are pruned to reveal their graceful trunks. Flowers are found on the edges or in gaps where there is enough sun for them to bloom. Blue-flowering ceanothus and the golden flowers of tree poppy are the showstoppers, but the white flowers of the other shrubs are lovely when seen close up, and they are often fragrant. When you consider that many of these plants also sport big red berries and attract a wide variety of colorful birds, you can see that evergreen chaparral has the potential to make an extremely attractive garden.

Chaparral has been little used in gardens because most people think that it can survive only if it is burned. Pruning can, however, replace fire in the home landscape. Those who live in an area where wildfires occur should plant nonflammable southern California woodland next to their homes–live oak, California bay, or western sycamore–with shady ground covers underneath.

Region 3	*Inland evergreen chaparral*
Elevation	*50 to 6,000 feet, between woodland and desert scrub*
Area	*Riverside, Santa Clarita, south- or west-facing slopes*
Temperature	*20s to above 100 degrees F*
Rainfall	*Averages 15 inches a year, mostly in winter*

Region 3 is very similar to Region 2, but it is drier, so coverage would likely be 80 to 90 percent, which allows enough sun for many more flowers. Probable components are chamise, California scrub oak, toyon, hollyleaf cherry, California fremontia, blue manzanita, chaparral whitethorn or woollyleaf ceanothus, sugarbush, lemonadeberry, and jojoba. For those in fire zones, live oak woodland should be used around the house.

In this view of the Mojave Desert at Red Rock, just north of Las Vegas, stunted Joshua trees and banana yucca are the accents in a ground cover of creosote, rabbitbrush (*Chrysothamnus nauseosus*), brittlebush, globe mallow, Apache-plume, blackbush (*Coleogyne ramosissima*), and numerous herbaceous flowers. It is still winter, too early for flowers, but rain is on the way. Note the desert floor of pebbles.

THE WARM DESERTS
(REGIONS 4, 5, 6, 7)

The warm deserts receive their meager precipitation in the form of rain as opposed to snow, and they suffer from heat more than from cold. Residents of all our southwestern warm deserts *think* they can grow palms, and many of them actually can, although the only population center where palms are native is around the Palm Springs area in the Lower Colorado Desert in southern California. The flatlands are predominantly creosote flats or desert grasslands, and the most exciting desert vegetation is on the foothills—saguaro and Joshua tree—or in the washes—desert willow and smoketree. This book deals only with those desert plant communities that are found below the pinyon pines.

Every desert plant that doesn't live in an oasis has a strategy for dealing with drought. Cacti, jatrophas, and hackberries store water in their trunks. The ephemeral wildflowers can take in as little as an inch of rain during the cool season, and on that meager amount they grow large enough to flower and make seed in the spring. The plants then die, passing on their genes in the seeds, which endure the summer. Ocotillo and other drought-deciduous plants drop their leaves and go dormant during hot, dry spells. Paloverdes drop their leaves but continue to make food with their green stems and trunks. The plants that stay leafy and green all summer, such as mesquites and acacias, have deep roots; some, such as desert holly, have heat-reflecting silvery leaves, and some, such as creosote, have waxy leaves that cut down on evaporation.

In a good spring, the deserts are alive with pink, yellow, orange, white, purple, and blue flowers (two good springs in a row is unlikely), and they are shades of green, silver, and khaki the rest of the year. The color of desert rocks and soil is significant because they, along with the sky, are the dominant hues.

Vegetation is scattered, making the soil, or desert pavement, highly visible. In contrast to chaparral, where shrubs touch and even intertwine, large desert shrubs not only do not touch, they usually have at least 4 feet between them. As you look at these desert scenes, notice that the saguaros, tree yuccas, and ocotillos—the tallest plants—space themselves evenly apart from each other. There are two exceptions. The ground-cover shrubs sometimes touch and form drifts that look continuous from a distance. And paloverdes, ephedras, and other trees and shrubs, acting as "nurse plants," allow saguaros or tree yuccas to grow up into their branches where they are safe from browsers.

Some desert washes (called arroyos in the Chihuahuan Desert) are barely visible indentations where rains run off, while others are deeper cuts that have extensive gravel deposits to trap and store floodwater. The shallow washes are lined with creosote, but the deeper ones with permanent stores of water are dominated by desert willow, mesquite, netleaf hackberry, cottonwood, willow, and giant reeds (*Phragmites australis* and *Arundo donax*). Underneath might be smaller shrubs, prickly pear, and flowers. Songbirds such as Scott's oriole and the blue-gray gnatcatcher take advantage of the leafy branches to build nests that are hidden from hawks and owls and are above the reach of coyotes and panthers.

Region 4	Mojave Desert
Elevation	3,000 to 5,000 feet (Joshua trees from 3,500 to 5,000 feet)
Area	Las Vegas (3,281 feet), Lancaster (2,340 feet), Bull Head City
Temperature	5 to 120 degrees F
Rainfall	Averages 4 inches a year with 3 percent soil penetration, mostly summer thunderstorms

LEFT: Joshua trees, the signature plant of the Mojave Desert, rightfully dominate the landscape of the Blasco home in Las Vegas. The front garden, designed by Jim Dalton of Phoenix, contains numerous other plants that do quite well here in the low-water-use zone: Torrey mesquite, Mojave yucca, Parry's penstemon, desert marigold, bursage, desert spoon, globe mallow, autumn sage, and Texas ranger. In back is a lawn ringed with a windbreak of cottonwoods.

The most distinctive feature of the Mojave Desert is the Joshua tree. In the foothills, such as on the outskirts of Las Vegas near Red Rock where new neighborhoods are going in, Joshua tree and ocotillo should be used for height. They are more durable than plants that are native to surrounding deserts, such as saguaro, palm, or paloverde, and just a small amount of irrigation will keep them looking pretty all year. On the heavier, siltier soil that was once part of the Colorado River drainageway, the best tree to use is Torrey mesquite. The Mojave Desert is rather sparse on the flats—mostly a scattering of shrubs and unreliable displays of ephemeral wildflowers. Those who garden there should imitate a wash habitat or borrow heavily from the Mojave Desert foothills. Plants from the Chihuahuan Desert are useful in courtyards because they have the necessary cold tolerance.

Region 5	*Lower Colorado Desert*
Elevation	*Below sea level to 1,000 feet*
Area	*Palm Springs (425 feet), Coachella Valley, Salton Sea, Yuma (160 feet)*
Temperature	*Rarely below freezing, generally 60 to 110 degrees F*
Rainfall	*Averages 2 to 4 inches a year, mostly in winter*

The Lower Colorado Desert is the hottest and driest of the warm deserts. Scientists use the name to define a huge portion of the Sonoran Desert, and in some books it extends from Phoenix, Arizona, to Needles, California, and a third of the way down the Gulf of California. For the purposes of this book, it designates the drainageway of the lower Colorado River before it combines with the Gila River and flows into the Gulf of California. Low elevation and low rainfall make native landscapes in Palm Springs look quite different from those in Phoenix, so here the term *Lower Colorado Desert* means there are no saguaros, the California fan palm might be native, and vegetation is so sparse that the envelope garden should be designed to imitate a wash. It will require a little bit of water. The well-loved, cold-tender smoketree with its midnight blue flowers will flourish in this garden. Its pale trunks and branches combine beautifully with the lime green ones of blue paloverde or the silver of ironwood. Torrey and screwbean mesquite, with their lime green foliage and golden flowers, are also extremely attractive and easy to grow, along with bladderpod and desert lavender. White bursage and burrobush (*Hymenoclea salsola*) mixed with desert Canterbury-bells and other spring ephemerals are the most common ground covers, but an ever-silver cover of desert holly and brittlebush is possible, and evergreen desert agave and dune marigold can be added with very little trouble.

ABOVE: Looking toward the Joshua Tree National Monument from the northern edge of the Lower Colorado Desert, the scene is dominated by creosote flats. Purple sand verbena and desert dandelion (*Malacothrix glabrata*) with white desert pincushion (*Chaenactis fremontii*) lend color in late March. It is so dry in the Lower Colorado section of the Sonoran Desert that cacti shrivel. Yet, as you can see, there are grasses and flowers where the desert floor is undisturbed—not blowing sand. RIGHT: Smoketree is distinctive to the warm washes of the Lower Colorado Desert. Here at Anza-Borrego Desert State Park in Borrego Springs, California, it is used with brittlebush and ocotillo. In early June, the brittlebush will no longer be covered with yellow daisies, and the smoketree will be a mass of midnight blue pea-shaped blossoms. The bare ground is the result of many children's feet happily exploring this beautiful garden.

Region 6	*Sonoran Desert*
Elevation	*Sea level (in Mexico along Gulf of California) to 5,000 feet*
Area	*Phoenix (1,090 feet), Carefree (2,567 feet), Tucson (2,389 feet), Casa Grande (1,391 feet)*
Temperature	*Rarely below freezing, generally 50 to 90 degrees F*
Rainfall	*Averages 4 to 12 inches a year, half in steady winter rains and half in late-summer thundershowers*

The signature plant of the Sonoran Desert is the saguaro. This tree-tall cactus dots the foothills at elevations between 1,500 and 3,500 feet. Where the saguaros grow, all the choicest vegetation of the Sonoran Desert comes together—bursage, fairyduster, chuparosa, brittlebush, globe mallow, desert marigold, dwarf white zinnia, and cacti. The plants grow thickly enough to seem generous but open enough to give any soul all the space and sky it

needs. This is the prettiest and most photogenic of our warm deserts.

Not every Sonoran Desert resident can landscape with saguaros, however. The plants are slow-growing, are federally protected, and don't live naturally on the flats of Phoenix and suburbs such as Scottsdale, Tempe, and Youngtown. But that doesn't mean that the native landscape will be boring. Ironwood and blue paloverde are the two most important indigenous trees, although these will do better with a swale to catch extra moisture. Companion plants are mesquite, acacia, ocotillo, cholla, prickly pear, Mormon tea, creosote, saltbush (*Atriplex*), bursage, white bursage, bush muhly, big galleta (*Hilaria rigida*), desert marigold, globe mallow, and California gold poppy, along with many other ephemeral wildflowers. With just a little irrigation, penstemon, agave, and other plants of the foothills can thrive as well.

Region 7	*Chihuahuan Desert*
Elevation	*1,200 to 4,000 feet on north-facing slopes, to 6,500 feet on south faces*
Area	*Las Cruces (3,896 feet), El Paso (3,762 feet), Big Bend*
Temperature	*5 to 100 degrees F (one recorded low of −8 degrees)*
Rainfall	*Averages 7 to 12 inches a year, mostly thunderstorms in late summer*

The Chihuahuan Desert is high and cold like the Mojave Desert, but it is older and moister and so has a more extensive palette of plants. It originated in Mexico and reached

ABOVE: The front garden of Joe and Lou Batnara's home in Tucson was left almost completely undisturbed by landscape designer Mary Rose Duffield. Ocotillo, saguaro, palmilla, creosote, and desert spoon, held together by a ground cover of bursage, are the natural, native components of this garden. It requires no water and almost no maintenance, and still looks good all year. **LEFT:** At Gonzales Pass in the high Sonoran Desert east of Phoenix, the most characteristic plant is the tall slender saguaro. Other prominent plants are ocotillo and cholla, held together by a myriad of soft, aromatic-leaved shrubs, flowers, and grasses.

its northern boundaries less than 8,000 years ago, and it is now expanding eastward as the climate gets drier. Frost-free winters are likely to happen only at low points along the Rio Grande River in the Big Bend area. Statistically, because of cooler summers and summer thunderstorms, the Chihuahuan Desert ought to be the most luxuriant of the warm deserts. However, many years the rains never appear, and, as in the Mojave, when they do arrive, they come with such force that the water runs off so quickly that it cannot penetrate the soil. Only a few species are hardy enough to bloom every year, and some have been known to stay dormant for 50 years, waiting for sufficient moisture.

The indicator plant of the Chihuahuan Desert is lechuguilla. It is a ground cover and does not stand out against the sky like saguaros or Joshua trees except when it sends up its long slender bloom stalk. Like most Chihuahuan Desert plants, it is able to grow in ground white with limestone. Other dominant plants are creosote, tarbush (*Flourensia cernua*), ocotillo, sotol (the Chihuahuan name for desert spoon), sacahuista, mariola, acacia, and skeletonleaf goldeneye.

Grasses used to be fairly abundant before overgrazing caused erosion and loss of organic matter. Grasses likely to be still present in tufts and patches are gramas, threeawns (*Aristida* spp.), tridens (*Tridens* spp.), and fluffgrass (*Erioneuron pluchellum*). Palmilla, Spanish bayonet, and other tree yuccas provide height in the foothills, and mesquites and desert willows are the trees of the arroyos.

RIGHT, ABOVE: The El Paso garden of Theresa Cavaretta truly reflects the desert. Ocotillo, littleleaf sumac, Spanish bayonet, claret-cup cactus, blackfoot daisy, red yucca, creosote and Mexican century plant (*Agave americana*) grow under a mulch of decomposed granite on either side of a dry stream of river rocks. **RIGHT, BELOW:** Lechuguilla, ocotillo, and creosote dominate this view of the Chihuahuan Desert at Big Bend National Park. The ground cover is composed of raspberry-colored krameria (*Krameria parvifolia*), plume tiquilia, and many other beautiful flowers and shrubs.

PART ONE

The best-designed native plant gardens are a balance between raw nature and human control. Nurturing a garden is like raising children: You have to find the right balance between giving them enough freedom to develop their own personalities while teaching them to live within the necessary limits set by society.

The vast majority of today's gardens are overly controlled. Everything is either lined up or mowed down. This is largely the legacy of the post–World War II generation of gardeners. At the end of the war, Americans felt not just victorious, but omnipotent, convinced that anything was possible, given enough science and engineering. They thought they could bend even the forces of nature to their wills–from changing the course of rivers to annihilating garden pests.

Many of us who belong to the Vietnam generation have learned a different lesson: We've learned that we are fallible and that technology is a two-edged sword which must coexist in harmony with nature, not attempt to subjugate it. Our generation's task seems to be to figure out the correct balance between what is actually under our control and what is best left to take care of itself.

We now have overwhelming evidence that conventional gardening is unkind to nature and creates sterile environments for songbirds, butterflies, and a host of other wildlife. We now realize that we cannot kill off half of nature and still have the other half remain healthy. And yet the old ways die hard, and we still feel guilty if our gardens don't look as though they are ready to pass military inspection.

Control is a heady thing, and most of us are reluctant to voluntarily give it up. A row of sculptured shrubs on either side of the front door may look rigid and ridiculous, but it does give visible expression to our power and handiwork, especially when so much in the garden, from the weather to the time we have available to cultivate, is beyond our ability to change.

A more sensible approach to garden design is to let nature take care of herself within our carefully prescribed limits. This doesn't mean letting weeds run amok; no one thinks a garden should look like a vacant lot. Instead, allow your garden to express itself while from time to time you prune a bit here, pick up there, and enjoy the many delightful surprises produced.

To give form to the garden, carefully position a few man-made features, such as a bench, a wall, or a walk. These permanent fixtures will give structure while the minimally groomed natural plantings fill in the spaces. These structures can have bold lines and straight edges, or they can be rustic or curving. Either way, the look can be relaxed rather than rigid. A broad, straight walkway where flowers and ground covers are permitted to dribble over the edges is not only entirely usable but also more interesting, and it will invite you to slow down to appreciate the scents and colors in the garden.

The structural framework is large and simple—the house and the driveway. Even a completely wild landscape, when seen against the clean lines of a house, is magically tamed. Add a little pruning and artistic placement of the largest plants, and it becomes a beautiful garden.

In the courtyard gardens, note how patio, arbor, paths, sitting areas, water features, steps,

Creating the Garden

and other man-made focus points determine the shape and flow of each one. These small theme gardens can be used singly, or several can be arranged into a larger space, as many rooms in a house.

To create the garden of your dreams, first decide where you want to walk, where you need privacy, and where you want visibility. Give yourself at least one sitting area and an outdoor eating area. Imagine the path to your front door as a series of beautifully composed pictures. Then arrange the plants according to the theme-garden plans or the indigenous charts at the back of this book.

By using the plant groupings found in the charts, and by relaxing your control over your garden, you will be going in an exciting new direction. But you will be well rewarded for your daring. When a garden is designed around natural habitats, the basic needs of keeping the plants alive by watering, weeding, fertilizing, and medicating are unnecessary. The gardener is free to give his full attention to aesthetics. Your garden will be softer, lovelier, and far more diverse than ever before. Your labors will be dramatically reduced. And you will be gardening not to keep up appearances for the neighbors, but to help preserve our environment for the next generation.

The natural Sonoran Desert that can be seen over the courtyard wall completely surrounds the Cliff Douglas home in Mesa, Arizona. The envelope of desert was fenced-off
and preserved during construction. Inside the courtyard, Douglas hand-waters about
once a week when temperatures are high. For visual harmony and ease of maintenance,
at least half of the courtyard species are native to the desert outside the walls. Foothill
paloverde, prickly pear, agave, and two Chihuahuan Desert plants—autumn sage and
cenizo—provide an evergreen backdrop for an array of colorful flowers: Baja fairyduster, brittlebush, globe mallow, and bougainvillea (native to Brazil) are the most
prominent in this view. The landscape was designed by Steve Martino. RIGHT: Bulldozing
the fragile desert for homesites destroys natural habitat, perhaps forever; here a razed
site outside Las Cruces, New Mexico.

OPE GARDEN

IN AN EARLIER BOOK, *REQUIEM FOR A LAWNMOWER,* I TOLD OF MY

twin epiphanies: first, the excitement of discovering native plants; and

then, a few years later, being exposed to a wonderful new way to use

them—working with the plants, not as individuals but as members of

a synergistic, harmonious community—just as they exist in nature.

Since then I've learned of another, equally exciting approach to

home landscaping. This relatively new concept, called the building

envelope, was conceived as a means of saving fragile habitats while

25

the land is under development. With the envelope plan, the land developer, whose work has so often destroyed habitat, can now be an environmentalist.

The term *building envelope* came about because the house, along with the driveway and other man-made structures, is in effect *enveloped* by the natural landscape; the house looks as if it has been gently set down in the midst of the undisturbed property. When building on raw wild land, all the land's characteristics are considered sacrosanct, and measures are taken to preserve not just the indigenous plant life but other site features such as outcroppings of rock, gullies and washes, even scenic views. The Cliff Douglas home in Mesa, Arizona, is an excellent example of how gracefully this concept can be employed.

The origins of the building envelope concept are unknown, but landscape architect Gage Davis is credited with introducing the concept to Arizona. In 1981 he and his associates designed Desert Highlands, an 850-acre golf-course community in Scottsdale. New home construction continues to this day at the community, and each property owner must utilize the building envelope; it is stipulated in the purchase agreement.

This is how the building envelope works: The lot is surveyed and marked into three specific zones. The house and access drive constitute the *private area.* Here, nonnative plants, even those requiring irrigation, are permitted. Next comes the *transition area,* a 10- to 20-foot buffer zone where workers and their equipment are confined during construction. Larger plants—trees, shrubs, and cacti—situated in both the private and transition areas, are boxed, moved to a holding area, and put on a drip irrigation system to be replanted on the site later. Even the top few inches of topsoil or desert floor can

At this private home in Scottsdale, Arizona, the landscape was preserved and designed by Marcus Bollinger and John Suarez. An enormous advantage to preserving the natural landscape is that you have a mature landscape instantly. Even though the house was not quite finished when we took this picture, the landscape already looks complete. A few large-sized paloverdes (both blue and foothill), a mesquite, and an ironwood were added to the disturbed areas around the driveway and up near the house. An indigenous pink fairyduster is in bloom in the foreground. The grasses seen here are not native, but they were already well established at the site and so were left.

be scraped off and preserved with its precious assortment of weathered rock, hoard of seeds, and nutrients. The ground cover of choice—white sage, black sage, coyote brush, grasses, bursage, turpentinebush, dalea, or whatever else is abundantly native—is usually grown by a local nursery by special arrangement when construction begins; that way, it's at planting size by the time it is needed for revegetation. The third zone is the *natural area,* and it is home to a wide range of wildlife, from roadrunners and hummingbirds to butterflies and horned lizards. There is also, of course, a full palette of native plants. The natural area is fenced off from the other zones, and workers, equipment, and materials are strictly banned. A contract can stipulate that the builder is financially responsible for any damage the crews may inflict on plants outside the fencing and in the holding area.

The natural, indigenous landscape that surrounds the house and driveway is by definition very low maintenance and exists, as it has always existed, on whatever water nature provides. As evidenced by landscapes in Desert Highlands and the nearby Boulders community, a natural landscape does not mean "living like a bear in the wilderness," as one garden writer once pronounced. Far from being ugly and unkempt, these are extremely attractive gardens.

Unfortunately, the building envelope is known and used by only a handful of builders, architects, and property owners. There are many places where the concept is sorely needed. As an example, in Riverside, Las Cruces, Santa Clarita, and El Paso, we saw vast acreages of viable habitat scraped clean to make room for housing developments. All the indigenous plant materials living in that soil were destroyed. After construction, the homesites will, of course, be landscaped, but the animals were lost and so was the chance to have a fully installed natural landscape of mature size.

THE ENVELOPE GARDEN PLAN

The envelope garden plan illustrates how a house can be set into an intact habitat, but it can also be used as a revegetation plan for homeowners wanting to convert a cleared lot or an inherited high-maintenance landscape to an indigenous one. Admittedly, revegetation requires a bit of work at the outset, but the end result will be well worth it. The new envelope will be on a drip irrigation system for a year or two, until the plants get established. And, depending on how many foreign weeds have invaded the property, getting rid of them will demand at least some time on hands and knees during the first few years when irrigation is needed. But once the roots of the native plants are established, the envelope landscape will take care of itself, just as if it had been there all along.

The plan is designed to be as universal as possible for Southern California and the Southwest. Turn to the Indigenous Charts at the end of the book, find your city, or the one closest to you, and note the plants with a *D* (for dry) in each plant category. These will give you a good start on your revegetation project. Once you have the system going, other desirable plants often show up, brought in by birds and other animals. The rule here is, if it looks good, survives on its own, and is not aggressive, let it stay. You can also gather seed and sow it yourself if you can't find specific plants at a nursery.

Within the envelope plan is more than one courtyard garden. A hummingbird garden, a fragrance garden, or a moonlight garden could be planted in the sunny walled courtyard. The less sunny inner courtyard might contain a thornless garden, a songbird garden, an outdoor room, or a curandera garden. (Examples of each are in the next chapter.)

The front of the property gives a true sense of place, and the back terraces might offer a splendid view of mountains and nature. But envelope landscapes are not limited to huge properties and estates; ordinary town lots also use this approach. If, instead of a glorious panorama, the only view is a neighbor's backyard, there are two choices: enclose the backyard and make it into a courtyard garden, or keep it natural. If the neighbor opts for a natural backyard, too, a marvelous sense of country living is created between your homes, even in the heart of the city.

For inspiration, look at a natural landscape that resembles, as closely as possible, your future garden. In chaparral, east- and north-facing slopes are cooler and moister than slopes facing south and west. In the desert foothills, a difference of a hundred feet in elevation can mean a change of habitat with a new plant palette.

Plants marked *W/D,* which require more water than rainfall alone can provide, can be

BELOW: The envelope of this private home in the Tobosa area of Las Cruces is the natural Chihuahuan Desert. In this view, photographed in September, are field bursage (*Ambrosia convertiflora*), honey mesquite, creosote bush, and prickly pear. A century plant (*Agave americana*) and a cowtongue (*Opuntia lindheimeri* var. *linguiformis*) were added for extra accents. This would not do for the purist, for these are not indigenous, but they are drought-tolerant. Inside the envelope—next to the house—are the less drought-resistant, nonnative nursery fare—an orange tree and a bird-of-paradise (*Caesalpinia pulcherrima*). But there are also a native Wheeler sotol (called desert spoon in Arizona), a cholla (*Opuntia imbricata*) loaded with yellow tunas, a nonnative saguaro (of questionable winter hardiness), and other cacti.

RIGHT: "I wish you could have seen the 'before'" writes Carol Wolcott of the revegetated garden surrounding her home in Carefree, Arizona. "Many boulders and large trees were brought in, and many plants were heavily pruned and nonnatives were removed." Except for the two fishhook barrel cacti, which are native only one county to the west, all the plants employed in the front garden are indigenous to this part of the Sonoran Desert. The design and spacing by landscape designer George Pingitore are in harmony with the natural rhythms of the desert. Decomposed granite makes a new desert pavement, as the original had been removed. BELOW RIGHT: Since landscape architect Jeff Powers's home in Laguna Beach, California, is next to chaparral, he had to plant a fire barrier of succulents in order to purchase fire insurance. So often, homeowners in this situation make a fence of prickly pears. Here, a naturalistic barrier of a variety of succulents is used so that the chaparral and garden blend into each other artistically. The few prickly pears are not rigidly lined up but are scattered like those on the hill, and they are interspersed with three kinds of agaves and a nonnative aloe. This type of barrier will not stop a fireball, but it is effective against less aggressive fires.

used on properties where swales collect extra rainwater from roofs or pavement. This gives desert residents a chance to imitate wash or arroyo habitats. Those who live in Yuma, Palm Springs, or Las Vegas should utilize swales in their gardens as much as possible; conditions are extremely harsh in these areas, and the most interesting plants tend to grow in the washes.

There are not an equal number of options in every plant category for every environment. Although in some deserts creosote bush must be used in every place on the plan that calls for a leafy evergreen, it will be an appropriate backdrop for the more colorful elements.

In the desert, just about any plant in each category will work, but in southern California near San Diego, Santa Barbara, Los Angeles, and Riverside, plant selection must be more finely calibrated. This is because these cities have two, three, even four distinct plant communities or habitats. True, all the plants listed under each city are indigenous within its boundaries, but they do not all belong in the same habitat. The habitats of southern California are coastal sagescrub, evergreen chaparral, oak woodland, and indigenous grassland. Sometimes, to make life really interesting, they are not always separate and distinct but can overlap and invade each other.

If you are in doubt about precisely which habitat to use, the easiest and most universal habitat for southern Californians to re-create is evergreen chaparral. This kind of chaparral is short on trees, although it often has patches of coast live oak in it. In the wild, evergreen chaparral is usually under 10 feet tall because it gets burned to the ground every 15 years or so.

The threat of fire is a serious consideration in California chaparral communities. Any property that backs onto regularly burned wild chaparral should not have an envelope garden full of chaparral. Concrete, rocks, or sand may be the safest option, but who would want to live with that kind of "landscape"?

What's called for is a reasonable landscape plan that is aesthetically pleasing and still low-risk. Here are some ideas based on guidelines proposed by area fire departments. The first

The Envelope Plan

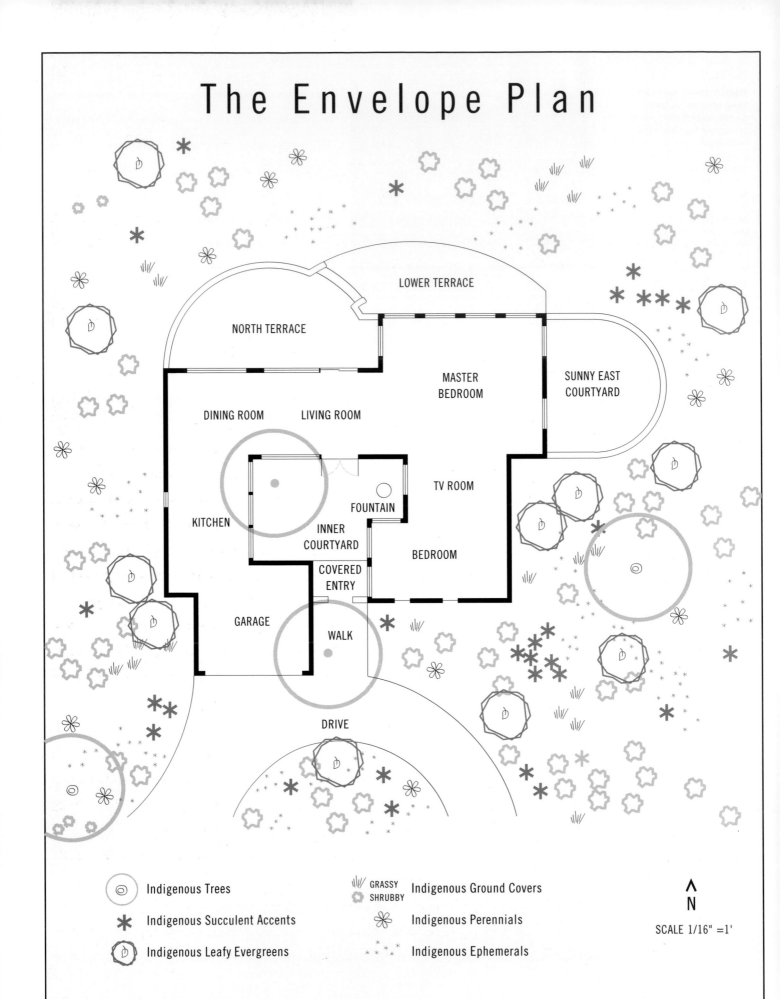

LOWER TERRACE

NORTH TERRACE

MASTER BEDROOM

SUNNY EAST COURTYARD

DINING ROOM LIVING ROOM

KITCHEN

TV ROOM

INNER COURTYARD

FOUNTAIN

BEDROOM

COVERED ENTRY

GARAGE

WALK

DRIVE

⊚ Indigenous Trees

✳ Indigenous Succulent Accents

🝔 Indigenous Leafy Evergreens

〰 GRASSY / SHRUBBY Indigenous Ground Covers

❋ Indigenous Perennials

∴ Indigenous Ephemerals

∧
N
SCALE 1/16" =1'

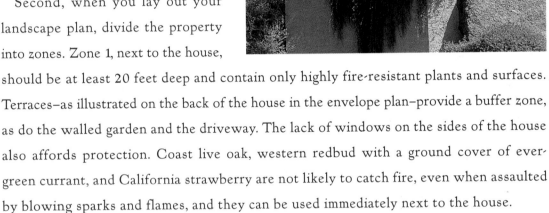

RIGHT: At the entrance to the home of landscape architect Phil Hebets in Skye Top, Troon Village, just north of Phoenix, Arizona, a driveway now separates this ironwood tree from the boulder-strewn hillside seen on the left. Marooned on its own high island by bulldozers, the tree was later protected with a stone-and-concrete retaining wall. In the giant planter thus created, other native flowering plants were added. BELOW: The Sonoran Desert, pure and undisturbed, comes right up to the edge of the pool with no other man-made interference at Mary Rose Duffield's home in Tucson. Architect Guy Greene would never claim to have actually invented the "negative edge" pool, but he knows of none that predates this one he designed in the early 1970s. Many gardeners feel compelled to meddle in a natural landscape so they can say they "designed" it, but I think full credit for design goes to those who know when to leave perfection alone. Even pruning here is unnecessary. The dead wood seen in this picture is an important lookout for desert animals. (We saw a roadrunner, a sparrow, and a ground squirrel each use it in turn, just in the time it took us to take this picture.)

has nothing to do with landscaping per se, but it's probably the most important measure you can take: Replace a combustible wood roof with a noncombustible material with a minimum UL rating of Class C, such as laminated fiberglass or Spanish tile. Neighborhoods where the homes are surrounded by expanses of lawn still burn–not because of the landscapes, but because sparks go from roof to roof.

Second, when you lay out your landscape plan, divide the property into zones. Zone 1, next to the house, should be at least 20 feet deep and contain only highly fire-resistant plants and surfaces. Terraces–as illustrated on the back of the house in the envelope plan–provide a buffer zone, as do the walled garden and the driveway. The lack of windows on the sides of the house also affords protection. Coast live oak, western redbud with a ground cover of evergreen currant, and California strawberry are not likely to catch fire, even when assaulted by blowing sparks and flames, and they can be used immediately next to the house.

Zone 2, a transitional area, can be planted with chaparral, although not nearly in the density in which the plants are found naturally. Plant the shrubs 18 feet apart, canopy to canopy, and keep them pruned up like small trees to cut down on dry undergrowth. Many of the hard chaparral shrubs–blue manzanita, San Diego summer holly, fremontia, toyon, hollyleaf cherry, lemonadeberry, and sugarbush–can eventually form small trees. For ground cover, use succulents such as dudleya and Our Lord's candle, penstemons, sages, and many of the shady ground covers such as elymus and Douglas iris.

In a large sunny area, a bit of southern California grassland–a combination of three needlegrasses, oniongrass, elymus, deergrass or littleseed muhly (*Muhlenbergia microsperma*), and Junegrass (*Koeleria cristata*)–might be the best solution. Flowers might be blue-eyed grass, California gold poppy, or purple owl's clover. It should be mowed or given a slow, cool, controlled burn *before* the fire season so that it is not flammable. Never burn without consulting local authorities or the local fire department for instructions and conditions.

Zone 3, the outer zone, is wild chaparral itself. Plan to spend a little time here each year pruning dead wood and thinning so that when the adjacent chaparral does burn, as it inevitably will, there will be little here to fuel the fire and endanger the rest of your property.

Of course, in a neighborhood where fire is unlikely, chaparral plants can be used thickly next to the house. Once they are established, they make a handsome landscape that is totally drought-tolerant. To use the envelope plan, substitute the treelike shrubs wherever the plan calls for trees and leafy evergreens. Substitute ceanothus and any of the other leafy evergreens on the chart for the succulent accents, and follow the plan from there on. Any of the indigenous vines can be trained to clamber over either a fence or a shrub.

Clip the shrubs annually to keep the landscape as low as burned chaparral, and replace the short-lived ceanothus from time to time. Shrubs pruned into trees, after 20 years or so, will create a woodland with shady ground covers replacing the ceanothus— a welcome habitat for songbirds.

GETTING STARTED

Use this book to draw up a wish list. Identify the most frequently occurring local plants as well as personal favorites among those that occur less often. Then find an area about the size of your garden that you particularly like. Armed with pencil and paper, go to that site and make observations that can be translated into your landscape.

For example, a study of a gently sloping hillside in the suburbs above El Paso—the lower Franklin Mountains—would find that the tallest plants are Torrey yuccas growing from 8 to 100 feet apart. Ocotillos, the next tallest plant, take up a space 6 feet wide and appear 10 to 20 feet apart. Between the ocotillos is a variety of succulent accents. Lechuguilla is usually in clumps about 8 feet wide and composed of a dozen rosettes, and these clumps are 20 to 60 feet apart. Prickly pear clumps are 4 to 6 feet wide and arranged 4 to 25 feet apart. Creosote bushes, the most prominent leafy evergreens, are about 6 feet wide and are found 8 to 30 feet apart. Small flowering shrubs such as dalea, plume tiquilia, and skeletonleaf goldeneye are 2 to 3 feet wide and arranged 4 to 15 feet apart. They are so numerous that they appear more like ground cover than do the smaller scattered clumps of grass and turpentine weed that are 1 to 2 feet apart.

Small flowers–perennials such as desert marigold and ephemerals–are scattered 1 to 2 feet apart in shallow swales or at the bottom of slopes. Littleleaf sumac, sotol, New Mexico agave, and mesquite are only occasionally seen, while Apache plume is commonly found in lower slope water courses and arroyos. The desert floor is covered with 4- to 6-inch rocks about 6 feet apart, with rocks under 2 inches across being most prevalent and just 2 to 6 inches apart.

Then, to translate this information into a reasonable indigenous planting plan for the lower Franklin Mountains, look at the envelope plan and its key list on page 30, and match the categories with appropriate indigenous plant materials. For instance, where it says trees, mark them either Torrey yucca or ocotillo. Where succulent accents are indicated, label them prickly pear or lechuguilla. Creosote can be the leafy evergreens, and the ground covers marked on the plan can be dalea, plume tiquilia, and skeletonleaf goldeneye. When you are finished, the result is an indigenous planting plan for an envelope landscape in the Franklin Mountains above El Paso.

The plan could also be used for a garden near San Diego. In this area, where coastal sage-scrub, desert, and chaparral are very close to each other, many cacti, agaves, and other succulent accents combine to make a special habitat called succulent coastal sagescrub. To imitate this habitat, ignore the trees, or use lemonadeberry or laurel-leaf sumac. Use all of the succulent accents listed under San Diego, but choose only jojoba and bladderpod from the leafy evergreen category. Cram in as many as you like of the sunny ground covers, perennials, and ephemerals.

For gardeners who quake at the thought of so many decisions, a professional native-plant person can help define the garden plan. There are many landscape architects, landscape designers, engineers, botanists, and environmentalists who are trained in revegetation techniques. Although the services are not inexpensive, the amount saved on replacing failed plants and redesigning can make them well worthwhile. If you can't find such a professional in the Yellow Pages, call your state native-plant society, local arboretum and nature center, native-plant nurseries, botany departments at universities, or the Nature Conservancy. (See the Directory on page 175 for addresses.)

Landscape architect Christy Ten Eyck created this traditional-looking fence of ocotillo cane attached to stretched chicken wire for Charlene Siler's backyard in Paradise Valley, Arizona. It provides a charming and effective transition to an arroyo dense with paloverde and Engelmann's prickly pear (*Opuntia engelmannii*). It is also an especially attractive way to keep toddlers and pets from wandering into the desert.

2 COURTYARD GARDENS AND PLANS

IN CONTRAST TO THE ENVELOPE GARDEN, WHICH CELEBRATES NATURAL BEAUTY, A COURTYARD GARDEN CEL-ebrates the harmonious interaction of plants and humans. These courtyard garden plans are all centered around a place to sit. Each has a theme, such as plants to attract hummingbirds, and endeavors to bring one of the most enviable aspects of Southwest gardening up close where it can be enjoyed in comfort.

The opportunities for special gardens is particularly high in Southern California and the warm South-west. Nowhere else in the United States do gardeners have so extensive a collection of silver-leaved trees, shrubs, and flowers. Add to this the charismatic night pollinators such as nectar-feeding bats and moths, and the entertainment value of a moonlight garden becomes irresistible. Another extraordinary garden for Southwesterners is the fragrance garden. Not only is there a profusion of sweet-scented nec-tar-bearing plants to attract butterflies and hummingbirds, but there is also a large palette of plants with spicy-scented oil glands in their leaves. One of the first things one notices about all southwestern native-plant gardens is that they have intense and extremely pleasant fragrances. This great number of herbs, combined with a still-living tradition of folklore from pre-Columbian residents, gives yet another special opportunity—the curandera garden. The songbird garden, like the hummingbird garden, brings together a delicious collection of superior bird-food plants. As the plants mature and the fruit becomes prolific, an especially fine assortment of birds will find your songbird garden irresistible and put it on their itinerary each year. And, since many migratory routes cross the Southwest, the variety of songbirds to be found in this part of the country is quite stunning.

Courtyards are popular in the Southwest because they combine privacy with beauty. It is not necessary, however, to have a walled courtyard to use these plans. The essential design elements can be transferred to an urban front yard or to any small space. Also, the basic shape of a particular plan does not have to coincide with an existing shape in the area to be landscaped. These plans purposely present a wide assortment of configurations that can be used. And each plan doesn't have to be married to a particular plant list—you can mix and match these theme gardens. For example, the patio design from the moonlight garden could be employed around an existing pool, and the plants used could be those from the hummingbird garden.

There is a photograph for each theme garden to help inspire you. But notice that the photographs do not illustrate the plans as drawn. The pictures were taken of actual gardens that have a high percentage of the plants chosen for each theme garden and are intended to give you one idea of how to combine these plants. The plans themselves give you another suggestion. Each plan is imaginary and created solely to showcase its theme. Any plan can be executed exactly as drawn, as careful attention has been paid to color scheme, bloom time, spacing for mature size, texture, aspect at different seasons, heights, position in relation to the sun, water and drainage requirements, and focal points.

In all cases, the plants are labeled by a number. Find the number on the list to discover the name of the plant. For more information and a picture of the plant, turn to the plant profile with that same number. This bypasses the index and is intended to save time and make these plans much easier to read for gardeners unfamiliar with these plants.

Please note, however, that often there are two plants suggested for each spot. In that case, the first number is for California chaparral, and the second number is for the deserts. In some plans, such as the hummingbird garden and the outdoor garden room, the plants work equally well for both desert and chaparral, with only a couple of carefully noted exceptions.

Curandera

A CURANDERA IS A HEALER, A MEDICINE WOMAN, SOMEONE WHOSE ROOTS IN THE NATURAL healing arts go back into antiquity. The ancient curandera had no corner drugstore; instead, she had thousands of native plants—a vast natural pharmacy! The roots, berries, barks, blossoms, leaves, and seeds of these plants became teas, salves, poultices, tonics, sedatives, diuretics, expectorants, and inhalants and were used to treat everything from mosquito bites to hiccups, from diarrhea to allergies, from bellyaches to skin rashes. They were even turned into soap, shampoo, fish bait, insect repellent, chewing gum, and mouthwash.

We are fortunate that much of this invaluable information still exists and is being documented, and that there are still many (although the number is sadly dwindling) Native American and Hispanic curanderas practicing and passing on this lore.

This herb garden is more medicinal than culinary. It is populated with a variety of native herbs and plants that contain remarkable properties for alleviating allergies, headaches, colds, and many other ills. It is *not* intended to be a substitute for the family doctor; rather, it is, like all gardens, primarily an aesthetic experience—in this case, one with historical and cultural connections that make it especially relevant to residents of Southern California and the Southwest.

Also, because this is a gardening book and not a medical primer, I have avoided specifics as to the healing properties that are attributed to these herbs, and I make no recommendations for their use. For that information, the reader can turn to three excellent reference books by Michael Moore: *Medicinal Plants of the Desert and Canyon West, Medicinal Plants of the Mountain West,* and *Los Remedios.* All are well documented and cover much more than folklore; many of the plants and curative properties Moore describes are being studied and used by the traditional medical community.

This particular garden was intended for a fairly small backyard, or as a portion of a large one—its total area should not exceed 40 feet on a side, or 1,600 square feet. In a desert home, it might be enclosed in a traditional ocotillo fence. Gardeners who live in California chaparral can use a plain wooden fence or wall. Some sort of enclosure is necessary to keep out

Artemisia (the blue-green lacy foliage) is useful for indigestion and stomach and menstrual cramps. It can also be used as a scent in a sauna. The leaves of salvia (the red-flowered plant) can be brewed into a tea to ease a sore throat, and the flowers can be used in salads and as a garnish. Ceanothus (scattered blue flowers—almost through blooming) makes an excellent home remedy for nosebleeds and is commonly used in Oriental diagnostic methods. A tea of chopped California gold poppy can be used as a mild sedative—but take it in small doses, as too much will give you a hangover. Navajos used to roast and eat the pods and seeds of western redbud (the very young tree with pink flowers). Not listed in the herbals but a lovely part of this picture are the large succulent rosettes of a green form of Britton's chalk dudleya (*Dudleya brittonii*) growing out of crevices in the rocky bank. This charming garden borders the entrance patio at the home of Jeff Powers in Laguna Beach, California.

Garden

Curandera Garden

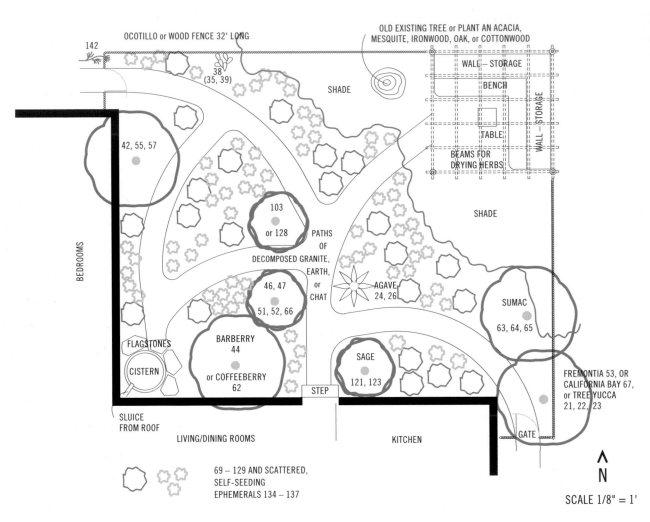

OCOTILLO or WOOD FENCE 32' LONG

OLD EXISTING TREE or PLANT AN ACACIA, MESQUITE, IRONWOOD, OAK, or COTTONWOOD

142

38
(35, 39)

SHADE

WALL – STORAGE

BENCH

TABLE

WALL – STORAGE

BEAMS FOR DRYING HERBS

42, 55, 57

BEDROOMS

103

or 128

PATHS
OF
DECOMPOSED GRANITE,
EARTH,
or
CHAT

SHADE

46, 47

51, 52, 66

AGAVE
24, 26

SUMAC

63, 64, 65

FLAGSTONES

BARBERRY
44

or COFFEEBERRY
62

CISTERN

SAGE

121, 123

FREMONTIA 53, OR
CALIFORNIA BAY 67,
or TREE YUCCA
21, 22, 23

STEP

SLUICE
FROM ROOF

LIVING/DINING ROOMS

KITCHEN

GATE

N

SCALE 1/8" = 1'

69 – 129 AND SCATTERED,
SELF-SEEDING
EPHEMERALS 134 – 137

C D Acacia (1)
C D Desert willow (8)
    D Ocotillo (9)
    D Ironwood (13)
C D Cottonwood (16)
C D Mesquite (17)
C   Oak (19) (61)
    D Joshua tree (21)
C D Yucca (22) (23) (40) (41)
C D Agave (24) (25)
C   Shaw's century plant (26)
    D Jatropha (35)
C D Prickly pear (38)
    D Jumping cholla (39)
C   Manzanita (42)
C D Barberry (44)

C   Ceanothus (46) (47)
C D Hopbush (51)
C D Apache-plume (52)
C   California fremontia (53)
C D Desert lavender (55)
    D Creosote bush (57)
C D Cenizo (58)
C   Coffeeberry (62)
C   Lemonadeberry, laurel-leaf
     sumac (63)
    D Littleleaf sumac (64)
C D Sugarbush (65)
C D Jojoba (66)
C   California bay (67)
C D Coastal sagebrush (69)
C D Buckwheat (76)

C   Sages (81) (97)
C   Iris (88)
C D Feather dalea (103)
C D Brittlebush (105)
C   St. Catherine's lace (109)
C D Sulphur flower (109)
C D Penstemon (117) (118) (119)
C D Sages (121) (122) (123)
C D Globe mallow (124)
C   Woolly bluecurls (128)
C D Verbena (129)
    D Desert onion lily (134)
C   Onion lily (134)
C D Fleabane daisy (136)
C D California gold poppy (137)
C   Clematis (142)

C Chaparral   D Desert

hungry rabbits—and curious toddlers; a number of the herbs have such strong properties that even a few leaves can have an effect. A medicinal herb garden, like a swimming pool, requires some commonsense precautions.

Part of this garden area must have direct sun; herbs need lots of it to best bring out their flavors and medicinal properties. If your backyard has an established old tree, take advantage of its shade and place the work area beneath its boughs. If you don't have a tree, plant one. Acacia, mesquite, ironwood, cottonwood, and oak not only provide shade but also have herbal properties themselves. Of course, you'll have to wait for this tree to grow up, so in the meanwhile put up a temporary roof, or ramada, made of beams or branches. You can also use some sort of shade cloth, but I prefer the more natural, rustic look.

The tops of several kinds of wild onions—stronger tasting than cultivated onions, were used to flavor food and as a source of vitamin C.

The work area measures approximately 10 feet square and contains a worktable and bench. Above the work area is an arbor with beams or poles for hanging the herbs to dry. The wall should be high enough to provide protection from the wind, but not as high as the arbor in order to ensure good air circulation around the curing herbs. A seat beneath the herbs offers a pleasant spot for viewing the garden while enjoying the pungent fragrances of the harvest.

In the other corner, where the roofs come together, is a cistern. A sluice from the roof guides rainwater into the cistern to be used for irrigation and also for washing and mixing.

I've indicated a network of paths throughout the garden, giving you easy access to the plantings. These can be of beaten-down earth, decomposed granite, or, in the Chihuahuan Desert, compressed caliche—the hard white alkaline residue that accumulates when there is not enough water to wash the minerals through the soil, known locally as "chat."

Some larger shrubs around the garden provide additional shade and visual interest, and there are a number of options, depending on the region. For example, for California chaparral, either barberry or coffeeberry can be planted by the house; they both take shade very well. But in the desert, select one of the desert barberries. When faced with choices, consult the plant profiles and pick the plant that best matches your locale and your needs.

Moonlight

FOR ROMANCE, AS ANY SONGWRITER OR LOVESTRUCK COUPLE KNOWS, A GARDEN NEEDS moonlight. That's why I placed the courtyard on the south side of the house–this gives you the greatest amount of time to watch the moon traverse the night sky.

The walls of the house, the walls of the garden, and the paving materials are all pale cream colored–a warm ivory white that shows well by moonlight without taking on the eerie blue of white surfaces at night. The wooden trim and the outdoor furniture are pale sage green–the true color of silvery foliaged plants–and the pots on the step are large and glazed with celadon, that lovely pale-green Chinese glaze. All the foliage in this garden is ever-green–or, more precisely, ever*silver*–so the change of seasons is marked by which flowers are in bloom at different times of year. Most of the blossoms are white to lavender–highly visible in moonlight. With the flowers comes a bonus: the night-pollinating creatures. It is quite exciting to see a large delicate hawk moth hover over a blossom and draw out nectar with its slender 5-inch tongue. It is equally thrilling to watch soft-furred bats fluttering their webbed-finger wings as they bury their heads into a saguaro flower or their tongues into an agave bloom.

Despite their "evil" B-movie reputation, bats are delightful creatures and are very necessary to our ecosystem. Saguaro and its cousins and the agaves depend primarily on nectar-feeding bats to pollinate their flowers and make fertile seeds for the next generation. The lesser long-nosed bat and the Mexican long-tongued bat are the principal species in the United States. Since these bats also eat the fruit as they migrate back to Mexico for the winter, they are an important vehicle for seed dispersal. The numbers of young saguaro and agaves are not as high as they should be, and the decline in numbers of pollinating bats is the main reason. Other species of bats, such as the Mexican free-tailed bats, have a great appetite for mosquitoes, and pallid bats feed half on nectar and half on insects.

The plan for the moonlight garden has been designed for chaparral and desert. The first number recommends a plant palette for the southern California chaparral, and the second number is for desert plants. Gardeners in the Chihuahuan or northern Mojave deserts may

The best time to sit outdoors is in the cool of the evening. The brilliant daytime colors don't show up, of course, but silvery foliage does. And so do white flowers that are pollinated by moths and bats. This silvery garden is lovely in daylight also. It was designed by landscape architect Nancy Wagner to match the soft gray exterior of an office building in Phoenix. Gray, pale blue, or white-foliaged plants are ironwood (which also has silvery trunks), desert spoon, pink fairyduster, Baja fairyduster (*Calliandra californica*), jojoba, brittlebush, pale blue-green desert agave, and pretty dalea.

Garden

Moonlight Garden

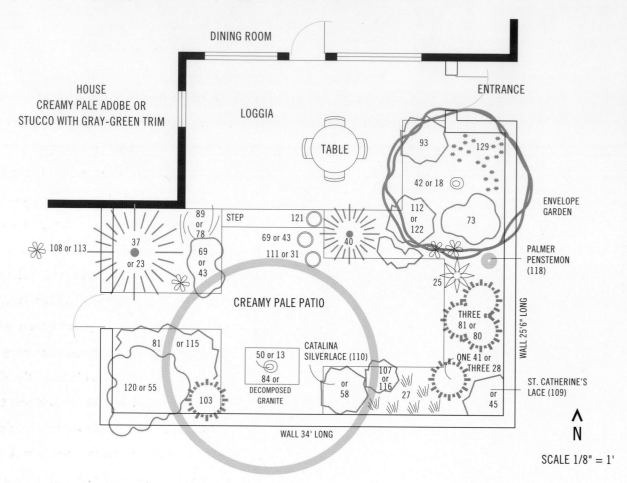

DINING ROOM

HOUSE
CREAMY PALE ADOBE OR
STUCCO WITH GRAY-GREEN TRIM

ENTRANCE

LOGGIA

TABLE

93   129

42 or 18

112
or
122   73

ENVELOPE
GARDEN

89
or
78   STEP   121

108 or 113   37
or 23   69 or 43

69
or
43   111 or 31   40

PALMER
PENSTEMON
(118)

25

THREE
81 or
80

WALL 25'6" LONG

CREAMY PALE PATIO

81   or 115

50 or 13

CATALINA
SILVERLACE (110)

84 or
DECOMPOSED
GRANITE

107
or
116

ONE 41 or
THREE 28

ST. CATHERINE'S
LACE (109)

120 or 55

103

or
58   27   or
45

WALL 34' LONG

∧
N

SCALE 1/8" = 1'

	WHITE FLOWERS						
C	D	Roemer acacia (1)		D	Palmilla (23)	C	California fescue (85)
C		Redshanks (2)	C	D	Desert agave (24)	C D	Elymus (89)
	D	Saguaro (4)	C	D	New Mexico agave, etc. (25)	C D	Desert marigold (99)
C	D	Desert willow–white (8)	C	D	Ajamete (27)	C D	Fairyduster selection (101)
C	D	Fragrant ash (10)	C	D	Desert spoon (28)	C D	Pretty dalea (103)
	D	Joshua tree (21)	C	D	Candelilla (31)	C D	Silver dalea (103)
	D	Tree yuccas (22) (23)		D	Wolf's beargrass (37)	C D	Brittlebush (105)
C	D	Texas falseagave (33)	C	D	Santa Rita prickly pear (38)	C D	Panamint daisy (106)
	D	Mojave yucca (40)		D	Banana yucca (40)	C	Zauschneria (107)
C		White lilac (46)		D	Our Lord's candle (41)	C	Seaside daisy (108)
C	D	Littleleaf cordia (49)	C		Blue manzanita (42)	C D	Sulphur flower (109)
	D	Arizona cottontop (74)	C	D	Desert holly (43)	C	St. Catherine's lace (109)
C	D	Starleaf Mexican orange (83)	C	D	Woolly butterflybush (45)	C	Catalina silverlace (110)
C		Island alumroot (87)			Channel Island tree poppy (50)	C	Golden yarrow (110)
C		Douglas iris selection (88)	C	D	Desert lavender (55)	C	Corethrogyne (111)
C	D	Mexican plumbago (93)	C	D	Boquillas silverleaf (58)	C	Evergreen lupine (112)
C	D	Blackfoot daisy (113)	C	D	Cenizo (58)	C D	Mesa greggia (115)
	D	Birdcage primrose (116)	C	D	Jojoba (66)	C D	Fragrant evening primrose (116)
C	D	Dwarf white zinnia (132)	C	D	Bursage (68)	C D	Palmer penstemon (118)
C		Onion lily (134)	C	D	Coastal sagebrush (69)	C D	Matilija poppy (120)
C		Pipestems, ropevine (142)		D	Gregg dalea (73)	C D	Cleveland sage (121)
			C	D	Chihuahuan bull muhly (78)	C D	Dorri sage (122)
		SILVERY FOLIAGE	C	D	Guayule, mariola (80)	C D	Globe mallow selection (124)
	D	Ironwood (13)	C		San Miguel mountain sage (81)		D	Plume tiquilia (127)
	D	Fremont cottonwood (16)	C		White sage (81)	C D	Goodding's verbena (129)
C	D	Smoketree (18)	C		Santa Catalina dudleya (84)	C D	Desert wild grape (146)
			C		Chalk dudleya (84)			

C *Chaparral*   D *Desert*

substitute more cold-hardy plants for ironwood (13), smoketree (18), candelilla (31), and desert lavender (55). If there is only one number, the plant indicated can be used by gardeners in both habitats.

This garden is strongly visual because banana yucca, Our Lord's candle, desert spoon, Wolf's beargrass, and palmilla are all spiky plants with stiff leaves that cast dramatic shadows. They, along with the blue manzanita (or smoketree) in the corner near the entrance gate and the Matilija poppy (or desert lavender) in the southwest corner, provide the height. Everything else is usually 4 feet tall or less and soft rather than crisp in texture.

Moth larvae will probably browse some of the seedpods and foliage, but they will not do serious harm and should be left alone. Fastidious gardeners who think everything must be untouched and "perfect" end up with sterile and unnatural-looking gardens. The reward for taking a more naturalistic viewpoint is that the larvae turn into attractive moths. The primrose moth has a special relationship with the fragrant evening primrose, as does the yucca moth with, logically, all the yuccas. The moths pollinate the flowers and lay their eggs at the same time; the plant produces fertile seeds so it can reproduce, and the moth larvae feed on some of the seeds when they hatch to give them a good

A saguaro flower is pollinated by two lesser long-nosed bats seeking nectar for dinner.

start on life. It's an elegant arrangement ensuring the continuation of both species. The queen and monarch butterflies have a similar relationship with ajamete and other milkweeds.

Nectar-rich flowers attract moths, butterflies, hummingbirds, and the black-and-orange tarantula hawk, which is really a wasp. These flowers are often fragrant, and the silvery foliage is usually aromatic. Since scents are often stronger at night, the moonlight garden will be both sweet and spicy.

This is a very drought-tolerant garden; silvery-leaved plants have a strong aversion to getting too wet. Maintenance will consist mostly of grooming and sometimes digging up and replanting. Many of these plants tend to wander around by root or seed, so the following year you may find that while you still have all the same plants, the layout of your garden is a little different. This is perfectly fine and nothing to worry about.

One last piece of advice: Don't delay too long in putting in a moonlight garden. Scientists confirm that the moon is gradually pulling away from the Earth, and in a million years or so it will not look nearly so romantic.

Thornless

ROAMING AROUND IN THE WILDS OF ARIZONA ONE DAY, OUR COMPANION STOPPED TO gingerly extract some sharp burrs. "Everything out here," he grumbled wearily, "either sticks you, stings you, stabs you, or bites you." Conversely, we have another friend who is fond of saying, "In nature, nothing is always always and nothing is never never." Exceptions abound. So I am pleased to report that it is quite possible to have a desert or chaparral landscape around your home that is both beautiful and safe, one you can enjoy without first donning shin guards and heavy work gloves.

The thornless garden is meant to be as safe as possible. If you are surrounded by dogs, cats, and small children, this is the kind of landscape you need. It is also ideal for gardeners who work long hours, never have enough money, and never have enough time. It doesn't feature a pool, because a pool uses a lot of water, involves regular maintenance, and means that the children have to be watched constantly. And it doesn't have a lawn, because a lawn wastes water, involves lots of work, and is not necessary for playing catch with the kids. Instead, children can play on the swing set and in the wading pool and the fort or playhouse, and still enjoy—and learn from—the endlessly fascinating natural world itself. The more indigenous species you use, the more flowers, scents, and seeds there will be to appreciate; the more butterflies, beetles, lizards, and other delightful creatures there will be to watch.

The garden starts right next to the house with the covered patio. It is somewhat skimpy as usual (contractors are always building on a tight budget), so there are additional patios for adult dining, children's toys, and just more room to stroll. Two trees give shade to these areas. Any of the trees or shrubs in list A on the plan will do—just look them up to find out which ones will grow best for you and then choose the two that fit your needs or taste.

This patio area—the left third of the backyard—is primarily for the adults. Plan to have a drip irrigation system here, and use selections from list B for screening and those from list C for knee-high interest. Right around the patio in the bare spaces on the plan, you can have decomposed granite for easiest upkeep. For a solid mat of green in the shade, use dudleya or strawberry or Mexican evening primrose. Where trees are too small to make shade, plant

Fleabane daisy, verbena, Indian blanket (*Gaillardia* spp.), desert marigold, and pretty dalea frame a garden path of decomposed granite at the Frieder home in Phoenix. Landscape architect Christy Ten Eyck created this scene. These are just a few of the many native plants that are drought-tolerant but also have no thorns, spines, poisonous leaves, or toxic berries that can harm children.

Garden

Thornless Garden

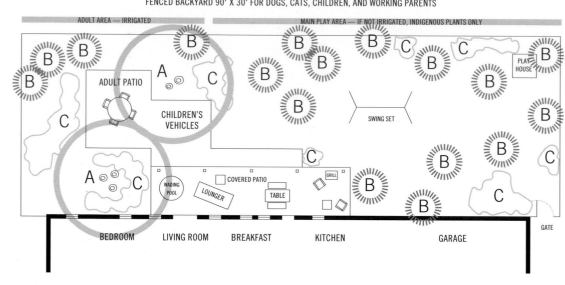

FENCED BACKYARD 90' X 30' FOR DOGS, CATS, CHILDREN, AND WORKING PARENTS

ADULT AREA — IRRIGATED

MAIN PLAY AREA — IF NOT IRRIGATED, INDIGENOUS PLANTS ONLY

ADULT PATIO

CHILDREN'S VEHICLES

PLAY HOUSE

SWING SET

WADING POOL

COVERED PATIO

GRILL

LOUNGER

TABLE

BEDROOM   LIVING ROOM   BREAKFAST   KITCHEN   GARAGE   GATE

N

SCALE 1/16" = 1"

A—MAY GET 20' BROAD OR MORE

C		Redshanks (2)	C		Flowering ash (10)	C		Manzanita (42)
C		Chamise (2)	C	D	Goldenball leadtree (11)	C		San Diego summer holly (48)
C	D	Netleaf hackberry (5)	C		Catalina ironwood (12)	C		Tree poppy (50)
C	D	Foothill paloverde (6)	C		Torrey pine (14)	C		Fremontia (53)*
C	D	Western or Mexican redbud (7)	C		Western sycamore (15)	C	D	Sugarbush (65)
C	D	Desert willow (8)	C	D	Cottonwood (16)	C		California bay (67)*
C	D	Fragrant ash (10)	C		Coast live oak (19)			

B—MAY GET 60' BROAD OR MORE

C	D	Most Mormon teas (30)	C	D	Hopbush (51)*	C		Coffeeberry (62)
C	D	Chuparosa (36)	C	D	Apache-plume (52)	C		Lemonadeberry (63)
C	D	Woolly butterflybush (45)	C	D	Desert lavender (55)	C		Laurel-leaf sumac (63)*
C		Santa Barbara ceanothus (46)	C	D	Bladderpod (56)		D	Littleleaf sumac (64)
C		White lilac (46)		D	Creosote bush (57)*	C	D	Jojoba (66)
C		Woollyleaf ceanothus (47)	C	D	Cenizo (58)		D	Desert broom (70)
C	D	Littleleaf cordia (49)	C		Baja birdbush (59)			

C—SMALL STUFF

C	D	Ajamete (27)	C	D	Oniongrass (77)	C	D	Mexican evening primrose (91)
	D	Candelilla (31)*	C	D	Muhly grasses (78)	C		Ferns (92) (94)
C	D	Red yucca (34)		D	Mariola, guayule (80)	C	D	Mexican plumbago (93)*
	D	Leatherstem (35)	C		Sages (81) (97)	C		Evergreen currant (96)
	D	Desert holly (43)	C		Columbine (82)	C		Snowberry (98)*
C	D	Coastal sagebrush (69)	C	D	Starleaf Mexican orange (83)			
C		Coyote brush (70)	C		Dudleya (84)	99 – 146 are safe except for
C	D	Grama grasses (71)	C		California fescue (85)	Globe mallow (124)*
C	D	Damianita or dogweed (72)	C		Strawberry (86)	
C	D	Gregg dalea (73)	C		Island alumroot (87)	*may have a chemical substance that
	D	Arizona cottontop (74)	C		Douglas iris (88)	causes a reaction in some people
	D	Turpentinebush (75)	C	D	Elymus (89)	
C	D	California buckwheat (76)	C	D	Bamboo muhly (90)	

C Chaparral   D Desert

Designed by landscape architect Ann Christoph, this bench, shaded by a western sycamore and surrounded by gentle flowers, ground covers, and native evergreens such as lemonadeberry, makes a safe retreat for Leah Heidenrich and her small children.

blue (or black) grama. Let it grow several inches high and become soft and billowy so that it needs mowing just a couple of times a year. Notice that there are subtle openings from the patios to a viewing area where the fence overlooks the front yard. The family dog will make such paths or openings anyway, so incorporate his routes into the garden design.

The right (or eastern) two-thirds of the backyard is the children's play area. Here the ground cover is decomposed granite. To allow children the freedom to dig, don't install an irrigation system in this area. Plant the shrubs from list B to give screening and lots of shelter for playing games. The spacing shown is for gardens without irrigation and planted with indigenous shrubs. The size of these shrubs drawn on the plan is the mature size for desert shrubs and the size typical for very young chaparral shrubs. Eventually chaparral shrubs will touch and give complete screening. From the back gate to the patio area, space the shrubs far enough apart to make a path wide enough for adults. For color and interest, add clumps and drifts from list C where indicated. Make sure that the playhouse/fort is buried in the wilderness and that there is plenty of space around the swing set for high swings and jumps.

Fragr

Just one Small's huisache can perfume an entire garden. Other flowers here are red Eaton's penstemon, pink Parry's penstemon, Indian blanket (*Gaillardia* spp.), desert lupine, and desert marigold. After a rain, the special fragrance of creosote bush permeates the garden. This courtyard is part of the Frieder home landscape in Phoenix designed by landscape architect Christy Ten Eyck.

ance Garden

SOUTHWESTERN PLANTS ARE, I BELIEVE, AMONG THE MOST FRAGRANT. MAYBE THIS IS nature's compensation for putting them in such demanding environments. Anyone who has ever walked in the desert after a rain knows the sharp, tarry, green-and-alive fragrance of creosote. California sagescrub is another heady olfactory experience. Its mint-leaved and mint-flowered sages combine with astringent coastal sagebrush (an artemisia) and nectar-sweet blossoms to make a special blend of scents that I find quite addictive. And then there is the perfume of huisache or Roemer acacia, each every bit as strong and romantic as the scent of orange blossoms. I think that it is this splendid mixture of floral perfume and herbal scents that makes the gardens of southern California and the Southwest so magical.

The leaves have herbal pungency because the special scent of the plant is stored in oil glands. This is an ancient way of conserving moisture that would otherwise be lost through transpiration, since oil doesn't evaporate as quickly as water. Also, some browsing animals are discouraged if they don't like the taste. The warmth (or heat) of the sun acts on these oils and sends out a wide range of scents, from tangy to sharp to mellow.

The sweetness of the flowers is released to attract pollinators—bees, hummingbirds, butterflies, nectar-feeding bats, moths, and the tarantula hawk.

None of these plants had us humans in mind at all during their evolution. Still, they give us so much pleasure that I have grouped together those that are the most intensely fragrant—at least to our noses. Most can be used anywhere in the areas covered by this book, but there are alternative suggestions for the few that have limitations.

The planting areas in this plan are all easily accessible from the patio and walk, and they should give you some good ideas on how to treat small spaces without lining up flowers in a rigid border. The loggia is both a covered porch and an entrance patio. The bench (from which the garden scents can be enjoyed) and olla (a large earthern jar, usually for water storage or cooking but used here to hold a collection of walking sticks) give interest by the front door in a dark, dry, airless space where plants would not thrive.

Fragrance Garden

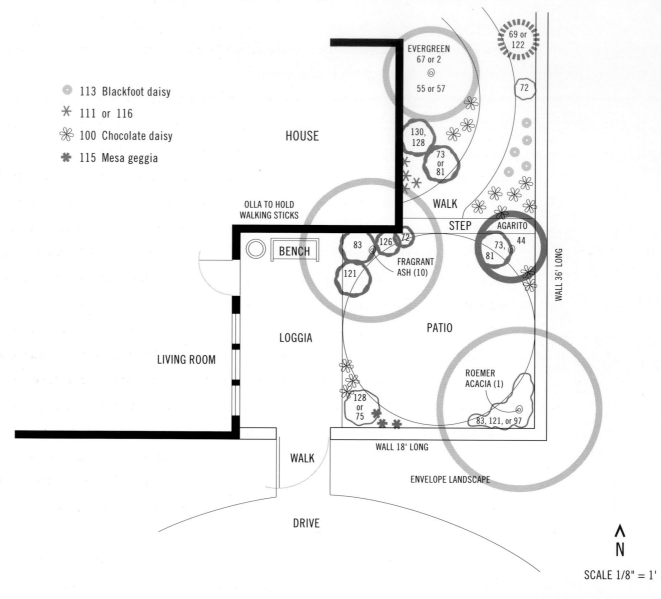

Legend:
- ⊙ 113 Blackfoot daisy
- ✳ 111 or 116
- ✳ 100 Chocolate daisy
- ✳ 115 Mesa geggia

Labels within plan: HOUSE, EVERGREEN 67 or 2, 55 or 57, 69 or 122, 72, 130 128, 73 or 81, WALK, OLLA TO HOLD WALKING STICKS, STEP, AGARITO, 73, 81, 44, BENCH, 83, 126, 72, FRAGRANT ASH (10), 121, WALL 36' LONG, PATIO, LOGGIA, LIVING ROOM, ROEMER ACACIA (1), 128 or 75, 83, 121, or 97, WALK, WALL 18' LONG, ENVELOPE LANDSCAPE, DRIVE, SCALE 1/8" = 1', N

C D	Small's huisache (1)*	
C D	Whitethorn (1)*	
C D	Roemer acacia (1)*	
C	Redshanks (2)*	
C D	Blue paloverde (6)*	
C D	Fragrant ash (10)*	
C D	Goldenball leadtree (11)*	
C D	Torrey mesquite (17)*	
C D	Tornillo (17)*	
C D	Red barberry (44)*	
D	Agarito (44)*	
C	Nevin's barberry (44)*	
C	Chaparral whitethorn (47)*	
C D	Desert lavender (55)*†	

D	Creosote bush (57)†	
C	California bay (67)*†	
C D	Coastal sagebrush (69)†	
C D	Damianita (72)†	
C D	Gregg dalea (73)*	
D	Turpentinebush (75)†	
C D	Starleaf Mexican orange (83)*†	
C	Sages (81) (97)*†	
C D	Chocolate daisy (100)*	
C	Brittlebush (105)*	
C	Corethrogyne (111)†	
C D	Blackfoot daisy (113)*	
C D	Mesa greggia (115)*	
C D	Fragrant evening primrose (116)*	

C	Matilija poppy (120)*	
C D	Sages (121) (122) (123)†	
C D	Mountain marigold (126)†	
C	Woolly bluecurls (128)†	
C D	Verbenas (129)*	
C D	Skeletonleaf goldeneye (130)†	
C D	Sand verbena (133)*	
C D	Onion lilies (134)†	
C D	Arroyo lupine (138)*	

* has sweetly scented flowers
† has aromatic foliage

C *Chaparral*   D *Desert*

The fragrance plants don't bloom all at once but have a sequence. For Californians, the first to bloom is the California bay, whose green flowers release their spicy scents in winter. Just as there is a hint of spring in the air, the agarito bursts forth into golden yellow flowers that are strongly sweet, but not cloying. The Roemer acacia will be next—a mass of creamy, fuzzy, globelike flowers that will delightfully perfume the whole garden area. Next in turn is the fragrant ash—a show of brilliantly white, fringelike flowers laden with a sweet scent as delicate as new-mown hay.

As the mildness of spring quickly heats up, blackfoot daisy and mesa greggia release their honey scents, which seem to be most intense in the hottest part of the day. Chocolate daisy really smells like chocolate, and one plant can make a garden into a Neuhaus shop. I used many in the plan because I'm a chocaholic, but for those of you who are not addicts, two plants would be sufficient. Always plant at least two of any of these low-growing, everblooming flowers, because they are short-lived. Two plants increases the likelihood of fertile seeds. They are best in masses, where they self-seed prolifically, with one seedling always there to replace an older plant that dies. If some seedlings appear where they aren't wanted, baby rosettes can always be transplanted in the fall.

In the blistering heat of full summer, blooms are scattered at best and fragrance will be appreciated only at night when you venture out of air-conditioning. This is a time when the foliage scents predominate, the oil glands having been activated by the intense heat of the day. Turpentinebush, bluecurls, starleaf Mexican orange, mountain marigold, skeletonleaf goldeneye, desert lavender, and the salvias are the aromatic-leaved plants drawn on this plan, although you will find others on the list. Their aromas become so concentrated during the summer that the leaves are too strong for cooking, but they still give the garden a freshness and an affirmation of life that are a welcome defiance to the heat that causes so many leaves, flowers, and creatures to go dormant.

As fall rolls around, cooler evenings invite many autumn flowers to appear and some spring flowers to bloom again. Canyon sage, canyon marigold, corethrogyne, and skeletonleaf goldeneye are primarily late-summer to winter flowering. In the Southwest, however, bloom times are not as rigid as they are in some climates; your fragrances may get scrambled. Plants are quick to take advantage of cooler temperatures, higher humidity, and actual rain—whatever time of year it happens. There is only one sure thing—on any day, in any month, all year long, there will be something sweet scented or aromatic in the fragrance garden.

Songbird

Songbirds are found in greatest numbers along creeks or wherever there is enough moisture for drinking and bathing and for trees to grow for nesting and cover. Under the trees are shade-loving ground-cover plants and flowers. All provide fruits, insects, nesting materials, or hiding places for songbirds. To imitate this environment, Roy and Ysabel Fetterman of Pasadena scooped out a short dry wash in their previously level front yard to collect rainfall. A bridge connects the simple foot paths that wind through the garden. In this scene, taken on the last day in March, Douglas iris, blue-eyed grass, red columbine, and woody morning glory are in bloom. In a bright spot of sunshine, there is a sun-loving bladderpod. This garden looks as charming in August as it does in the spring, even though the Fettermans rarely water or weed.

A GARDEN IS FOR ALL THE SENSES, AND NOT THE LEAST OF THEM IS THE SENSE OF HEAR-ing. Unfortunately, the garden sounds most commonly heard are power mowers, leaf blowers, and electric pruners. These are the tools that shape the typical American landscape. The yard becomes an artifact, overly controlled and out of synch with nature. It is not a welcoming environment for wildlife–least of all songbirds.

Songbirds contribute to our enjoyment of a garden on many levels. First, obviously, are the trilled and warbled melodies of thrushes, kinglets, blackbirds, warblers, northern mockingbirds, California thrashers, and sparrows. Some people learn to recognize the distinctive calls and songs of the different species and can even identify individual birds by their voices. Of course, appearance is an equally important part of the show. So, for colorful plumage, look for orioles and goldfinches, and in the fall, if you're lucky, a vireo, western tanager, or lazuli bunting. Finally, when the garden becomes a welcoming habitat, and not just a brief stopover, songbirds offer an entirely new range of delights: the pleasures of observing their courtships, rivalries, and playful antics and of emotionally sharing the struggles of a nesting pair in raising their young.

In southern California and the Southwest, where winters are mild, songbirds are present in great numbers all year round as long as they have cover–leafy refuges to nest or hide in–and plenty to eat. In spring they build nests, lay eggs, and hatch their young. They feed their babies high-energy food–bugs. This is one big reason why spraying toxic chemicals on caterpillars, spiders, and beetles is a terrible idea; it destroys a valuable source of protein for the nestlings and thereby reduces the songbird population. Of course, another reason is that caterpillars become butterflies, spiders weave wonderfully geometric webs and ensnare mosquitoes, and beetles, many of them a gorgeous iridescent green or blue, serve a variety of housekeeping functions.

The greater portion of a songbird's diet consists of fruits, seeds, and berries. Grass seed, hackberry and redbud seed, and wild currants, cherries, and strawberries are favorites. The smaller seeds and softer fruits are easier to eat. By late summer, the young birds have learned

Garden

Songbird Garden

SCALE 1/8" = 1'

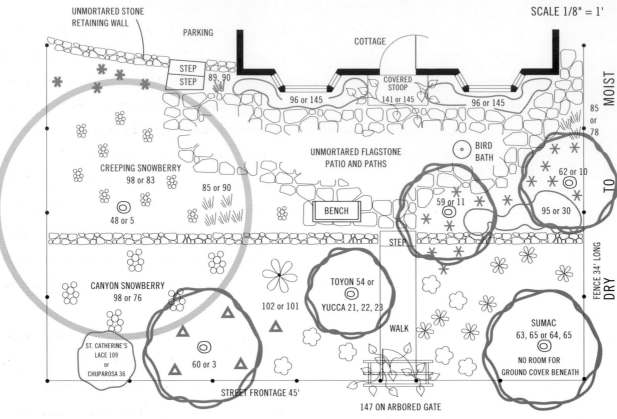

Sulphur flower (109) or desert holly (43)

Coast sunflower (104) or California poppy (137)

Grasses and ephemerals

Hummingbird sage (97) or brittlebush (105)

California strawberry (86) or Mexican evening primrose (91)

CALIFORNIA SONGBIRD GARDEN

Tall–Moist* and Sunny
Western redbud (7)
California flowering ash (10)
Catalina ironwood (12)
Torrey pine (14)
Western sycamore (15)
Fremont cottonwood (16)
Channel Island summer
   holly (48)
Catalina cherry (60)
Coffeeberry (62)
Lemonadeberry (63)
California bay (67)
Woody morning glory (141)

Short–Moist* and Shady
California fescue (85)
California strawberry (86)
Fuchsia flowering
   currant (95)
Evergreen currant (96)
Creeping sage (97)
Creeping snowberry (98)

Tall–Dry† and Sunny
Redshanks (2)
Coast live oak (19)
Blue manzanita (42)
Refugio manzanita (42)
Ceanothus (46) (47)
San Diego summer holly (48)
Tree poppy (50)
Fremontia (53)
Toyon (54)
Baja birdbush (59)
Hollyleaf cherry (60)
California scrub oak (61)
Lemonadeberry (63)
Laurel-leaf sumac (63)
Sugarbush (65)
Coast sunflower (104)
Sulphur flower (109)
St. Catherine's lace (109)
Desert wild grape (146)

Short–Dry† and Shady
California buckwheat (76)
Beach strawberry (86)
Elymus (89)
Hummingbird sage (97)
Canyon snowberry (98)
Giant correopsis (102)

DESERT SONGBIRD GARDEN

Tall–Moist* and Sunny
Netleaf hackberry (5)
Granjeno (5)
Mexican redbud (7)
Fragrant or California
   flowering ash (10)
Goldenball leadtree (11)
California fan palm (20)
Red barberry (44)
Hopbush (51)
Sugarbush (65)
Canyon grape (146)

Short–Moist* and Shady
California buckwheat (76)
Starleaf Mexican orange (83)
Bamboo muhly (90)
Mexican evening primrose (91)
Thicket creeper (145)

Short–Moist* and Sunny
Deergrass (78)
Fleabane daisy (136)

Tall–Dry†and Sunny
Canotia (3)
Saguaro (4)
Ocotillo (9)
Tree yuccas (21) (22) (23)
Chollas (39)
Desert holly (43)
Desert lavender (55)
Littleleaf sumac (64)

Short–Dry†and Sunny
Claret-cup cactus (29)
Mormon tea (30)
Chuparosa (36)
Beavertail (38)
Desert holly (43)
Bush muhly (78)
Mariola, guayule (80)
Pink fairyduster (101)
Brittlebush (105)
California gold poppy (137)

* *irrigation once a month to once a week*
† *irrigation no more than once a month and by drip only;*
   no sprinklers

how to find their own food, with San Diego summer holly providing the main fresh fruit in southern California. Otherwise, their diet consists primarily of grasshoppers and other insects, and even small lizards.

Fall brings in birds that nested farther north or up in the mountains, so there has to be several times more food to go around. Lots of fresh fruits and nuts ripen at this time—acorns, snowberry, sugarbush and other sumac berries, tunas from cacti, coffeeberry, wild grape, buckwheat seeds, and more grass seeds. Some of these, such as coffeeberry and cac-

Cactus wrens usually build their nests in cholla, but here one has chosen a paloverde.

tus fruits, are soft and juicy, as are the spring fruits; they must be eaten quickly before they spoil. Most are drier and have a longer shelf life, providing a steady source of nourishment through the winter. These fruits attract the smaller, more polite birds. Store-bought sunflower seeds attract the scrub jay, the raven, and European starlings, which are often humorous characters to watch but are definitely the raucous, rougher element in bird society.

This plan can be adapted for both chaparral and desert. In southern California, it will be a shady garden, where the shade-loving flowers and grasses provide as much food as do the trees and shrubs. In the desert, it will be sunnier, attracting those birds that prefer open spaces.

The particular inspiration for the layout of this plan was a cottage garden in Laguna Beach shown to us by its landscape architect, Jana Ruzicka, whose lovely Czech surname means "little rose." We took no photos here because it was primarily a nonnative rose garden, yet it displayed the perfect setting for a bird garden, with a tiny meadow along the drive and a steep drop to a creek behind the house.

On the plan, imagine that the street is quite a bit higher than the cottage. A low fence or wall next to the curb surrounds the front yard, which is entered through a front gate under a tiny arbor draped with drought-tolerant wild grape. The path and the whole upper tier of the garden slope gently for about 12 feet down to a stone retaining wall, which has been left unmortared to allow spiders, lizards, and other creatures important in songbird habitats to thrive in the crevices between the stones.

In the chaparral version of this plan, a lemonadeberry on the right shields the house from the street. Although pruned on the street side because of traffic, it is allowed to grow quite large on the garden side, where it is so dense that nothing grows beneath it. Birds love

sumacs for both cover and food. To the left of the path is a toyon, pruned up to be treelike so you can walk under the shelter of its branches. To its left, closer to the street, is a hollyleaf cherry. Underneath the toyon is a ground cover of beach strawberry, and underneath the cherry is a ground cover of hummingbird sage. These ground covers will not remain pure without some effort, since a forest of bird-planted toyons, cherries, and all the other seeds from the garden will appear there to be weeded out each year. This should be done in the winter when the soil is wet and it's easy to pull them out by the roots.

In the desert version, littleleaf sumac is as large and dense as the lemonadeberry, but there

the resemblance ends. Instead of small shady trees, there is space and sunlight. A tree yucca towers over the path, and a canotia by the fence provides both nesting within its thorns and ripe seed. If a canotia is too cold-tender for you, use an ocotillo to attract orioles; they sip nectar from its flowers. Underneath are sunny ground covers–brittlebush, desert holly, fairyduster–and a sprinkling of California gold poppy.

The lower level contains plants that require more moisture. In chaparral, use Channel Island summer holly, coffeeberry, and Baja birdbush. In the desert, here is an opportunity to enjoy fragrant ash, goldenball leadtree, and the shade of a large hackberry. The chaparral trees are evergreen. The desert trees have bright flowers and delicate shade in the summer; they are bare-branched in winter but are still decorated with dangles of nourishing seed.

The walk on the lower level is replaced by a flagstone patio. The front door is in a direct line with the gate at the street and is also covered with an arbor or a little roof. For chaparral gardeners, this structure could support a woody morning glory, which would not only frame the doorway with pale pink blossoms for many months of the year but would also produce a steady supply of little tan capsules that contain the tiny seeds that are just the right size for finches. Desert gardeners could use thicket creeper, with its blue berries, red stems, and red fall color. Where it is unsupported by the arbor, it will creep along the foundation of the house to make a ground cover.

A birdbath should be set on the patio far from a tree or any other place where a cat can lurk unseen. If cleaning out the bath and replenishing the water every day sounds like too much work, consider a fountain, a tiny shallow pool, or a disguised emitter that drips into a dish. There are lots of ways to provide the water songbirds need. Just follow these guidelines: The water must be fresh; it must be shallow enough for bird bathing; and it must be out in the open where predators have no place to hide within pouncing distance. Be sure to keep the birdbath clean and free of debris. Of course, if a neighbor already has a birdbath, or there is some other reliable source of water within a block or so of your garden, then you won't have to provide water for your birds.

Next to the house and by the driveway, plant an abundance of grasses, low shrubs, and flowers, and then be sure to let them go to seed in the fall to produce a bounty for songbirds migrating through your area to their winter homes farther south.

Except during periods of drought, this garden can survive on normal rainfall. But it will look its best if watered once a month when the weather is hot and dry. Except for the birdbath, maintenance need be no more than an annual weeding out of bird-planted seedlings and pruning out dead wood or ungraceful growth on the shrubs.

Hummingb

HUMMINGBIRDS ARE A VISUAL DELIGHT IN YOUR GARDEN. BUT TO ATTRACT AT LEAST some of the 13 species native to the Southwest, you have to give them what they are looking for—nourishment. Not the colored sugar water many people put in those feeders. That is hummingbird junk food and has no real food value. A hummingbird's metabolism requires more—much more.

Consider this: If an average-size man had the same metabolism as a hummingbird, he would have to consume 370 pounds of potatoes a day! No wonder hummingbirds zoom along close to the ground, keeping an eye peeled for food. Even hovering, they beat their wings at a remarkable 50 to 75 flaps *per second*.

Admittedly, a feeder will attract a lot of hummingbirds to your garden because the volume of sugar to water is so great. But what hummingbirds are really looking for is nectar—rich in proteins, trace minerals, and vitamins. Zoos have discovered that hummingbirds maintained on sugar water alone are not able to reproduce. When given a choice between sugar water and nectar (and we have friends who have experimented with this), most hummingbirds will choose the nectar. The best source of nectar is brightly colored native flowers—the kind recommended for this garden.

The plants for this hummingbird garden are generally suitable for both desert and chaparral. This garden is designed for quiet enjoyment, so I have drawn in a swing hanging from a small arbor. Chaparral gardeners can use campo pea on one side of the arbor, and island snapdragon on the other. Although it is a bush, this snapdragon can be trained to twine up the posts like a vine. Desert gardeners should substitute chuparosa for island snapdragon, and simply forget about an alternative for the campo pea; two arbor vines would look too "busy" for the more sparse desert look.

The color scheme for the garden is bright and red—all shades of red. Purple- and pink-reds are represented by desert willow, Parry's penstemon, autumn sage, and California buckwheat. Orange-reds are found in Eaton's penstemon, ocotillo, agave, zauschneria, chuparosa, and mountain sage, and bladderpod is pure yellow. Claret-cup cactus might be either

Although young, this private garden in Tustin, California, designed by Jeff Powers, is already full of perennial color. Visible at the entrance gate are a western redbud, just out of bloom, and two silvery-leaved natives—artemisia and zauschneria, often called California fuchsia. To the right is a mixture of penstemons and salvias, whose spires of red, pink, salmon, or purple (varying from month to month) provide nectar for hummingbirds from March to Thanksgiving.

Hummingbird Garden

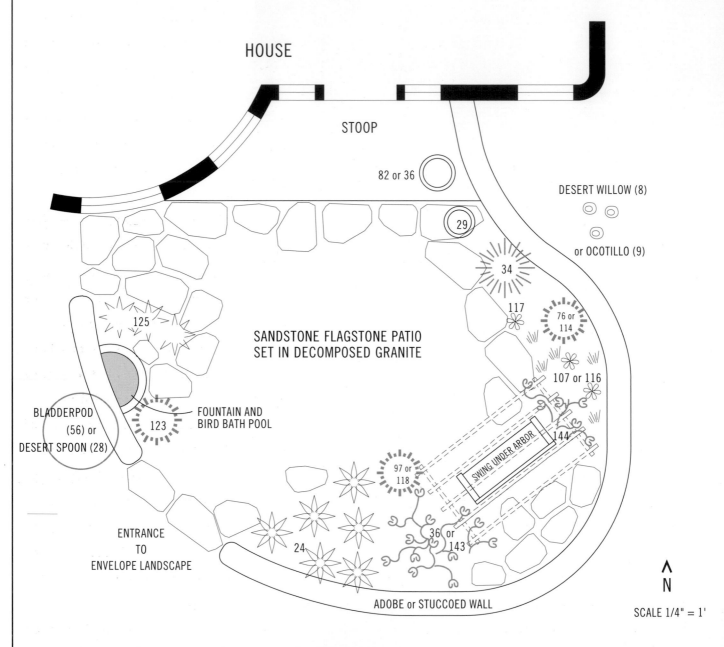

HOUSE

STOOP

82 or 36

29

34

117

76 or 114

107 or 116

125

SANDSTONE FLAGSTONE PATIO
SET IN DECOMPOSED GRANITE

DESERT WILLOW (8)

or OCOTILLO (9)

123

FOUNTAIN AND
BIRD BATH POOL

BLADDERPOD
(56) or
DESERT SPOON (28)

144

SWING UNDER ARBOR

97 or
118

24

36 or
143

ENTRANCE
TO
ENVELOPE LANDSCAPE

ADOBE or STUCCOED WALL

N

SCALE 1/4" = 1'

D Saguaro (4)	C D Desert lavender (55)	C Monkeyflower (114)
C D Paloverdes (6)	C D Bladderpod (56)	C D Fragrant evening primrose (116)
C D Desert willow (8)	C D California buckwheat (76)	C D All penstemons (117) (118) (119)
D Ocotillo (9)	C Sages (81)	C D Sages (121) (122) (123)
C D Agaves (24) (25)	C Columbines (82)	C D Scarlet betony (125)
C D Desert spoon (28)	C Douglas iris (88)	C Woolly bluecurls (128)
D Claret-cup cactus (29)	C Fuchsia flowering currant (95)	C Island snapdragon (143)
C D Red yucca (34)	C Hummingbird Sage (97)	C Campo pea (144)
C D Chuparosa (36)	C D Pink fairyduster (101)	
D Woolly butterflybush (45)	C Zauschneria (107)	

C *Chaparral*   D *Desert*

orange- or purple-red, and hummingbird sage and campo pea are pure dark red. As long as orange and purple shades of red are equally intense, they work well together, bringing out depths and highlights in each other.

A fountain provides the extra humidity and moisture preferred by autumn sage and especially by scarlet betony. In fact, there is a floater in the catch pool that activates a drip valve when the water level drops because of evaporation. Whenever more water drips into the pool, another valve drips on the scarlet betony. All the other plants are drought-tolerant, usually requiring irrigation only once a month to keep on blooming.

The exception is desert willow. It is placed outside the garden where it can be nestled into the side of a swale and where runoff from the roof can be channeled to it. It also has several drip irrigation valves buried just below ground level at intervals over its roots to keep it blooming all summer. For the envelope concept in the desert, use ocotillo instead. An existing tree that exudes healthy sweet sap in the summer can also be used by hummingbirds.

Hummingbird plants bloom most abundantly in spring and fall at hummingbird migration times, but they always have a small supply of blooms on hand during the warm and hot months, and they often have flowers during the winter as well for those few hummingbirds that winter over.

The hummingbird garden may in fact attract more butterflies than hummingbirds. As the tongues of butterflies are not as long as a hummingbird's beak, flowers that are very long, slender, and tubular are pollinated only by hummingbirds or by long-tongued moths.

Chuparosa and ocotillo withstand sun, drought, and throngs of visitors at the Anza-Borrego Desert State Park in Borrego Springs, California. Nectar-bearing honey mesquite, in the background, is important for butterflies and butterfly larvae. The other plants visible in this picture are golden-flowered brittlebush, a favorite browse of chuckwalla—a charmingly fat-tummied lizard—and the hummingbird plant desert agave.

Garden Room

A patio, an arbor, a wall or trellis, some vines, some pots, a table and chairs—it all makes an invitingly cool and shady nook for dining, visiting, observing nature, or simply enjoying a little peace and quiet, and maybe a good murder mystery. This drinking and bathing pool—open for wild animals to enjoy—is part of a covered eating area that overlooks the natural desert.

IN SOCIETIES WE CONDESCENDINGLY call primitive, people live inside their shelters only when climate and nightfall dictate. Their days are spent mostly outdoors, working, playing, communing with nature. We of course are "civilized," and so we spend most of our hours indoors, breathing recycled air and watching TV. One reason may be that we feel there is nothing outside for us; our conventional landscapes offer little to satisfy our senses and souls. This plan is designed to help change our attitudes about outdoor living.

The garden is small—just 10 feet by 20 feet—and is divided into two equal "rooms" and completely paved as a patio. It could be at an apartment or condominium or part of a tiny yard. Or it could be an intimate entrance on a large estate.

Surrounded by soft, peach-colored stucco walls, with cream limestone trim around windows and doors, the floor is covered with soft pink Mexican tiles. The foliage in the earthen pots is either silver or very dark green. The flowers are red,

Outdoor Garden Room

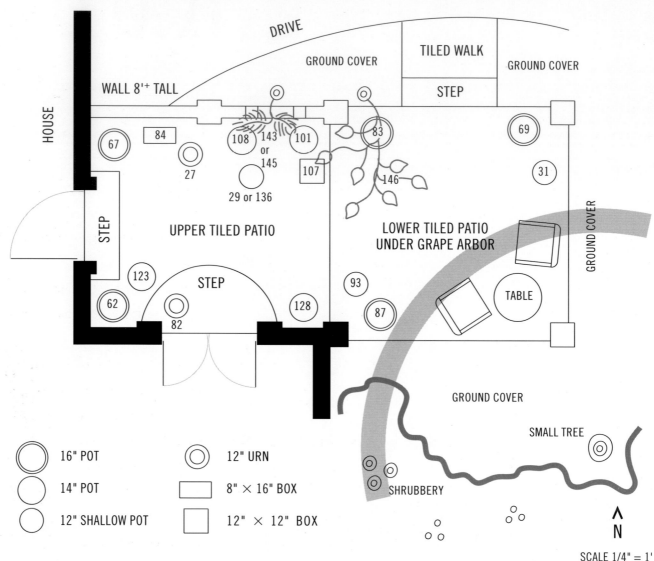

DRIVE

GROUND COVER

TILED WALK

GROUND COVER

STEP

WALL 8'+ TALL

HOUSE

67 84 27 108 143 or 145 101 107 29 or 136 146 83 69 31

STEP

UPPER TILED PATIO

LOWER TILED PATIO UNDER GRAPE ARBOR

123 62 82 STEP 128 93 87

TABLE

GROUND COVER

GROUND COVER

SMALL TREE

SHRUBBERY

N

SCALE 1/4" = 1'

16" POT   12" URN

14" POT   8" × 16" BOX

12" SHALLOW POT   12" × 12" BOX

FOR PLANTER, WINDOW, LOW TRELLIS, OR RETAINING WALL

C   Island morning glory (141)
C   Spring morning glory (141)
C   Island snapdragon (143)
C   Campo pea (144)
C D Thicket creeper (145)

FOR ARBOR, TALL TRELLIS, OR FENCE

C   Woody morning glory (141)
C   Pipestems (142)
C   Ropevine (142)
C D Desert wild grape (146)
C D Canyon grape (146)

C *Chaparral*   D *Desert*

POT PLANTS: Can be used anywhere, as long as you water and take them in the house if it gets too cold or too hot

Ajamete (27)
Claret-cup cactus (29)
Mormon tea (30)
Candelilla (31)
Chuparosa (36)
Desert holly (43)
All cenizos (58)
Coffeeberry (62)
California bay (67)
Coastal sagebrush (69)
Grama grasses (71)
Damianita (72)
Gregg dalea (73)
Guayule (80)
All sages (81) (97) (121) (122) (123)
Red columbine (82)
Starleaf Mexican orange (83)
Dudleyas (84)
Island alumroot (87)

Coffeeberry fern (92)
Mexican plumbago (93)
Desert marigold (99)
Chocolate daisy (100)
Pink fairyduster (101)
Daleas (103)
Zauschneria (107)
Seaside daisy (108)
Sulphur flower (109)
Corethrogyne (111)
Blackfoot daisy (113)
Monkeyflower (114)
Mesa greggia (115)
Mountain marigold (126)
Plume tiquilia (127)
Woolly bluecurls (128)
Wright's verbena (129)
Skeletonleaf goldeneye (130)
Fleabane daisy (136)

RIGHT: This seaside daisy called 'WR', a hybrid between *Erigeron glaucus* and an unknown erigeron, resides in a 14-inch glazed pot with a bottom saucer on a shady deck at the Santa Barbara Botanic Garden. We found it to be in bloom on our April visit and again in September. BELOW RIGHT: Candelilla in a 10-inch terra-cotta pot with no saucer withstands Texas sun and heat reflected from Margaret Kennedy's concrete patio. BELOW: This pot of island alumroot has been living under a shady tree in Pasadena, at Roy and Ysabel Fetterman's home, for 15 years. It requires one watering a week during the summer.

pink, and white; these colors set off best against the soft stucco and look more welcoming than yellow and blue, but any number of color schemes can work here.

The left (west) side of the patio is enclosed on two sides by the walls of the house and on a third side by a wall at least 8 feet high containing a Spanish-style window. Cascading over the sill of this window is island snapdragon. In the desert, replace the snapdragon with thicket creeper. Arranged around the perimeter of the west "room" are pots in varying sizes and shapes, which can be filled with plants of different heights and colors.

The right (east) side of the patio is a step lower but similarly tiled. It also has large and small patio pots, but these contain shade-tolerant plants, since this room has a roof—a wooden arbor covered with a large wild grape vine. One vine is quite enough, as it grows large and hangs over the sides, making a curtain of green. This room is supposed to feel cool and shadowy, so depending on the availability of space, surround it with a green wall of shrubbery. The nearest shrub on the plan is planted at least 5 feet away. Shrubbery gives a more crowded feeling than a smooth upright wall does. A small tree

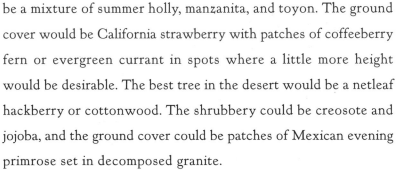

can be added to help shade the arbor. In southern California chaparral, the tree could be Catalina cherry, while the shrubbery might be a mixture of summer holly, manzanita, and toyon. The ground cover would be California strawberry with patches of coffeeberry fern or evergreen currant in spots where a little more height would be desirable. The best tree in the desert would be a netleaf hackberry or cottonwood. The shrubbery could be creosote and jojoba, and the ground cover could be patches of Mexican evening primrose set in decomposed granite.

This is not a low-maintenance garden; pots require watering at least once a day when temperatures are high and humidity is almost nonexistent. Still, the area is small and the pleasures of such a garden are sufficiently rewarding.

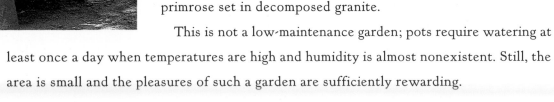

3 PLANTING AND MAINTE

Habitats can change dramatically even in a small space, as in this swale garden at Rancho Santa Ana Botanic Garden in Claremont, California. The short yellow meadow foam (*Limnanthes douglasii* ssp. *sulphurea*) vividly claims the bottom of this dry wash, where extra moisture is available, while the drier edges attract Ithuriel's spear (*Triteleia laxa*), Douglas iris, wild onion lilies, dudleya, and California gold poppy.

NATIVE PLANTS ARE ALL TOO OFTEN THE VICTIMS OF THEIR OWN GOOD PRESS. WHEN gardeners realize how hardy natives are, many of them reach a "logical" but erroneous conclusion: that natives can be brought into a landscape situation, stuck straight into the ground, and then ignored. The truth is, no matter how hardy a native plant is, it must go through a period of adjustment to its new home. And this requires giving it a degree of coddling, just as you would any newly acquired exotic plant. Unless careful steps are taken to allow the new native to acclimate itself, it will very likely be dead within a week. Native plants and native-plant gardens ultimately need less work than exotic plants and gardens, but getting them started is essentially the same. It is necessary to water any newly installed plant until it grows a network of roots so extensive it can support itself on rainfall alone. But because native plants are more drought-tolerant and independent than nonnatives, there are some major differences in planting and irrigation.

Aeration Air, which is necessary for all roots, can be driven out of soil by either compaction or watering. Compaction is caused by construction or heavy traffic. Use an aerator, a tiller, or a pitchfork to fluff the soil. A planting hole dug in untreated compacted soil will act like a patio pot, causing the roots of your plant to wrap around and around and never penetrate into the surrounding earth. Desert and chaparral plants are accustomed to high levels of oxygen–more than typical nursery fare–and they cannot tolerate soggy soil at any time, even for short periods. Plant them on a slope or a swell, never a swale. Swales are shallow depressions that catch rainwater and allow it to sink in. The natural topography of even seemingly flat landscapes is actually made up of gentle swells and swales. Plants that must always have perfect drainage–such as fremontia and cacti–grow on the swells.

This newly planted garden for Charlene Siler in Paradise Valley, Arizona, which was designed by Christy Ten Eyck, imitates the Sonoran Desert. The plants are widely spaced, with trees in the swales and cacti on the mounds. Decomposed granite prevents blowing sands, hides the drip irrigation system, retains moisture, allows air to reach root systems, makes weeds easy to pull, and provides the perfect hiding places for flower seeds so they can germinate before being eaten by birds or other desert animals. Cages of chicken wire protect especially tasty plants from being devoured by rabbits until they are large enough to survive an aggressive nibble. Across the back is 30 to 40 feet of mature creosote screening. These shrubs are planted up to 10 feet apart and not lined up, so they will look as though nature had placed them there.

Maximizing Water Many desert and chaparral plants thrive only along washes, arroyos, and streams or in ravines where water accumulates. These plants appreciate extra water and need to be planted in the swales. So contour the garden in such a way that rain running off the roof, patio, or driveway is channeled to these swales.

Spacing This can be critical in the deserts. Desert plants space themselves far apart so that they don't have to compete with each other for water. The envelope plan (page 30) illustrates sensible spacing. There should be at least 3 to 5 feet between the *mature* large desert shrubs. When desert shrubs are crowded together for screening, either they will remain stunted or they will require a drip irrigation system.

Irrigation In the wild, trees and leafy evergreens are usually small, not because of genetic characteristics, but simply because low rainfall prevents them from growing larger. But when more water is available, as in a home landscape, they can grow up to twice the size they attain in the wild. But be careful–a drought-tolerant plant that becomes accustomed to this luxurious irrigation regimen can then no longer be supported by rainfall alone. The plant will either die or sacrifice huge hunks of itself to stay alive. Large existing trees that have gotten large on their own are best left unwatered, just as long as the topography directing rainfall to them has not been changed. Magnificent old coast live oaks, saguaros, or tree yuccas are often killed by misguided watering. Rather than introducing a ground cover that needs

regular watering under a large tree, it is usually best to make a patio of decomposed granite or to use indigenous ground covers only. If you start with a nursery-grown tree and train it to the watering schedule you plan to follow, then a lusher ground cover may be used.

California chaparral plants are extremely sensitive to irrigation during the summer. Wet soil at that time provides the right conditions for water molds to kill the root system. Because the roots have rotted, they cannot take up water, and the plant wilts. "Aha!" says the gardener. "This plant needs water." And so the cycle is repeated and worsened. Studies have shown that the best way to keep these plants looking fresh in August is to water them during the traditional winter-to-early spring rainy season. Install new plants in the fall for the same reason. If rainfall is normal or above average, clearly watering is not necessary. But if rainfall is below average or if showers are spaced so far apart that drought stress is occurring, or if the rain was a real frog strangler that came down hard and ran off so fast that moisture had no chance to soak in, then you and your garden hose must make up the difference.

RIGHT: Yuccas indiscriminately dug from the wild are on their way to market. BELOW: A small bubbling fountain at the Frieder residence in Phoenix, Arizona, is not only charming, it is environmentally correct. It has a recycling pump to minimize water loss.

In the Southwest and southern California, drip irrigation systems are far more preferable than sprinkler systems, which leave too much moisture on the foliage, making the plants vulnerable to fungal diseases. The primary advantages of drip irrigation systems are that they use water more efficiently and that they are normally hidden beneath the surface, out of sight. Most professional landscapers install the systems with several outlets per tree and one for each small plant. Some lines are temporary and are turned off and forgotten once the plants have become established. Other systems are designed to be long-term. In both cases, the irrigation system is completely installed before the top mulch is laid down.

Mulches Mulches are important for holding in moisture and for protecting surface roots from extremes of heat and cold. They are also useful for trapping oxygen, preventing erosion, and maintaining a tidy appearance. Two to four inches of rock mulch is the usual application, with most landscapers favoring decomposed granite. If you saved your desert

surface by using an envelope installation (see page 30), this too would go on top of the irrigation system. There are other crushed-rock options besides decomposed granite, and these will change depending on where you live; to match the color of the natural soil, select a local variety to maintain a sense of place in the landscape. In southern California, mulches made of twigs and shredded bark are often used instead of rock.

Water Features When you live in a dry region, water becomes more than a commodity. It is a symbol of survival, a buffer against the harshness of nature, and as such must be displayed to give constant reassurance. Maybe that's why there are so many swimming pools and fountains here. A water feature for the garden that won't brand the owner as a profligate or an environmental philistine is a small recirculating fountain. Buy or make one that measures just 2 to 6 feet across and can be turned on only when someone is in the garden to enjoy the soothing sound of running water, along with the cooler air that results from evaporation.

Propagating, Growing, and Rustling Most native plants in a nursery that have been labeled "nursery-propagated" are very likely exactly that and have not been dug up illegally from the wild. Natives labeled "nursery-grown," however, are not necessarily "nursery-propagated." "Nursery-grown" indicates that the plant may have been dug from the wild, then potted at the nursery and grown there for a few weeks. Be wary of buy-

LEFT: Ron Gass shows off a supply of 5-gallon Boquillas silverleaf at Mountain States Wholesale Nursery in Glendale, Arizona. This nursery, owned by Ron and Maureen Gass, has pioneered the growing of native trees, shrubs, and flowers on a vast scale. ABOVE: Phil Hebets designed the public-area gardens for Troon Village, a middle-class community in Carefree, Arizona, including the Skye Top Clubhouse. The modestly sized front and back gardens of the homes are also supposed to be as native and natural as possible. The homeowner to the left obviously got the main idea and followed through. Unfortunately, the public areas, with their poodled shrubs and stubbed trees, have fallen prey to old-fashioned ideas of pruning.

ing a large specimen; it's probably from a poacher, not a grower. Demand to see a state or federal permit, and check with a county agricultural extension agent.

The reason a number of states have laws against taking these plants from their habitats is that so many of them are endangered. In fact, the habitats themselves are fragile and can be damaged, even destroyed, by reckless plant rustlers. In some cases, entire areas have been virtually denuded of native plants. The temptation to "plant-nap" mature plants is especially strong with slow-growing cacti and yuccas.

And yet there are those who say that the real danger to plants and habitats comes not from commercial plant poachers but from ordinary homeowners who see a particularly attractive specimen while out for a hike, dig it up, and take it home, sincerely believing that just one can't hurt. There are only two occasions when harvesting plants from the wild is acceptable: when they are in a place that will be torn up for a new highway or a building site and they would die without your intervention, and when an abundant plant not labeled as endangered is on private land and you have the owner's permission to take one.

Availability   One of the most common questions asked by beginner native gardeners is, "Where can I find native plants?" Most nurseries today carry few if any, but with more and more municipalities, highway departments, and landscape architects and designers, as well as ordinary citizens, specifying and using native plants, a young but energetic native-plant industry has begun to grow. A few wholesalers and a multitude of small nurseries are propagating native plants, giving us an extremely impressive variety to choose from—about twice as many species as you'll find in this book. Many are now being grown in large quantities and large sizes and are dependably available year after year. (The Directory on page 175 lists a selection of these sources.)

Pruning After a landscape has become established and mature, pruning becomes a significant issue. The way it is done can make or break the natural look you've been striving for. Native shrubs can be adapted to any landscape style—even the clipped look of the formal garden. However, I think this manicured approach does a disservice to the plants and keeps them from looking the way nature intended. A softer, more natural look is doubly rewarding: the shrubs look more beautiful as they achieve the shape that nature intended for them, and pruning will be an annual chore instead of one that needs to be done monthly or weekly.

Many gardens are so small that shrubs must be trained to grow to a size smaller than is natural. Eric Johnson, a landscape architect in Palm Desert, California, devised an ingenious method to retrain city maintenance crews to prune desert shrubs in a more natural style, and it is a good method for the home gardener as well. It works because it is based on traditional techniques. First, the worker prunes the shrub just the way he was trained—into a rounded ball. Then, instead of leaving the job that way, Johnson has him cut *every other* branch back to the first big V. The shrub still has a conventionally rounded shape—at least for the time being—but all those V-cuts now give it a softly irregular, more natural shape. Moreover, the shrub now needs pruning less often to look good, saving crew time and taxpayer money.

Many shrubs, especially large ones, become treelike in their old age. You may want to hasten this process, especially for shrubs such as manzanita and Baja birdbush; these have such beautiful bark, it would be a pity not to show it off. To do this, choose a few of the longest, cleanest, and prettiest stems—these will become the trunks. Cut all the others off at ground level. These stumps will irritate you by continuing to sprout for a year or so, but keep after them; they will eventually give up. With a new shrub, choose three to five stems that are growing outward away from each other and let them become your trunks. Proportions are prettiest when you have two-thirds leafy and one-third trunk if you need screening, but make it two-thirds trunk for a small tree situated alongside a path, so the branches will arch overhead. Maintaining the same plant as a 5- to 6-foot shrub will result in its either being in the way or being pruned until it looks like an unattractive tight cluster of sticks with a thin veneer of leaves.

California chaparral leafy evergreens have a natural cycle of shedding old stems and growing new ones. Since the old stems remain until burned, this can make mature, unburned chaparral look messy and half dead—which is not very attractive. If you buy land in this condition, go through and prune out only the dead wood. Some old shrubs with multitrunks will become treelike, and smaller ones will remain shrubby, but all will now be graceful and fully alive. You will be astonished and extremely pleased by the end result, which should be

To save public money and to introduce people to the beauties of native plants, city landscape architect and author Eric Johnson converted this grassy parkway in Palm Desert, California, to this colorful, water-saving, easy-maintenance garden. It has been an immense success—water savings have been enormous, and nearly every day someone calls the city to find out the name of a particular plant. To help maintenance crews learn new ways, Johnson devised an easy method for natural pruning. First, crews prune the shrub into the rounded shape they're used to, but then they pick-prune out every other branch. This keeps the shrub small, and the more natural shape looks good with fewer prunings per year. The Baja fairydusters in the picture have been shaped by this method.

maintained with yearly pruning. Leaving a picturesque dead trunk and hiding a pile of brush in an out-of-the-way corner are just two ways to help wildlife and also keep the garden attractive.

Generally, the best time to prune is spring or fall, when plants have a chance to recover. Summer pruning is almost always a mistake, often resulting in the death of the plant. Lack

of shade over the roots can deplete the plant's food reserves, making successful regrowth difficult if not impossible. Moreover, the sun can scorch the freshly exposed stems, further weakening the plant. Any plant that is looking slightly disheveled in the spring should be cut back right after blooming; this will give it a chance to let fresh growth toughen up before summer. In California, winter pruning can also prove fatal. When temperatures are cool and humidity is high, diseases are easily spread by pruning shears from one plant to another.

Whenever you cut off the tips of branches, you are affecting flowering and fruiting. Learn which plants flower on "new wood," which means they can bloom on twigs that appeared only a month or so earlier, and which bloom only on "old wood," or last season's growth. These old-wood shrubs are best pruned right after blooming, because that gives them a whole year to grow new flower-bearing twigs.

With fruit-bearing plants, however, some of the dead flowers at the branch tips must be left undisturbed to ensure a fruit crop for songbirds.

Once established, native plants can live entirely on their own. They will look better with an occasional watering in times of drought, and their beauty will be enhanced by sensitive pruning that cleans up dead material and shows off sculptural form. But even if you go off on vacation or for whatever reason simply ignore them, the odds are they'll still be around for you to make amends.

PART TWO

The building blocks of any garden are the actual plants. These profiles are designed to give gardeners the information they need to pick the right plant for any given situation. The headings in the upper portion of each profile provide all the information necessary to make this decision. Additional information, as well as personal observations and landscaping tips, can be found in the text that follows the headings. The profiles are then grouped into landscape categories to facilitate designing the garden.

HEADINGS

Common Name refers to the name or names by which the plant is most commonly known. Most plants have at least one common name, especially those plants that capture the popular imagination. If there are several common names, the one listed first is the one used elsewhere in this book. In those occurrences, it is not followed by the Latin name, because the Latin name can be found in the profile. A Latin name appearing in the text indicates a plant that may not be mentioned elsewhere in this book.

Under the heading **Latin Name** are names always printed in italics, because most of them are derived from Latin or Greek. For example, *velutina* in *Prosopis velutina* means the mesquite that is velvety, and *Baileya multiradiata* means the baileya with a multitude of radiating flower parts. Often plants are named for prominent plantsmen. *Baileya* honors Liberty Hyde Bailey (1858–1954), a horticulturist from Cornell University and one of the authors of the 1930 edition of *Hortus*.

The heading called **Native Habitat** is possibly the most important, for the information given there provides the biggest clue as to where the plant ought to be grown. If the native habitat of a plant includes the very area where you live, that plant is sure to thrive in your garden as long as it doesn't get overwatered. (For a quick summary of plants native to the metropolitan area closest to you, consult the charts of indigenous plants at the back of the book.) Occasionally, the notation RARE, ENDANGERED, THREATENED, or UNCOMMON will appear here. These are legal terms indicating that the few plants remaining in the wild are protected by the federal government.

For plants not native to your area, consult the heading **Regions of Use**. Under that heading are listed the regions where that plant has already proved successful in gardens. There are seven regions. Region 1 starts at the Pacific Ocean, and Region 7 is the Chihuahuan Desert. Consult the map on page 168 to find the number for your region. Also read the section "A Sense of Place" starting on page 13 to get a sense of how the individual plants fit into the regional landscapes.

Under **Soil**, the next heading, the soil described is fairly uniform throughout most of the Southwest in that it is alkaline, of low organic content, well drained, and dry compared with that found anywhere else in the United States. Limestone, caliche, serpentine, gypsum, clay, sand, and decomposed granite are local variations. Of course, swamps and springs are excluded from this characterization.

The heading recommending the optimum amount of irrigation is entitled **Water**. "None" indicates that the plant, when used in its native habitat, requires no supplemental water after the two-year establishment period. (See "Planting and Maintenance" for details.) Under the heading **Sun or Shade**, the plant's preference is indicated by sun symbols: ● for shade all day, ◑ for morning sun and afternoon shade, ◐ for morning shade and hot afternoon sun, and ○ for full sun all day long.

Selected Plants

Height × Width denotes both the maximum dimensions, which are often achieved in the garden where a plant is provided with optimal irrigation and care, and the plant's usual size in the wild. Parents are especially concerned with thorns, spines, and saw-toothed leaves. The heading entitled **Protective Mechanisms** provides this information as well as lists poisonous properties if they exist.

The heading **Related Species** does not give every relative of the profiled plant but only some of those garden-worthy species that are native to the seven regions.

LANDSCAPE CATEGORIES

The profiles are organized into landscape categories, starting with trees defined as the tallest plants around. Next are the succulent accents with their dramatic silhouettes that remain green all year. Leafy evergreen shrubs are third in importance. It is only after these elements are in place that the garden designer is ready to add the shorter ground covers and flowers. The vines, with their special uses, are the last category of profiles.

1 TREES

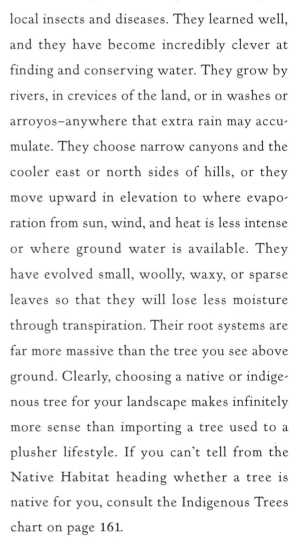

"STATELY," "MAJESTIC," AND "TOWERING" ARE not words one thinks of when describing trees that are native to the warmest, driest regions of southern California and the Southwest. Frankly, most would be called shrubs in many other parts of the country, being multitrunked and generally under 30 feet tall–some barely reaching over 10 feet. What is remarkable is that they manage to survive so well in these harsh conditions, to thrive with only minimal care.

Over the millennia, these natives have had to adapt to months of drought every year, soil with no humus, blistering heat, abrupt onsets of cold, harsh winds, freak storms, and local insects and diseases. They learned well, and they have become incredibly clever at finding and conserving water. They grow by rivers, in crevices of the land, or in washes or arroyos–anywhere that extra rain may accumulate. They choose narrow canyons and the cooler east or north sides of hills, or they move upward in elevation to where evaporation from sun, wind, and heat is less intense or where ground water is available. They have evolved small, woolly, waxy, or sparse leaves so that they will lose less moisture through transpiration. Their root systems are far more massive than the tree you see above ground. Clearly, choosing a native or indigenous tree for your landscape makes infinitely more sense than importing a tree used to a plusher lifestyle. If you can't tell from the Native Habitat heading whether a tree is native for you, consult the Indigenous Trees chart on page 161.

RIGHT: A saguaro provides a lookout perch for a hawk high above the Sonoran Desert shrubs and flowers. **BELOW:** At the Sonoran Desert Museum in Tucson, blue paloverde provides light shade for teddybear cholla, prickly pear, agave, purple threeawn (*Aristida purpurea*), brittlebrush, and annual dogweed.

1 *Common Name*	Roemer acacia
Latin Name	*Acacia roemeriana*
Native Habitat	Limestone hills 1,000 to 4,500 feet in Chihuahuan Desert
Regions of Use	1, 2, 3, 4, 5, 6, 7
Soil	Dry, decomposed granite, sand, clay loam, limestone, low organic content, well drained
Water	Once or twice a month in summer
Sun or Shade	○
Height × Width	Maximum: 20 feet × 25 feet with 16-inch-caliper trunk. Usual: 10 feet × 15 feet
Protective Mechanisms	Prickles
Leaves or Stems	Green, winter-deciduous
Ornamental Value	White fluffy balls of fragrant flowers, pinkish flat beans
Other Value	Nectar and pollen for bees and butterflies, nesting sites, seeds eaten by game birds, beans ground into pinole
Related Species	Small's huisache (*A. farnesiana* var. *smallii*), whitethorn (*A. constricta*), catclaw acacia (*A. greggii*)

Roemer acacia has creamy flowers so intensely fragrant that one tree can perfume a large garden. Another advantage is that it is not as prickly as the other acacias described here. It prefers deep soil, good drainage, and occasional irrigation. The fragrant golden flowers of huisache (WEE satch) (1, 5) have made it a favorite landscape tree in the tropics for centuries. **Small's huisache** (1, 2, 5, 6) is different from the main species because it endures the light frosts of such locations as Phoenix. In Las Vegas and El Paso, use the cold-hardy **whitethorn** (3, 4, 5, 6, 7). Besides fragrant yellow flowers, it might have red bean pods, purple winter branches, and no white thorns. For naturalizing in Southwest deserts, I recommend **catclaw acacia** (1, 2, 3, 4, 5, 6, 7), although not for use close to the house, however, because of its recurved spines. Usually described as a shrub, catclaw tends to form thickets, although occasionally it will become a tree.

....

2 *Common Name*	Redshanks, ribbonwood
Latin Name	*Adenostoma sparsifolium*
Native Habitat	Dry slopes or chaparral 1,000 to 6,500 feet in southern California coastal and mountain ranges and Baja California
Regions of Use	2, 3
Soil	Dry, decomposed granite, sand, low organic content, well drained
Water	None to once a month
Sun or Shade	○
Height × Width	Maximum: 20 feet × 20 feet. Usual: 12 feet × 15 feet
Protective Mechanisms	Aromatic oils discourage some browsers
Leaves or Stems	Evergreen, light green, aromatic, needlelike
Ornamental Value	Red shaggy bark, 4-inch clusters of fragrant white (rarely pink) flowers in late July or early August
Other Value	Flowers used by butterflies and bees, fruits eaten by songbirds and game birds
Related Species	Chamise (*A. fasciculatum*)

Because its upright branches appear so low on the trunk, you could be fooled into thinking that **redshanks** is a multi-trunked tree. These branches are soft red with lavender undertones, and the bark shreds off attractively in long ribbons. To use redshanks effectively in your landscape, place one well-pruned tree where its branches show up against the walls of your house or courtyard. Then plant drought-resistant, low-growing ground covers underneath, so you don't hide these branches. Mojave yucca and Our Lord's candle are companionable accents. Where redshanks grows in southern California chaparral, it grows quite thickly intermixed with **chamise**. Chamise (1, 2, 3), far more common than redshanks, is slightly shorter, has darker foliage, and flowers earlier.

3		
Common Name	Canotia, crucifixion thorn	
Latin Name	*Canotia holacantha*	
Native Habitat	Canyons, dry slopes, and mesas from 2,000 to 4,000 feet in upper Sonoran Desert, rare in Mojave Desert	
Regions of Use	4, 5, 6	
Soil	Dry, decomposed granite, sand, low organic content, well drained	
Water	None to once a month	
Sun or Shade	○	
Height × Width	Maximum: 20 feet × 15 feet with 12-inch trunk. Usual: 12 feet × 8 feet	
Protective Mechanisms	Spine-tipped branches	
Leaves or Stems	Green scales	
Ornamental Value	Evergreen texture of branching	
Other Value	Cover for nesting birds	

Canotia (kuh NO shuh) sports a yellow-green "witches'-broom" of branches above shaggy gray trunks–great texture for a desert garden. It is literally a mass of thorns, so weak-wooded and brittle that it can be pulled apart with bare hands. But if you are careful in handling this fragile tree, you'll find it a worthwhile plant to salvage or to add to your landscape. According to Phil Hebets of Cave Creek, Arizona, its roots allow it to be transplanted easily, but it is extremely sensitive to overwatering after being established. Brittlebush, bursage, desert marigold, verbena, and Parry's penstemon easily grow beneath it, as will dwarf white zinnia and globe mallow. At higher altitudes, you might also find turpentinebush, California buckwheat, lupine, fairyduster, blackfoot daisy, Nevada goldeneye, and deergrass, along with palmilla and sugarbush. Similar in appearance are **allthorn** (*Koeberlinia spinosa*), found in the Chihuahuan Desert and the Sonoran Desert around the Gulf of California (careful, its thorns cause swelling), **crucifixion thorn** (*Castelamoryi*), found in the Colorado Desert, and **crucifixion thorn** (*Holacantha stewartii*) in Big Bend, Texas.

....

4		
Common Name	Saguaro	
Latin Name	*Carnegiea gigantea (Cereus giganteus)*	
Native Habitat	Mostly below 4,500 feet in Sonoran Desert east of the Colorado River and the Gulf of California	
Regions of Use	6	
Soil	Dry, decomposed granite, low organic content, well drained	
Water	None best, once a month in summer acceptable	
Sun or Shade	○	
Height × Width	Maximum: 50 feet × 15 feet. Usual: 20 feet × 12 feet	
Protective Mechanisms	Spines	
Leaves or Stems	Evergreen, yellow-green	
Ornamental Value	Height and form, white flowers in late spring, green to maroon fruit in June	
Other Value	Flowers used by nectivorous bats at night and bees and hummingbirds during the day; fruits (green outside, red inside) are eaten by nectivorous bats, songbirds, game birds, humans, foxes, ringtails, and other mammals; woodpeckers and carpenter birds make	

Saguaro (suh HWAR o) is the indicator plant of the true Sonoran Desert–which simply means, when you see a saguaro growing naturally, you know which desert you're in. Where conditions are right, it forms saguaro forests, with the mature trees standing 30 to 70 feet apart. Although saguaro is found growing by the beach along the Gulf of California in Mexico, in the United States it grows naturally only in the foothills and low mountains of the Sonoran Desert in Arizona–not in the flatlands around Phoenix.

Countless huge saguaros have been killed by being transplanted in adjacent deserts. In the Lower Colorado Desert, for example–which is much drier than the Sonoran–saguaros need a permanent drip system. The first year at least, they need to be individually hosed down every day to prevent them from shriveling up. But giv-

Related Species	homes in the trunks; birds of prey build nests in the branches; fallen logs house lizards and beetles Organpipe cactus (*Stenocereus thurberi*) and senita (*Pachycereus schottii*)

ing them too much water is dangerous; they can literally burst. The Mojave Desert is too dry and too cold for saguaros, which must have above-freezing temperatures during the day. They can endure frost only at night according to Phil Hebets, a tree expert and landscape architect in Arizona. Frost-damaged saguaros take years to die, and it's a slow, painful way to go. The Chihuahuan Desert is not only too cold, it's also too humid, making the saguaros susceptible to a fungus. When you realize all this, it's obvious why the saguaro is native to only certain parts of the Sonoran Desert.

Buy only nursery-propagated saguaros. Those transplanted from the desert have only a 50 percent survival rate and, as mentioned earlier, to remove them is against the law. To rescue and then replant a saguaro that is endangered by construction, first get a permit. Keep the saguaro in a large box like the ones that house desert trees, and make sure the north-facing side continues to face north, so that the cactus won't get sunburned. Saguaros dug for sale are usually sold bare root.

Saguaros dug from the wild are valuable and desirable because they are so big, and the saguaro has a reputation for being very slow-growing. In the desert, it is. It is estimated that the average growth rate is 2 inches or less a year. Some speculate that most saguaros are 75 years old before they begin to branch. A pampered nursery-propagated plant, however, might grow 18 inches in only one year in a greenhouse with irrigation and perfect drainage. Giving your baby saguaro some irrigation will certainly speed its growth, but understand that it tolerates less water than do paloverde and ironwood. Don't plant it in a swale, or plan to irrigate it more than once a month after it is established. If it gets too much water, the base will become brown, a sure sign that it is beginning to rot. If it continues to get too much water, it will certainly die. All members of the saguaro family have a symbiotic relationship with nectar-feeding bats.

....

5 *Common Name*	Netleaf hackberry, palo blanco, acibuche
Latin Name	*Celtis reticulata*
Native Habitat	Arroyos, canyons, seeps, and washes below 6,000 feet from California to Mexico and Texas
Regions of Use	1, 2, 3, 4, 5, 6, 7
Soil	Dry to moist, decomposed granite, sand, clay loam, limestone, low to some organic content, well drained
Water	Once or twice a month in hot, dry weather
Sun or Shade	○
Height × Width	Maximum: 75 feet × 75 feet. Usual: 15 feet × 25 feet
Protective Mechanisms	None
Leaves or Stems	Green, winter-deciduous
Ornamental Value	Attracts songbirds in fall and winter
Other Value	Winter fruits eaten by songbirds, game birds, and other animals; larval plant for butterflies; cover for quail
Related Species	Granjeno, desert hackberry, huasteco (*C. pallida*)

What most southwestern gardeners like best about **netleaf hackberry** is that, unlike other desert trees, it looks like most people's idea of a tree. There are no fancy flowers or thorns, just a straight trunk, up to a foot in diameter; plain and simple leaves that stay on all summer; and spreading branches that form dense shade. It also lives to be more than 100 years old, has both a taproot and shallow lateral roots, and is reported to be strongly resistant to cotton (Texas) root rot. **Granjeno** (5, 6), not native to California, is less winter-hardy but far more drought-tolerant and can be grown many places in the Chihuahuan and Sonoran deserts without supplemental water. It is normally a spiny shrub that forms thickets, making it good for erosion control. If you put it in a garden and water it, you can wind up with a very pretty 20-foot tree.

6 *Common Name*	Blue paloverde
Latin Name	*Cercidium floridum*
Native Habitat	Washes mostly below 3,500 feet in Sonoran and Colorado deserts
Regions of Use	1, 2, 3, 5, 6
Soil	Dry to moist, decomposed granite, sand, clay loam, low organic content, well drained
Water	None to once a week
Sun or Shade	○
Height × Width	Maximum: 25 feet × 30 feet. Usual: 15 feet × 25 feet
Protective Mechanisms	Spines only on succulent new growth
Leaves or Stems	Pale blue-green trunks, drought- and cold-deciduous
Ornamental Value	Evergreen branches, golden yellow flowers two weeks in April, fragrant
Other Value	Soil stabilizer; flowers used by bees for honey and by butterflies and tarantula hawks; seeds eaten by doves, pack rats, and other desert wildlife; beans ground into pinole
Related Species	Foothill paloverde, littleleaf paloverde (*C. microphyllum*)

The two paloverdes are the best-loved trees of the Sonoran Desert. Even without leaves or flowers, their green trunks and branches are a handsome sight. In fact, these stems share nutritional chores with the leaves, accounting for 40 percent of the tree's annual photosynthesis. **Blue paloverde** has pale blue-green trunks and is common in the washes of the lower Sonoran and Colorado deserts, along with prickly pear, ironwood, and creosote. It is faster growing, shorter lived (20 to 40 years), and better adapted to watered gardens. First to flower, it is the showier of the two and the only one that is fragrant. **Foothill paloverde** (1, 2, 3, 5, 6) has lime green trunks and commonly grows among saguaro, pink fairyduster, penstemons, globe mallow, brittlebush, chuparosa, and other desert flowers. Its flowers are pale creamy yellow and appear two weeks later than those of blue paloverde.

· ·

7 *Common Name*	Western redbud, pata de vaca
Latin Name	*Cercis occidentalis*
Native Habitat	300 to 4,500 feet in California foothill woodlands and chaparral and in isolated pockets at 4,000 to 4,500 feet in Sonoran and Mojave deserts
Regions of Use	1, 2, 3, 4
Soil	Dry to moist, decomposed granite, sand, clay loam, low to high organic content, well drained
Water	Once or twice a month in hot weather
Sun or Shade	◑ ◐ ○
Height × Width	Maximum: 25 feet × 30 feet. Usual: 20 feet × 20 feet
Protective Mechanisms	None
Leaves or Stems	Glossy blue-green, heart-shaped, winter-deciduous
Ornamental Value	Purple, pink, or white flowers in late March or early April on old wood; rosy seedpods in May
Other Value	Soil stabilizer, flowers used by bees, seeds eaten by birds, browsed by deer, larval plant for butterflies
Related Species	Mexican redbud (*C. canadensis* var. *mexicana*)

In the spring, before it leafs out, **western redbud** is at its showiest, covered with purply pink (not red) flowers. To make a big statement, plant several of them together. Choose ones that have been grown from seed, so there is a beautiful blending of paler and darker pinks. This is far lovelier than having all the redbuds the exact same color. Western redbud requires one or two deep waterings a month during the summer, at least for the first four years, so beneath them plant a colorful mixture of flowers that can take extra water—Douglas iris, seaside daisy, penstemon, mountain marigold, blue-eyed grass, onion lily, island alumroot, and Mexican evening primrose. **Mexican redbud** (2, 3, 4, 6, 7), similar in size and growth habit to western redbud, is native to limestone areas of the Big Bend of Texas and the Chihuahuan Desert in Mexico in the 12- to 20-inch rainfall belt. Its leaves are ruffled and velvety.

8 *Common Name*	Desert willow
Latin Name	*Chilopsis linearis*
Native Habitat	Desert washes below 5,000 feet in Colorado, Mojave, Sonoran, and Chihuahuan deserts
Regions of Use	2, 3, 4, 5, 6, 7
Soil	Dry to moist, decomposed granite, sand, clay loam, limestone, low to some organic content, well drained
Water	Twice a month to once a week in summer
Sun or Shade	○
Height × Width	Maximum: 40 feet × 40 feet. Usual: 15 feet × 20 feet
Protective Mechanisms	None
Leaves or Stems	Green, winter-deciduous, sometimes drought-deciduous, slow to leaf out in spring
Ornamental Value	Trumpet-shaped flowers 2 to 3 inches long in white to rose to purple, often two-toned and ruffled, after rains
Other Value	Flowers used by butterflies, hummingbirds, and bees; larval plant for white-winged moth in late spring to early summer; seeds eaten by birds

Flowers from mid-spring to fall make **desert willow** a favorite with gardeners from Texas to the California coast. An old tree has graceful, thick, twisty trunks, whereas a young one tends to have too many trunks unless it is carefully pruned. It grows so quickly that you might have to reshape it three times the first year, but probably not at all by the fifth year. Not a true willow, desert willow got its name because of its delicate, slender, willowlike leaves. These provide shade light enough to extend the bloom time of flowers growing down below, while still allowing them plenty of sunshine. If desert willow is planted in a swale that gets extra runoff from rain and receives an occasional summer rain, it will not need additional irrigation. But summer watering definitely improves its overall appearance and its frequency of bloom. Without supplemental water, it might become drought-stressed and defoliate.

---

9 *Common Name*	Ocotillo
Latin Name	*Fouquieria splendens*
Native Habitat	Rocky slopes below 5,000 feet in Chihuahuan, Colorado, Mojave, and Sonoran deserts down to beaches on Gulf of California
Regions of Use	2, 3, 4, 5, 6, 7
Soil	Dry, decomposed granite, sand, limestone, low organic content, well drained
Water	None to once a month in summer
Sun or Shade	○
Height × Width	Maximum: 25 feet × 15 feet. Usual: 12 feet × 10 feet
Protective Mechanisms	Spines
Leaves or Stems	Green leaves for a short time after rain, stems are evergreen with occasional irrigation
Ornamental Value	Red to orange flowers after rain, green stems
Other Value	Flowers used by hummingbirds, butterflies, orioles, and bees; nesting for songbirds; living fences

Ocotillo has a very shallow root system, enabling it to flower and attract hummingbirds after even the briefest summer shower. It is common in all the deserts covered in this book. In the Chihuahuan Desert, ocotillo and tree yuccas tower over creosote, lechuguilla, prickly pear, dalea, coldenia, littleleaf sumac, desert spoon, skeletonleaf goldeneye, and various flowers and grasses. In the Sonoran, it is equally at home with saguaro and paloverde where the understory might consist of creosote, bursage, teddybear cholla, globe mallow, and brittlebush. In the Mojave, it stands tall with the Joshua tree, and its understory might be creosote, Mojave yucca, turpentinebush, Mormon tea, and Apache-plume. Besides providing height, another popular landscape use is living fences. Plant the upright canes 2 to 6 inches apart in a narrow slit trench and wire them together. Ocotillo has a delightfully improbable-looking cousin in Mexico called boojum (*F. columnaris*) (5, 6), which resembles a pale upturned carrot.

10	Common Name	Fragrant ash, flowering ash
	Latin Name	*Fraxinus cuspidata*
	Native Habitat	On rocky hillsides, even west-facing, between 2,400 and 7,000 feet in Chihuahuan and Great Basin deserts
	Regions of Use	1, 2, 3, 4, 6, 7
	Soil	Dry, decomposed granite, sand, clay loam, limestone, low to some organic content, well drained
	Water	Once a month to once a week
	Sun or Shade	◑ ○
	Height × Width	Maximum: 18 feet × 20 feet. Usual: 12 feet × 12 feet
	Protective Mechanisms	None
	Leaves or Stems	Dark green, cold-deciduous
	Ornamental Value	White flowers in spring, fragrant
	Other Value	Fruits eaten by birds, browse
	Related Species	California flowering ash (*F. dipetala*)

Fragrant ash is close kin to *Chionanthus* species, the stunning fringe trees of Asia and the southeastern United States. But unlike these trees, it is well suited to the Southwest. Its intensely fragrant, pure white flowers hang in 3- to 4-inch clusters that almost literally cover the tree. A fragrant ash in bloom can be spotted on a hillside half a mile away. Down on the desert floor, fragrant ash should be used only in irrigated courtyards. Still, it needs less water than many trees currently recommended by the nursery trade. It can bloom at the same time as littleleaf sumac, columbines, goldenball leadtree, Carneros yucca, mesa greggia, and shrubby dogweed. **California flowering ash** (1, 2, 3), only occasionally fragrant, is native between 400 and 3,700 feet in foothill woodland and chaparral communities from the Sierra Nevada to Orange County. Like fragrant ash, it will not tolerate extremely dry conditions, but it needs only a minimum of water to thrive and look its best. It grows with California scrub oak, western redbud, coffeeberry, sugarbush, toyon, chaparral whitethorn, and hollyleaf cherry.

11	Common Name	Goldenball leadtree
	Latin Name	*Leucaena retusa*
	Native Habitat	Dry canyons of Guadalupe Mountains south to Mexico in Chihuahuan Desert and east to central Texas, mostly at 3,000 to 6,500 feet
	Regions of Use	1, 2, 3, 4, 5, 6, 7
	Soil	Dry, decomposed granite, sand, clay loam, limestone, low to some organic content, well drained
	Water	Once or twice a month in summer
	Sun or Shade	◐ ◑ ○
	Height × Width	Maximum: 25 feet × 25 feet. Usual: 15 feet × 20 feet
	Protective Mechanisms	None
	Leaves or Stems	Bright green, winter-deciduous
	Ornamental Value	Golden fluffy balls of flowers after rains, fragrant
	Other Value	Flowers used by butterflies and bees, seeds eaten by songbirds and game birds, a favorite browse of cattle and deer

Goldenball leadtree grows fairly quickly in a garden setting. Its leaves are a fresh chartreuse, which contrasts well with silver foliage or very dark green leaves. The flowers appear all during the warm season after rains. They are also triggered by watering, so if your tree receives irrigation once or twice a month, it should bloom almost continually. Goldenball leadtree has a reputation for being weak-wooded and easily damaged by winds. For this reason, it is usually grown as a multitrunked tree, the rationale being that several stems offer less wind resistance than would a single trunk at the mercy of a large, top-heavy crown. While many landscapers will use this tree only in a protected courtyard or against a sheltering wall, other gardeners have told me that they think this reputation is largely undeserved; their trees have survived fairly severe storms with no damage.

12		
Common Name	Fernleaf Catalina ironwood	
Latin Name	*Lyonothamnus floribundus* ssp. *asplenifolius*	
Native Habitat	RARE, oak woodland and chaparral below 1,700 feet on Santa Catalina, Santa Rosa, and Santa Cruz islands	
Regions of Use	1, 2, 3	
Soil	Dry, decomposed granite, sand, clay loam, low to rich organic content, well drained	
Water	Once a month	
Sun or Shade	◐ ◑ ○	
Height × Width	Maximum: 60 feet × 35 feet. Usual: 20 feet × 15 feet	
Protective Mechanisms	None	
Leaves or Stems	Evergreen dark green, shiny, aromatic	
Ornamental Value	12-inch clusters of white flowers in June (ill-smelling to some people), thick shredding bark	
Other Value	Seeds eaten by birds, grazed and browsed	
Related Species	Catalina ironwood (*L. f.* ssp. *floribundus*)	

Catalina ironwood (1, 2, 3) has slender leaves with scalloped edges, whereas its sister, **fernleaf Catalina ironwood**, has much fancier leaves. Both are rare in the wild and found only in the Channel Islands, where most seedlings are nibbled to death by animals. Since these trees are relatively short-lived–staying around less than 50 years–it is crucial to their survival in the wild that they continually have young trees coming up. Because they are narrow trees, they can squeeze into tight spots next to house walls or in cramped courtyards where you need height but you don't have room for much width. If you have a larger property, you could use a tiny grove of them to screen utility lines or some other tall eyesore. Leaf and bark litter make the soil beneath them unusually rich for southern California. Good plants to grow underneath are island alumroot, coffeeberry fern, evergreen currant, fuchsia flowering currant, and snowberry. Only the fernleaf Catalina ironwood is readily available in nurseries.

13		
Common Name	Ironwood, tesota, palo de hierro	
Latin Name	*Olneya tesota*	
Native Habitat	Desert washes and creosote scrub, usually below 2,000 feet in lower Sonoran and Lower Colorado deserts	
Regions of Use	1, 2, 3, 5, 6	
Soil	Dry, decomposed granite, sand, clay loam, low organic content, well drained	
Water	None to once a month	
Sun or Shade	◐ ○	
Height × Width	Maximum: 30 feet × 40 feet with 18-inch-diameter trunk. Usual: 15 feet × 15 feet	
Protective Mechanisms	Recurved spines	
Leaves or Stems	Gray, evergreen–rarely winter-deciduous	
Ornamental Value	Silverly trunk and leaves, some trees have rosy flowers	
Other Value	Flowers used by bees; beans eaten by animals; browse for bighorn sheep, mule deer, pack rats, and wild horses; cover for desert wildlife	

Ironwood is not fond of cold weather and freezes back at 20 degrees F. For that reason, it used to be considered an indicator plant of climates warm enough to grow orange trees. It is a highly prized element in those low, hot landscapes because its silvery bark and leaves are a handsome complement to many desert color schemes. Its flowers appear in May just as new leaves replace the old, and usually the blooms are so pale that they are unnoticeable. But, occasionally, in the Colorado Desert, you will see a tree with beautiful rosy purple flowers as showy as those of redbud. Today nursery-propagated trees are finally becoming available, either single- or multitrunked. Because ironwood is naturally slow-growing, continue to water yours for several years after getting it established to speed up its growth rate. But don't overdo it–experiments have shown that lots of water is no more helpful than just a little.

14	*Common Name*	Torrey pine
	Latin Name	*Pinus torreyana*
	Native Habitat	THREATENED, soft sandstone canyons, coastal scrub, chaparral below 500 feet in Del Mar and Torrey Pines State Reserve near San Diego and on Santa Rosa Island
	Regions of Use	1, 2, 3
	Soil	Dry, decomposed granite, sand, low organic content, well drained
	Water	Once a month
	Sun or Shade	○
	Height × Width	Maximum: over 100 feet. Usual: 40 to 70 feet × 35 feet
	Protective Mechanisms	None
	Leaves or Stems	Evergreen, aromatic, gray-green, five needles per bundle
	Ornamental Value	Fragrance
	Other Value	Habitat for American robin, northern mockingbird, wrentit, scrub jay, California towhee, pine siskin, Nuttall's woodpecker, northern flicker, vireos, and warblers

Pines can survive in the high desert but not in the low. **Torrey pine** survives in southern California chaparral, with less than 11 inches of rain a year, but only on the coast where temperatures are cooler and there's ample fog to provide moisture. It does very well in cultivation and seems to be both smog-tolerant (no small consideration) and fast-growing. Too much water causes a root fungus; not enough and Torrey pine will be attacked by insects. Unfortunately, there may be no possibility of selecting cultivars that are resistant to these problems, because all 6,000 trees left on the mainland are genetically almost identical. The 1,500 trees on Santa Rosa look different; they are multitrunked and have darker green foliage. To help adjust watering to just the right amount, plant natives underneath. For a conservative, evergreen look, use lemonadeberry, laurel-leaf sumac, chamise, California or Nuttall's scrub oak, toyon, tree poppy, jojoba, Mojave yucca, and dudleya.

15	*Common Name*	Western sycamore
	Latin Name	*Platanus racemosa*
	Native Habitat	Streamsides and canyons, usually below 4,000 feet in central, southwestern, and Baja California
	Regions of Use	1, 2, 3
	Soil	Moist, decomposed granite, sand, clay loam, high organic content, seasonal flooding okay
	Water	At least once a week
	Sun or Shade	○
	Height × Width	Maximum: 100 feet. Usual: 50 feet × 50 feet
	Protective Mechanisms	None
	Leaves or Stems	Large, velvety, winter-deciduous, attacked by anthracnose
	Ornamental Value	Smooth white or pale lime bark mottled with tan
	Other Value	No information

Without a continuous supply of water, **western sycamore** becomes drought-stressed and falls prey to anthracnose, its leaves turning brown and crispy as early as mid-spring. It's really suitable only for properties that have a stream running through. Otherwise, plant it in a hollow where it will benefit from the runoff from a roof, patio, or driveway. On the coast, away from the drying heat and blessed with moisture-laden fog, it is easier to manage. Under its somewhat heavy shade, use hollyleaf cherry and California bay for screening, and make a shady flower garden employing evergreen currant, fuchsia flowering currant, red columbine, hummingbird sage, island alumroot, coffeeberry fern, and California strawberry. Set a few boulders among them to show off their delicate foliage and to provide cool, damp places to shelter roots. Then place a bench or loveseat beneath the tree to give yourself a cool, comfortable place to enjoy your garden.

16 *Common Name*	Fremont cottonwood, Gila cottonwood, alamo
Latin Name	*Populus fremontii*
Native Habitat	By rivers, arroyos, seeps, and irrigation ditches below 6,000 feet in the Sonoran, Colorado, and Mojave deserts west to Santa Catalina and San Nicholas islands
Regions of Use	1, 2, 3, 4, 5, 6, 7
Soil	Dry to moist, decomposed granite, sand, clay loam, low to high organic content, well drained or seasonally flooded
Water	None to once a month when dry
Sun or Shade	○
Height × Width	Maximum: 90 feet × 120 feet. Usual: 30 feet × 40 feet
Protective Mechanisms	None
Leaves or Stems	Pale blue and velvety or green and shiny, winter-deciduous
Ornamental Value	Shade, sound of the leaves
Other Value	Soil stabilizer, larval plant for butterflies, aspirin tea from inner bark or leaves
Related Species	Rio Grande cottonwood, alamo, guerigo (*P. wislizenii* or *P. fremontii* var. *wislizenii* or *P. deltoides* ssp. *wislizenii*)

Cottonwoods are so tall that they look quite silly in desert foothill gardens. They look best in washes and arroyos with desert willow, mesquite, or California fan palm, and they are also appropriate for windbreaks or shade down on the flats. Their leaves tremble and spin like those of their cousins the aspens, and they make a wonderful sound when the wind blows through them. Once established, cottonwoods are surprisingly drought-tolerant. Their roots never turn down available water, however. They won't cause a plumbing leak, but if you have one, your cottonwood roots are sure to find it. The males are more desirable ornamentally, because they don't have cottony seed and they do have showier flowers–3- to 6-inch-long tails of vivid red or yellow. The more drought-resistant specimens of **Fremont cottonwood** have very pretty pale blue, velvety leaves. **Rio Grande cottonwood** is the one with golden fall color in the Chihuahuan Desert.

....

17 *Common Name*	Torrey mesquite, western mesquite, mezquite
Latin Name	*Prosopis glandulosa* var. *torreyana*
Native Habitat	Anywhere the water table is high, below 5,000 feet in Chihuahuan, Mojave, Sonoran and Lower Colorado deserts
Regions of Use	2, 3, 4, 5, 6, 7
Soil	Dry to moist, decomposed granite, sand, clay loam, low to some organic content, well drained
Water	Once a month
Sun or Shade	○
Height × Width	Maximum: 37 feet × 50 feet. Usual: 20 feet × 30 feet
Protective Mechanisms	Thorns
Leaves	Lime green, winter-deciduous, slow to leaf out in spring
Ornamental Value	Yellow flowers in late spring, fragrant, sometimes seedpods are scarlet
Other Value	Soil stabilizer; flowers used by butterflies and bees; beans eaten by birds and mammals
Related Species	Honey mesquite (*P. g.* var. *glandulosa*), velvet mesquite (*P. velutina*), tornillo or screwbean mesquite (*P. pubescens*)

Mesquites make outstanding shade trees. There are several species, but **Torrey mesquite** is so hybridized with honey mesquite that it might be futile to make a distinction. Both also hybridize with velvet mesquite. And recently Argentine (*P. alba*) and Chilean (*P. chilensis*) mesquites, equally promiscuous, have added their genes to the mix. Basically, Torrey mesquite has yellow-green foliage and shaggy bark; **velvet mesquite** (2, 3, 4, 5, 6, 7), native only to the Sonoran Desert, has velvety gray foliage and velvety beans, and it is almost thornless when mature; and **honey mesquite** (2, 3, 4, 5, 6, 7) has weeping foliage and is native only to the Chihuahuan Desert, although cattle have recently brought it farther west. **Tornillo** (1, 2, 3, 4, 5, 6, 7) is quite different–daintier with clusters of straw-colored corkscrew bean pods and rich golden flowers.

18		
Common Name	Smoketree, smokethorn dalea, Corona-de-Cristo	
Latin Name	*Psorothamnus spinosus* (formerly *Dalea spinosa*)	
Native Habitat	Dry sandy washes and creosote scrub around Gila and Colorado river systems in southwestern Arizona and southeastern California, below 1,500 feet in Mojave, Lower Colorado, and lower Sonoran deserts and into Sonora and Baja California	
Regions of Use	5, warm parts of 6	
Soil	Dry to moist, decomposed granite, sand, low organic content, well drained	
Water	None to once a week in hot, dry weather	
Sun or Shade	○	
Height × Width	Maximum: 25 feet × 30 feet. Usual: 15 feet × 15 feet	
Protective Mechanisms	Spines, aromatic wood	
Leaves or Stems	Occur only after winter rains	
Ornamental Value	Pale branches, midnight blue flowers in May or June	
Other Value	Flowers used by bees	

Smoketree got its name because the density of its extremely pale blue-gray branches–not the leaves or flowers–make the tree look as if it is enveloped in smoke. The leaves appear for only a short time, and the magnificent dark purple-blue flowers bloom for only about a week in early summer. The smooth, pale, almost white trunks and limbs are photogenic all year long. Smoketree doesn't transplant well because it has deep roots for tapping underground water. It is not difficult to grow from seed planted in early spring, as long as you puncture the hard seed coat first and sow the seed in its native soil. A seedling grows very quickly with irrigation, and the tree will soon reach higher than your head. To avoid watering after the smoketree is established and grown to a suitable size, plant it in a slight swale where it gets extra water, and mulch with decomposed granite. For brilliant spring color underneath, sow seeds of sand verbena, desert Canterbury-bells, and other wildflowers that grow in nearby washes.

··

19		
Common Name	Coast live oak, encina	
Latin Name	*Quercus agrifolia*	
Native Habitat	Chaparral and woodland, usually below 3,000 feet from Outer North Coast Ranges to Baja California	
Regions of Use	1, 2, 3	
Soil	Dry, decomposed granite, sand, clay loam, low to some organic content, well drained	
Water	None to once a month	
Sun or Shade	○	
Height × Width	Maximum: 80 feet × 70 feet. Usual: 40 feet × 40 feet	
Protective Mechanisms	Small spines on leaves	
Leaves or Stems	Evergreen, dark green, gets new leaves each spring	
Ornamental Value	Large trunks and spreading branches	
Other Value	Acorns eaten by squirrels and strong-beaked birds, cover for nesting songbirds, larval plant for butterflies	

Coast live oak is relatively slow-growing and can live well over 100 years. Nursery-propagated oaks adapt nicely to garden conditions and grow 1 to 3 feet a year if watered. Old specimens found on land being developed are adapted to natural cycles of rain and drought. These giants are valuable, and contractors and homeowners frequently–and wisely–try to save them. To do this successfully, protect the roots from the following: trucks and cars that compact the soil; paint, concrete wash, and other building fluids that poison the soil; bulldozers that scrape off the feeder roots, topsoil, and ground covers; overwatering that forces oxygen out of the soil and suffocates the tree; and regrading and piling soil over the roots, which also drives out oxygen. If grading or draining elsewhere on the site lowers the water table, give the tree periodic deep waterings, being sure to let the soil dry out in between. A dirt, gravel, or unmortared stone patio over the roots allows them to breathe. Native drought-resistant ground covers such as Douglas iris, evergreen currant, fuchsia flowering currant, island alumroot, and snowberry are also good.

20 *Common Name*	California fan palm
Latin Name	*Washingtonia filifera*
Native Habitat	Below 2,500 feet in canyons and near springs in Kofa Mountains near Quartsite, Arizona, and usually below 3,500 feet north and west of the Salton Sea and on the southern margin of the Mojave Desert in California and in northern Baja
Regions of Use	2, 3, 5
Soil	Moist but not wet, decomposed granite, sand, clay loam, low to some organic content, well drained
Water	None on coast to once a week in desert
Sun or Shade	○
Height × Width	Maximum: 75 feet × 45 feet. Usual: 25 feet × 15 feet
Protective Mechanisms	Hooked spines on leaf stems
Leaves or Stems	Evergreen, huge, fan-shaped, pleated and divided halfway to the center and then fringed with brown threads
Ornamental Value	Dramatic texture
Other Value	Fruits eaten by many animals, flowers used by bees, cover

The **California fan palm** and its taller, more slender cousin, the Mexican fan palm (*W. robusta*), have been used for more than a century to give southwestern landscapes a subtropical feel. Records show California fan palm trunks reaching 30 inches in diameter. Dead fronds left untrimmed form a shaggy vase-shaped skirt. If they are pruned off but the leaf-stalk bases are left, the trunks have a coarse, braided appearance. With stalks trimmed completely, the trunks look smooth and slender. Some California fan palms seem to self-prune naturally. Fan palms grow slowly, so most landscapers dig mature trees for clients who need instant gratification. But even very young palms, with no visible trunks, are extremely attractive. The main problem with palms is that they are often used in desert or chaparral landscapes where they are too tall and lush-looking for the surrounding vegetation. In an oasis, they grow naturally in groves–not in avenues–along with cottonwood, desert lavender, Torrey mesquite, and Cleveland penstemon.

. . . .

21 *Common Name*	Joshua tree
Latin Name	*Yucca brevifolia*
Native Habitat	Between 2,000 and 6,000 feet in the Mojave Desert and slightly west to Antelope Valley, California; north to Goldfield, Nevada; east to Wickenburg, Arizona; south to Joshua Tree National Monument
Regions of Use	3, 4, 5
Soil	Dry, decomposed granite, sand, low organic content, well drained
Water	None or once a month
Sun or Shade	○
Height × Width	Maximum: 32 feet × 34 feet. Usual: 20 feet × 20 feet
Protective Mechanisms	Spines
Leaves or Stems	Evergreen
Ornamental Value	White to cream flowers–do not bloom every spring
Other Value	Nesting for songbirds, doves, and lizards; dead trunks house woodpeckers and flickers; larval plant for butterflies and yucca moth

Joshua tree is the only tree that survives on the open Mojave flatlands. A young tree will have a single spike for about 20 years, until it blooms. Then two branches form beneath. More branching occurs after each blooming. After having the dead leaves removed, an old trunk develops a dark, corky bark that's similar to a live oak trunk. In California, Joshua trees might be found in chaparral with scrub oaks and manzanitas. In Arizona where they meet saguaros, they are called *Y. b.* var. *jaegeriana* because they branch closer to the ground, making a bushier, less treelike shape. The Joshua tree population is declining rapidly, with thousands of mature ones bulldozed each year by developers. Luckily, a number are rescued annually by local nurseries and offered for sale. Oddly, very few seem to be used in Las Vegas landscapes, where they make sense. Instead, there are many saguaros–which don't. To grow a Joshua tree from seed, plant it in a shrub such as Mormon tea to protect it from ground squirrels, jackrabbits, and other herbivores.

22	*Common Name*	Carneros yucca, palma samandoca, palma barreta
	Latin Name	*Yucca carnerosana*
	Native Habitat	Between 3,000 and 5,000 feet in Chihuahuan Desert in the Big Bend area in Texas and in Mexico
	Regions of Use	2, 3, 4, 5, 6, 7
	Soil	Dry, decomposed granite, sand, clay loam, limestone, low organic content, well drained
	Water	None to once a month
	Sun or Shade	○
	Height × Width	Maximum: 20 feet × 8 feet. Usual: 10 feet × 8 feet
	Protective Mechanisms	Spines on tips of leaves
	Leaves or Stems	Evergreen, dark green, broad
	Ornamental Value	Evergreen tree, white lilylike flowers in early spring to early summer once every three to seven years
	Other Value	Flowers used by yucca moths, larval plant for butterflies, nesting sites for birds and lizards
	Related Species	Spanish bayonet (*Y. faxoniana*), Torrey yucca (*Y. torreyi*), beaked yucca (*Y. rostrata*), Thompson yucca (*Y. thompsoniana*); all can be used in 2, 3, 4, 5, 6, 7

These broad-leaved yuccas with swordlike leaves are all native to the Chihuahuan Desert. **Carneros yucca** holds its flowers far above its leaves. If it is irrigated, the lower leaves might not die back, so that instead of a clear trunk with a crown of leaves, spiky green leaves extend all the way to the ground. **Spanish bayonet** has the same dark green leaves but gets a tall trunk and buries its flowers among the topmost leaves. The species seen in El Paso is **Torrey yucca**. It most resembles Spanish bayonet except that its trunk is shaggy and less attractive. Many believe that **beaked yucca** is the prettiest of the southwestern yuccas. It has smooth leaves and iridescent white flowers, but you must wait 15 years for them. **Thompson yucca** blooms when it is very young, sometimes before it starts developing a trunk. Its leaves are often a lovely pale blue. It needs more water than do the other yuccas in this entry. Botanists are still trying to sort out these yuccas, and there is much disagreement. I have followed *A Field Guide to Texas Trees*, by Benny J. Simpson.

23	*Common Name*	Palmilla, palmella, soaptree yucca, amole
	Latin Name	*Yucca elata*
	Native Habitat	Deserts, grasslands below 4,500 feet in Chihuahuan and Sonoran deserts
	Regions of Use	3, 4, 5, 6, 7
	Soil	Dry, decomposed granite, sand, clay loam, limestone, low organic content, well drained
	Water	None to once a month
	Sun or Shade	○
	Height × Width	Maximum: 30 feet × 20 feet. Usual: 10 feet × 8 feet plus a 3- to 6-foot flower stalk
	Protective Mechanisms	Spines
	Leaves	Evergreen, silver to pale blue-green
	Ornamental Value	White flowers in late spring, not every year
	Other Value	Flowers pollinated by yucca moths; nesting for lizards, beetles, spiders, and birds; larval plant for butterflies

Where nursery-propagated **palmilla** is unavailable, it must be grown from seed. Unlike other tree yuccas, palmilla has a huge tuberous taproot that only a skilled professional can dig with success. Fresh seed, pressed into the soil and barely covered with sand, germinates quickly as long as soil temperatures are between 60 and 70 degrees F. A piece of horizontal tuber will also usually root easily. A word of caution: Dusky wood rats think that very young, leafy palmillas are irresistible, so protect yours with a chicken-wire cage or a prickly shrub for a year or so. Its leaves are narrow and a very pale blue-green, like Wheeler sotol, but the edges are covered with fine white hairs rather than sawtooth spines. When young and trunkless, palmilla fans out in a ball that needs a space at least 4 feet in diameter. With monthly irrigation and deep loose soil, it will easily reach 10 feet in 10 years.

2 SUCCULENT ACCENTS

Chuparosa, Mexican fence-post, and foothill paloverde provide an evergreen screen for the end wall of the tennis court at the Cliff Douglas home in Mesa, Arizona (designed by landscape architect Steve Martino).

THIS MOST IMPORTANT CATEGORY of plants includes cacti and yuccas as well as other species with thickened stems or leaves designed for storing water. This is how they cope with extreme drought; this is also how they remain evergreen in an arid habitat where rainfall averages 2 to 16 inches a year. These succulents are an integral part of all the natural landscapes from the coastal chaparral of San Diego County to the Gulf of Mexico. Creating a true southwestern garden without at least one succulent accent is like preparing an authentic Mexican dinner and omitting the salsa.

These plants are rugged individuals. Unlike forest or chaparral plants that often crowd up against one another and rarely get to develop their own shapes, these accents always stand alone. Their roots might be covered with rocks or low ground covers, but their fattened stems and leaves stand out—rigid, uncompromising, and defiant of sun, rain, drought, nibbling pack rats, and browsing deer.

Residents of the Southwest are particularly fond of succulent accents, and these are often the only native plants saved on a site or deliberately planted.

Succulent accents are sometimes very picky about where they grow. A mass of, say, barrel cactus may appear in one spot on a piece of property, while a plot of land just a few hundred yards away will have just a few, or maybe none at all. Some succulents will thrive on the north side of a hill but eschew the southern slope.

Many of these plants are endangered or threatened in the wild. The good news is that all of these succulents are grown commercially, and with careful irrigation and perfect growing conditions, these plants can achieve in one year what normally takes them 10 years to attain out in the wild. This

means that you should be able to purchase fairly large nursery-propagated plants for a reasonable sum of money.

The indigenous chart tells you in which city (or cities) a particular succulent is native, but it does not tell you if that succulent is able to make it all on its own without extra water in all *parts* of that city–those parts being flats, washes, and foothills. As an example, desert spoon, agave, and cacti are rare on desert flats because it is a little too dry for them there. They are more at home along the edges of washes and in foothill neighborhoods.

ABOVE: Much of the creosote bush was left when the home of Russell and Dinah Jentsen in the Tobosa area of Las Cruces, New Mexico, was built, along with some of the prickly pear (*Opuntia* ssp.). Because this area has long been abused, bursage, grasses, flowers, and rocks do not form a secure desert floor, and there are problems with blowing sand. Most of this landscape is evergreen and looks the same all year. ABOVE LEFT: Santa Rita prickly pear, bursage, blackfoot daisy, barrel cactus, and Shaw's agave make a tiny, unwatered but colorful focal point by the entrance to the tennis court at Cliff Douglas's Mesa, Arizona, home. BELOW LEFT: The owner of this home near Phoenix opted to have her cactus garden, designed by Marcus Bollinger and John Suarez, stark and sculptural—unsoftened by bursage.

Be very cautious about watering these plants in your garden. They will definitely need water and careful attention to get established, but don't overdo it. You are far more liable to rot these plants than have them die of drought. Shriveling is a sign of drought. Turning brown is more likely a sign that the roots are rotting because of being too wet. Never put these plants at the bottom of a swale.

Our succulent accents range from knee-high to tree-size. Those with strong trunks are usually classified as trees by botanists. The ones in this chapter are usually shorter than people–although not always. Some bloom every few years and send up a bloom stalk like a TV antenna or a highway billboard. Some develop trunks and become treelike if they reach a ripe enough old age. Others, such as Wolf's beargrass, are naturally huge at ground level, a suitable scale for corporate headquarters or palatial houses. And still others are small enough for the tiniest courtyard garden.

24 Common Name	Lechuguilla
Latin Name	*Agave lechuguilla*
Native Habitat	On limestone hillsides below 7,500 feet in Chihuahuan Desert, mostly along the Rio Grande River in the United States
Regions of Use	2, 3, 4, 5, 6, 7
Soil	Dry, decomposed granite, sand, limestone, low organic content, well drained
Water	None or once a month
Sun or Shade	○
Height × Width	Maximum: 18 inches × 2 feet, with 9-foot flower stalks
Protective Mechanisms	Very long spines at ends of leaves
Leaves	Evergreen, yellow-green, succulent
Ornamental Value	Evergreen texture, red or yellow flowers once in early summer after rain
Other Value	Flowers used by nectivorous bats, hummingbirds, butterflies, hawk moths, and small bees; browse for deer, javelina, and lechuguilla gopher; larval plant for butterflies
Related Species	Desert agave (*A. deserti*), Schott's agave (*A. schottii*)

Lechuguilla is considered to be the indicator plant of the Chihuahuan Desert; it is native only there. The leaves, at first glance, seem to be only a foot high. In fact, each leaf is topped by about 6 inches of almost invisible spine. The central root produces numerous baby lechuguilla rosettes called offsets, which eventually form a clump about 8 feet square. Place the starter rosette at least 6 feet from a path (for safety) and 10 feet from long-lived shrubs such as creosote, ocotillo, or cenizo so the garden won't end up looking overcrowded. Once the clump is three years old, you should get at least one flower stalk per summer. To fill in the 8-foot square for the short term, plant wildflowers. Two other clump-forming agaves are **Schott's agave** (2, 3, 5, 6), which is native to the Sonoran Desert and has creamy flowers, and **desert agave** (2, 3, 4, 5, 6, 7), which has pale yellow flowers and is native below 5,000 feet in the Mojave and Colorado deserts.

- -

25 Common Name	New Mexico agave
Latin Name	*Agave neomexicana*
Native Habitat	Between 5,000 and 7,000 feet in Chihuahuan Desert–Franklin and Guadalupe mountains, Coahuila, Mexico
Regions of Use	2, 3, 4, 5, 6, 7
Soil	Dry, decomposed granite, sand, limestone, low organic content, well drained
Water	Once a month
Sun or Shade	◐ ○
Height × Width	Usual: 2 feet × 2 feet, with much taller bloom stalk
Protective Mechanisms	Spines on edges of leaves
Leaves	Evergreen, smooth pale blue-green trimmed and tipped with black spines
Ornamental Value	Leaves; yellow flowers once, in spring
Other Value	Nectar in flowers gathered by nectivorous bats, hummingbirds, and butterflies; larval plant for butterflies
Related Species	Havard agave (*A. havardiana*), Parry agave (*A. parryi*), Palmer agave (*A. palmeri*)

New Mexico agave is a good choice for most gardens because it is not too large. **Havard agave** (2, 3, 4, 5, 6, 7) (Chihuahuan Desert), **Parry agave** (2, 3, 4, 5, 6, 7), and **Palmer agave** (2, 3, 4, 5, 6, 7) (both of the latter in the Sonoran Desert) are very similar. All have wide, elegant, pale bluish green leaves, tipped with black. These handsome agaves are most often found on mountain slopes in high deserts where they find a little more rain and cooler temperatures. They form individual rosettes until flowering. Instead of lechuguilla's bottlebrush flowers, these have tall stems that branch out horizontally to hold golden yellow scrubbrushes. After they bloom, usually in 8 to 20 years, they set seed and die; after they've turned brown, baby agaves (offsets) come up around the base. Leave the offsets to start a colony of agaves, or cut them free with a clean knife, allow them to air-dry, and then plant them where you wish.

26 *Common Name*	Shaw's century plant
Latin Name	*Agave shawii* ssp. *shawii*
Native Habitat	RARE, coastal sagescrub below 1,500 feet in San Diego County and Baja California
Regions of Use	1, 2, 3, 5, 6
Soil	Dry, decomposed granite, sand, low organic content, well drained
Water	None
Sun or Shade	◑ ○
Height × Width	Maximum: 3 feet × 5 feet, not counting a 12-foot bloom stalk. Usual: 2 feet × 2 feet
Protective Mechanisms	Spiny teeth along edges of leaves
Leaves	Evergreen, dark green
Ornamental Value	Purple buds, bronze-red to yellow flowers in cool weather
Other Value	Flowers used by nectivorous bats and butterflies

Shaw's century plant is small and crisp and has very dark green leaves. It tends to form a colony of neatly rounded rosettes up to about 18 inches wide. Each rosette is made up of leaves arranged like the petals of a rose. A large ongoing colony has rosettes of varying sizes and will look slightly different each year as some of its members bloom, die back, and leave spaces. In a tiny garden, plan to maintain no more than three to five rosettes. But given some elbow room in a large garden, Shaw's century plant can form a ground cover over a space 8 feet square or more. Individual rosettes can also be planted in the crevices of a stone wall or in a patio pot. A rosette will grow for several years until it gets large enough to flower. The bloom stalk looks like a giant asparagas as it starts to shoot up. When it gets to be about 6 feet tall, it branches, with rounded clusters of bronzy flowers developing at the end of each branch for a sculptured, exotic flower display. Some companion plants are Baja birdbush, tree poppy, Nuttall's scrub oak, California buckwheat, San Miguel mountain sage, jojoba, and San Diego dudleya.

27 *Common Name*	Ajamete, rush milkweed
Latin Name	*Asclepias subulata*
Native Habitat	Desert washes in creosote scrub below 3,000 feet in Sonoran Desert and below 2,000 feet in Mojave and Colorado deserts
Regions of Use	3, 4, 5, 6, 7
Soil	Dry, decomposed granite, sand, clay loam, limestone, low organic content, well drained
Water	Once a month in hot weather
Sun or Shade	◑ ○
Height × Width	Maximum: 5 feet × 2½ feet. Usual: 3 feet × 2 feet
Protective Mechanisms	Stems contain latex
Leaves or Stems	Leafless; if unwatered, stems green only in spring
Ornamental Value	Small creamy white flowers, 4-inch silk-filled pods
Other Value	Larval plant for butterflies, flowers source of nectar for butterflies and tarantula hawks

Ajamete is one of the most attractive and drought-resistant of the southwestern milkweeds. It has upright stems that are hued very pale green to almost white. Ajamete is usually short and dense and somewhat resembles candelilla, even though they are not related at all. Use it in a flower garden to attract butterflies, or use it as an evergreen accent where you want something light and grassy in texture. It also does well in a large patio pot. Give your ajamete just a little water in the summer to keep it green. If it is a blistering summer and the air gets unusually hot and dry, your ajamete may fade to an attractive parchment tan. Don't worry. It will revive when the temperature drops and cooling rains fall. If some stems don't green up again, trim them out to maintain a groomed appearance. Where ajamete grows along washes, it is often quite abundant, so if you are simulating an arroyo, you can use drifts of it (nothing lined up, please) as you would use clumps of bunch grass or reed.

28	Common Name	Desert spoon, sotol, desert candle
	Latin Name	*Dasylirion wheeleri*
	Native Habitat	Between 3,800 and 6,000 feet in Chihuahuan Desert
	Regions of Use	3, 4, 5, 6, 7
	Soil	Dry, decomposed granite, sand, clay loam, limestone, low organic content, well drained
	Water	None (in El Paso and Las Cruces) to once a month
	Sun or Shade	○
	Height × Width	Maximum: 7 feet × 4 feet. Usual: 2 feet × 2 feet, not counting bloom stalk
	Protective Mechanisms	Spines along edges of leaves
	Leaves	Evergreen
	Ornamental Value	Texture, yellow flowers on 15- to 20-foot stalks
	Other Value	Flowers visited by hummingbirds; browsed by bighorn and cattle in droughts; used to make liquor, rope, and mats; roasted and eaten like artichokes

Desert spoon looks similar to agaves, but its leaves are much narrower, and it doesn't die after flowering. It is also similar to nolinas, although its leaves are stiffer and less grasslike. And, like yuccas, it might form a trunk—3 feet is typical on very old specimens. Desert spoon, called sotol in the Chihuahuan Desert, has been popular in southwestern and southern California landscapes for many years, mostly for the way the spiny edges of the leaves catch the light. But there's another reason—the lovely pale blue color, which echoes other pale, gray, or silvery-leaved desert plants. In its native habitat, these might include mariola, plume tiquilia, prickly pear, desert marigold, and California poppy, all set off by the darker foliage of creosote, ephedra, Spanish bayonet, ocotillo, and skeletonleaf goldeneye and the pale dormant gold of desert grasses. In a garden where winters are milder, you might use it with cenizo, New Mexico agave, ajamete, and candelilla, along with flowers such as brittlebush, mesa greggia, blackfoot daisy, and dwarf white zinnia.

29	Common Name	Claret-cup cactus, Mojave mound
	Latin Name	*Echinocereus triglochidiatus*
	Native Habitat	Mostly below 5,000 feet in Chihuahuan, high Sonoran, and Mojave deserts with saguaro or Joshua tree
	Regions of Use	1, 2, 3, 4, 5, 6, 7
	Soil	Dry, decomposed granite, sand, limestone, low organic content, well drained
	Water	None or once a month in summer
	Sun or Shade	◐ ○
	Height × Width	Maximum: 1 foot × 4 feet. Usual: 8 inches × 18 inches
	Protective Mechanisms	Spines
	Leaves or Stems	Thick, succulent stems; evergreen
	Ornamental Value	Scarlet to wine red flowers in spring or early summer
	Other Value	Flowers used by hummingbirds and butterflies; fruits eaten by songbirds, game birds, and desert mammals

Claret-cup cactus is popular with gardeners because of its small size and its long-lasting, generous blooms. Soil composition, not genes, seems to determine whether your claret-cup cactus will have orange-red flowers or purple-red ones. Although slow-growing in the wild, where drought keeps the stems wrinkled most of the year, claret-cup can form a significantly sized colony in five to eight years with regular irrigation. Be careful not to overwater: high humidity can cause fungal diseases, and moist soil can rot out the base of the plant. Even though your claret-cup might be only 2 inches across at first, put it in the middle of a 5-foot circle. Plant large shrubs and accents, such as creosote or cholla, far enough away so that their mature size will not encroach on the 5-foot circle. Small, short-lived flowers such as desert marigold, blackfoot daisy, dwarf white zinnia, mesa greggia, and any of the ephemerals are perfect for filling the space while your claret-cup is growing to maturity.

30 *Common Name*	Mormon tea, jointfir, ephedra, canutillo, longleaf teabush
Latin Name	*Ephedra trifurca*
Native Habitat	In creosote bush scrub or on the edges of washes below 7,000 feet in Sonoran, Mojave, and Chihuahuan deserts
Regions of Use	3, 4, 5, 6, 7
Soil	Dry, decomposed granite, sand, limestone, low organic content, well drained
Water	None to once a month in summer
Sun or Shade	◑ ◐ ○
Height × Width	Maximum: 15 feet × 15 feet. Usual: 4 feet × 6 feet
Protective Mechanisms	Spine at tip of stem
Leaves or Stems	Evergreen stems, yellow-green, scale leaves
Ornamental Value	Texture of stems, yellow flowers on males in spring
Other Value	Cones eaten by quail and other birds and small mammals; browse for bighorn, deer, and cattle; tea made from fresh or dried stems for arthritis and syphilis (no proof it works)
Related Species	*E. nevadensis, E. californica, E. fasciculata, E. coryi*

Mormon tea is the name given to a number of different species of ephedra prevalent throughout the Southwest and quite similar in appearance. These are the most heat-tolerant ones. You'll find them as dependable as creosote, but they are generally shorter and denser. Use any Mormon tea that is native to your area as a background shrub or evergreen accent, even one tucked up under a desert tree. Protect it from being nibbled to death while it is young; browsers love it. *E. trifurca* is the only one with spines and is the largest. *E. nevadensis* (1, 2, 3, 4, 5) grows with Joshua trees, and *E. californica* (1, 2, 3, 4, 5) tolerates the most moisture. Two of the smaller ephedras are a little different. Running ephedra, *E. coryi* (3, 4, 5, 6, 7), native to the eastern edge of the Chihuahuan Desert in Texas and partial to sand, can be a 6- to 12-inch-high ground cover with supplemental irrigation, and *E. fasciculata* (4, 5), native farther west and more drought-tolerant, is a prostrate form that can be massed to make a knee-high ground cover.

. . . .

31 *Common Name*	Candelilla
Latin Name	*Euphorbia antisyphilitica*
Native Habitat	Dry limestone slopes below 3,800 feet in Chihuahuan Desert, especially along Rio Grande River
Regions of Use	5, 6, 7
Soil	Dry, decomposed granite, sand, limestone, low organic content, well drained
Water	None to once a month in summer
Sun or Shade	◐ ○
Height × Width	Maximum: 3 feet × 4 feet. Usual: 18 inches × 18 inches
Protective Mechanisms	Milky juice toxic to browsers, may cause dermatitis on some humans
Leaves or Stems	Pale blue-green stems, waxy, evergreen in mild winters
Ornamental Value	Stems
Other Value	Commercial source of wax, harvesting has caused destruction of millions of plants in the wild

Candelilla, whose common name means "little candle," looks like a cluster of slender, pale green, waxy tapers. Its small size and polite character make it an ideal accent plant for courtyard gardens where winters are relatively mild, such as in Phoenix. It is winter-hardy in El Paso and Las Cruces only with protection, and likely to freeze back to the roots in those places every few years. If severely frozen, it takes a long time to recover. For wet winters or hard frosts, use candelilla as a pot plant and bring it inside for the winter. It can thrive for many years in a large patio pot with a drainage hole and, while outdoors, no bottom saucer. Indoors, it's fine to use a saucer, but don't allow water to stand in it. Planted outside, candelilla looks great in a rock garden among boulders. In the Trans Pecos areas of Texas, where it is native, it grows on limestone bluffs with lechuguilla, sotol, leatherstem, brown spine prickly pear, and Texas falseagave.

32	Common Name	Fishhook barrel cactus
	Latin Name	*Ferocactus wislizenii*
	Native Habitat	Deserts and grasslands, usually between 1,000 and 5,000 feet in Chihuahuan and eastern Sonoran deserts
	Regions of Use	3, 4, 5, 6, 7
	Soil	Dry, decomposed granite, sand, limestone, low organic content, well drained
	Water	None to once a month
	Sun or Shade	○
	Height × Width	Maximum: 11 feet × 2 feet. Usual: 2 to 5 feet × 1 foot
	Protective Mechanisms	Hooked spines
	Leaves or Stems	Evergreen
	Ornamental Value	Orange flowers in late summer, yellow fruit
	Other Value	Flowers used by bees, fruits eaten by many animals
	Related Species	California barrel cactus, visnaga (*F. cylindraceus,* formerly *F. acanthodes*); Coville barrel cactus (*F. emoryi*)

Barrel cacti prefer temperatures above 15 degrees F, and they require dry, fast-draining soil and full sun. However, protect the west side of a new transplant for a week to prevent sunburn. Barrel cacti are such strong focal points that it's best to use just one and surround it with open ground or low-growing desert flowers. For height next to it, use ocotillo, saguaro, or any tree yucca, so you won't be tempted to overwater. Barrel cacti are available grown from seed; please don't illegally dig one from the wild. There are basically two large barrel cacti native to the southwestern United States—**fishhook barrel cactus** in the eastern half and **California barrel cactus** (1, 2, 3, 4) in the western half. They meet in the middle near Phoenix and Tucson. California barrel has red spines and yellow flowers in the spring, while fishhook barrel has orange to red (sometimes yellow) flowers in very late summer. **Coville barrel cactus** (6) is native only where the other two meet. Its flowers bloom in midsummer and mostly are red in Arizona and yellow in Mexico.

....

33	Common Name	Texas falseagave, guapilla
	Latin Name	*Hechtia texensis*
	Native Habitat	Dry, limestone hills in Chihuahuan Desert below 3,700 feet
	Regions of Use	4, 5, 6, 7
	Soil	Dry, decomposed granite, sand, limestone, low organic content, well drained
	Water	None to once a month in summer only
	Sun or Shade	◐ ○
	Height × Width	Maximum: 2 feet × 3 feet. Usual: 18 inches × 2 feet
	Protective Mechanisms	Red, recurved spines
	Leaves or Stems	Evergreen, yellow-green, succulent
	Ornamental Value	White to peach flowers in spring, red to orange fall color
	Other Value	No information

Benny Simpson

Texas falseagave (false agave) makes handsome and succulent evergreen clumps that are finer in texture than agave but coarser than ajamete. The foliage is usually knee high and lime green. In fall, it often turns red or orange on the edges, which contrasts beautifully with the lime green center. The flowers, which appear after spring rains, are white, flushed with peachy tones, and quite profuse. As far as I know, Texas falseagave has not yet been used in landscapes—so you can be a trendsetter. Considering how attractive it is in the wild, despite drought damage, it should be quite spectacular in a garden with just a little grooming and watering during the summer. Near Boquillas Canyon in the Big Bend area of Texas, three other succulents are frequently seen with it: candelilla, brownspine prickly pear, and leatherstem. Nearby, you can find chino grama grass (*Bouteloua breviseta*) and mesquite trees. Texas falseagave often seeks rock crevices, where its roots get protection from extreme heat and cold.

34 Common Name	Red yucca
Latin Name	*Hesperaloe parviflora*
Native Habitat	Limestone hills, arroyos and mesquite thickets in Chihuahuan Desert, infrequent to rare in the wild
Regions of Use	1, 2, 3, 4, 5, 6, 7
Soil	Moist to dry, decomposed granite, sand, clay loam, limestone, low to high organic content, well drained
Water	None to once a week
Sun or Shade	◑ ○
Height × Width	Maximum: 3 feet × 5 feet. Usual: 2 feet × 3 feet
Protective Mechanisms	None
Leaves or Stems	Evergreen
Ornamental Value	Shrimp pink to dark salmon flowers on 3- to 5-foot stems
Other Value	Flowers used by hummingbirds

Red yucca is not a true red–the flowers are salmon to coral, and the stems are flamingo pink. The succulent leaves are completely spineless and are irresistible to deer and rabbits, which might explain why it is so rarely found in the wild. It is extremely easy to grow in a garden as long as you protect young plants with chicken-wire cages. Red yucca starts blooming in mid-spring. With weekly supplemental irrigation, it will bloom all summer– a boon to hummingbirds. To make a handsome specimen by a path or doorway, plant one red yucca in the center of a 6- to 8- foot circle. This will allow a comfortable amount of space around the tips of the leaves. It should reach maturity in less than five years. On a large irrigated project, red yucca can be massed 3- to 4-feet apart; doing this seems to produce shorter plants. You can also use red yucca in a large planter. Giant hesperaloe or samandoce (*H. funifera*), a common feature of watered southwestern gardens, is native to northeastern Mexico and Val Verde, Texas, where rainfall is higher. It might get 6 feet tall, not counting the bloom stalks, which are pale shrimp pink.

....

35 Common Name	Leatherstem, sangre de drago
Latin Name	*Jatropha dioica* var. *graminea*
Native Habitat	Limestone slopes below 4,000 feet in Chihuahuan Desert
Regions of Use	4, 5, 6, 7
Soil	Dry, decomposed granite, sand, limestone, low organic content, well drained
Water	None to once a month in summer
Sun or Shade	◐ ◑ ○
Height × Width	Maximum: over 3 feet. Usual: 2 feet × 3 feet
Protective Mechanisms	None
Leaves or Stems	Purple rubbery stems, leaves frost-deciduous
Ornamental Value	Stems, red fall color of leaves
Other Value	Seeds eaten by white-winged doves, coagulant for small cuts and bleeding gums, juice used as a red dye on leather
Related Species	Limberbush (*J. cuneata*), ashy limberbush (*J. cinerea*), heartleaf jatropha (*J. cardiophylla*)

It's not hard to identify jatrophas; nothing else has fat, rubbery, maroon stems. They are somewhat winter-tender and are not native west of Arizona, although they can be grown in the Lower Colorado Desert. **Leatherstem** has orange roots that travel horizontally to form colonies, but in a garden it is usually maintained as a small shrub. Frost turns the tiny leaves bright red–very pretty in contrast with the wine red stems. **Limberbush** (5, 6) is similar but larger, usually 3 to 6 feet tall, and is found in the lower Sonoran Desert. It drops its leaves during periods of drought, but they're so tiny you won't miss them. Its stems used to be cut to make basket handles. When cut, the stems bleed a clear fluid that instantly turns red. New stems come up from the roots. **Ashy limberbush** (5 and warm 6), a huge woody shrub 10 feet × 15 feet, has silvery stems. **Heartleaf jatropha** (5, 6) only 1 to 3 feet tall, has shiny heart-shaped leaves.

36 *Common Name*	Chuparosa
Latin Name	*Justicia californica* (formerly *Beloperone californica*)
Native Habitat	Washes and arroyos below 4,000 feet in Sonoran and Colorado deserts
Regions of Use	1, 2, 3, 5, 6
Soil	Dry, decomposed granite, sand, clay loam, limestone, low organic content, well drained
Water	None to once a month
Sun or Shade	◐ ◑ ○
Height × Width	Maximum: can clamber up a tree or make a mound 8 feet × 8 feet. Usual: 5 feet × 5 feet
Protective Mechanisms	None
Leaves or Stems	Stems evergreen, gray-green or yellow-green, leaves drought- and cold-deciduous
Ornamental Value	Red (rarely yellow) flowers, spring, summer, and fall
Other Value	Flowers used by hummingbirds, butterflies, orioles, warblers, and goldfinches; seeds eaten by quail and house finches; larval plant for butterflies

You'd like **chuparosa** if it did nothing more than just sit there–it's spineless, reliably evergreen, well mannered, frequently in bloom, and a good choice to put right by the front door. Gardeners use it most often as a low evergreen shrub, but it can also qualify as a flower or a vine. It drapes itself nicely in a planter or patio pot and will clamber up into the branches of a tree or onto the railings of a staircase. The biggest show of blooms is in March through May, but a few flowers are always open for hummingbirds, who really home in on it. It gets frost-damaged below 25 degrees F but bounces right back if the roots are unhurt. A Mexican relative of chuparosa, often sold as *J. sonora,* messily seeds out everywhere, so I don't recommend it.

....

37 *Common Name*	Wolf's beargrass
Latin Name	*Nolina parryi* ssp. *wolfii*
Native Habitat	In Joshua tree or pinyon/juniper woodlands in California between 3,500 and 6,000 feet in or adjacent to Mojave Desert
Regions of Use	1, 2, 3, 4, 5, 6
Soil	Dry, decomposed granite, sand, clay loam, low organic content, well drained
Water	None to once a month
Sun or Shade	◑ ○
Height × Width	Maximum: 8 feet × 10 feet, 15 feet when in bloom
Protective Mechanisms	Sharp saw-toothed edges on leaves
Leaves or Stems	Silver, evergreen
Ornamental Value	Huge size, creamy white flowers on male plants in spring
Other Value	Flowers used by bees, seeds eaten by small mammals, cover for lizards, larval plant for butterflies
Related Species	Bigelow nolina (*N. bigelovii*), mesa sacahuista (*N. erumpens*), Texas sacahuista (*N. texana*)

Nolinas make excellent landscape plants for southwestern gardens. They have the soft visual texture of grass, but they are lower-maintenance because they're evergreen and more drought-resistant. Sometimes leaves at the bottom turn tan, but these can be trimmed out. Most nolinas have the capability of developing trunks in their old age, as high as 6 feet in some cases. **Wolf's beargrass** is the largest and most dramatic, although **mesa sacahuista** and **Bigelow nolina** are also large. Others are a handy size for patio and courtyard gardens. **Texas sacahuista** is the smallest–only 2 feet tall. Once established, the roots of nolinas are massive and deep. The Chihuahuan nolinas (called sacahuistas) have their flowers partly buried in the leaves instead of held high like the Mojave nolinas. When nolina is used as an accent, give it a lot of space so the ends of its leaves don't get cramped. Rocks, flowers, other succulents, and true grasses look good around it. If you use masses to achieve a soft, grassy look, be careful–the edges of the leaves can cut.

38	
Common Name	Beavertail
Latin Name	*Opuntia basilaris*
Native Habitat	Creosote bush scrub below 3,000 feet in Sonoran and Colorado deserts, below 6,000 in Joshua tree woodland in Mojave Desert
Regions of Use	1, 2, 3, 4, 5, 6, 7
Soil	Dry, decomposed granite, sand, clay loam, low organic content, well drained
Water	None to once a month
Sun or Shade	◐ ○
Height × Width	Maximum: 4 feet × 4 feet. Usual: 1 foot × 2 feet
Protective Mechanisms	Short spines (glochids) in dark red bumps
Leaves or Stems	Evergreen
Ornamental Value	Magenta to rose (rarely white) flowers, purply green fruit
Other Value	Flowers used by bees, fruits eaten by birds and mammals
Related Species	Santa Rita prickly pear (*O. violacea* var. *santa-rita*), brownspine prickly pear (*O. phaeacantha* var. *major*)

There are many southwestern prickly pears. **Beavertail** is a favorite because it is small, has large showy flowers, and lacks long spines. However, it is covered with tiny polka-dot clusters of short, hairlike spines that can be quite painful to touch and hard to remove. Another garden-worthy prickly pear is a beautiful but cold-tender species with violet-colored pads. There are several varieties, but **Santa Rita prickly pear** (1, 2, 3, 4, 5, 6) is the one most often found in nurseries. Give it room to form a 4- to 6-foot-wide clump. The lavender color seems to deepen in response to either cold or drought. **Brownspine prickly pear** (1, 2, 3, 4, 5, 6, 7), native to the Chihuahuan, Sonoran, and Mojave deserts, has long, attractive, red-brown spines; yellow flowers with red centers; and bright magenta fruits. It's easy to grow any prickly pear from a pad. On a revegetation project, plant the pads irregularly from 4 to 25 feet apart.

39	
Common Name	Jumping cholla
Latin Name	*Opuntia fulgida*
Native Habitat	Flats, slopes below 4,000 feet in southern Arizona and Mexico
Regions of Use	6
Soil	Dry, decomposed granite, sand, low organic content, well drained
Water	None to once a month
Sun or Shade	○
Height × Width	Maximum: 7 feet × 4 feet. Usual: 4 feet × 3 feet
Protective Mechanisms	Spines
Leaves or Stems	Evergreen, succulent
Ornamental Value	Silvery fuzzy spines, pink summer flowers, chainlike fruits in fall
Other Value	Nectar for honey; nesting for cactus wrens and roadrunners; joints used by wood rats to protect their nests; fruits eaten by songbirds, game birds, antelope, and desert bighorn sheep
Related Species	Teddybear cholla (*O. bigelovii*), buckhorn cholla (*O. acanthocarpa*), tree cholla (*O. imbricata*), staghorn cholla (*O. versicolor*), and others

Jumping cholla, like the more famous teddybear cholla, has a single trunk and short branches. It looks soft and fuzzy, but it can be really nasty. Carry a comb; if attacked, comb the joint (or joints) off your clothes or skin. **Teddybear cholla** (3, 4, 5, 6) has even more spines, lime-yellow flowers in the spring, and small spiny fruits that get gobbled up by animals as soon as they ripen in the fall. **Staghorn** (5, 6) and **buckhorn** (3, 4, 5, 6) are native to high Sonoran deserts and have longer, more slender joints; multitrunks; and exceptionally attractive branching. The colorful **tree cholla** (4, 6, 7)–a Chihuahuan plant–has magenta flowers and pure yellow, long-lasting fruits, and it boasts a very pretty silvery-spined variety (5, 6). All the chollas spread aggressively by fallen joints, so keep them raked up. Otherwise, you'll end up with a cholla thicket–a formidable thought.

40		
Common Name	Mojave yucca	
Latin Name	*Yucca schidigera*	
Native Habitat	Creosote bush scrub below 8,000 feet in southern Mojave Desert and coastal sagescrub and chaparral in San Diego County and Baja California	
Regions of Use	1, 2, 3, 4, 5, 6, 7	
Soil	Dry, decomposed granite, sand, low organic content, well drained	
Water	None to once a month	
Sun or Shade	◑ ○	
Height × Width	Maximum: 15 feet × 8 feet with a trunk. Usual: 5 feet × 4 feet, including flower stalk	
Protective Mechanisms	Spines at ends of leaves	
Leaves or Stems	Evergreen	
Ornamental Value	White and maroon flowers	
Other Value	Flowers pollinated by yucca moth and eaten by some animals; seeds eaten by many animals; larval plant for butterflies; leaves used for arthritis, sandals, and rope	
Related Species	Banana yucca, datil, blue yucca (*Y. baccata*)	

Mojave yucca belongs to two wildly different plant communities–Joshua tree woodland near Las Vegas and coastal scrub in San Diego County. In the Mojave, use it with Joshua tree and banana yucca. Add brittlebush and Goodding's verbena for spring color, and Sonoran goldeneye and turpentinebush for fall flowers. Near San Diego, mix Mojave yucca with Torrey pine and lemonadeberry, and use Cleveland sage and coast sunflower for spring color. Corethrogyne, zauschneria, and woolly bluecurls can be planted for fall flowers. **Banana yucca** (1, 2, 3, 4, 5, 6, 7) is a beautiful soft blue and is less than 4 feet tall with no trunk, making it a convenient size for most gardens. It likes to form colonies as it matures, however, so it's best to leave a 10-foot-square spot for it to expand in. Water it occasionally in the hot, low desert cities. Its native habitat is on grassy hillsides with Joshua tree, saguaro, Wheeler's sotol, barrel cactus, or New Mexico agave.

....

41		
Common Name	Our Lord's candle, foothill yucca	
Latin Name	*Yucca whipplei*	
Native Habitat	Chaparral, coastal and desert scrub between 1,000 and 4,000 feet in southern California and northern Baja California	
Regions of Use	1, 2, 3, 5	
Soil	Dry, decomposed granite, sand, clay loam, low organic content, well drained	
Water	None or once a month	
Sun or Shade	○	
Height × Width	Maximum: 5 feet × 6 feet with 10-foot flower stalk. Usual: 3 feet × 5 feet with 6-foot flower stalk	
Protective Mechanisms	Spines at ends of leaves	
Leaves or Stems	Silvery evergreen	
Ornamental Value	Silvery foliage, creamy white flowers (once only)	
Other Value	Pollinated by pronuba moth, larval plant for pronuba moth	

Our Lord's candle is more like an agave than the other yuccas in that it blooms only once. Unlike an agave, the leaves are very narrow. It might be mistaken for a Wheeler sotol, except that the long spines occur only at the ends of the leaves, not all along the edges. The foliage, a beautifully rounded spiky ball of pale silvery leaves, looks handsome for four to eight years before it gathers up enough energy to bloom. The flowers start blossoming when the stalk is only a foot or two above the leaves, and they continue for several weeks in late spring, ultimately producing about 6 feet of blooms. After the seed has finished ripening, the whole plant turns brown. Like both yuccas and agaves, Our Lord's candle propagates itself by offsets as well as seeds. Cut the parent plant back to the ground and hope for pups. There are four subspecies; ssp. *percursa* is different from the others because it produces offsets before flowering, gradually forming colonies, and its flowers are sometimes scented as sweetly as orange blossoms.

3 LEAFY EVERGREEN SHRUBS

At this garden in Malibu, designed by landscape architect Paul Nota, toyon is pruned up like a tree, while coffeeberry, ceanothus 'Eleanor Taylor', and a nonnative arbutus are pruned as shrubs.

LEAFY EVERGREEN SHRUBS FORM THE BACKBONE OF MOST GARDENS. FOR THE BETTER part of this century, they were used as formal foundation plantings or hedges. But since the 1980s, landscapers have been massing a number of low-growing evergreen shrubs together to create a knee-high ground cover. I especially like a tall screen of evergreen shrubs

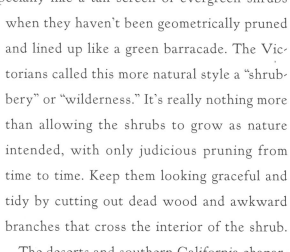

when they haven't been geometrically pruned and lined up like a green barracade. The Victorians called this more natural style a "shrubbery" or "wilderness." It's really nothing more than allowing the shrubs to grow as nature intended, with only judicious pruning from time to time. Keep them looking graceful and tidy by cutting out dead wood and awkward branches that cross the interior of the shrub.

The deserts and southern California chaparral communities both boast a wide variety of beautiful evergreens. Because these environments are so hot and dry, nature gave the leafy evergreens several clever ways to reduce transpiration. Some plants have thick leaves impregnated with aromatic, spicy oils to prevent moisture from escaping from the leaves. Some have leaves so heavily varnished and glossy that they reflect light and reduce absorbed heat. The leaves on others are velvety with soft pale gray fuzz that holds on to moisture.

Colors range from dark green to pale blue-green, gray, and silver to warmer shades of yellow-green, bright green, and even khaki, while gardens containing these shrubs are rich with scents that are spicy and invigorating.

In addition, some shrubs have large or flamboyant flowers; others have colorful fruits. All provide a safe haven for wildlife from predators, the summer's scorching sun, and the cold winds of winter.

In the deserts, you'll find these evergreen shrubs growing with an assortment of succulent accents, all spaced very far apart and able to show off their true shapes. While this is aesthetically pleasing, the reason is practical: there simply isn't enough rainfall to support a tightly packed community. Roots near the surface of the soil must extend way beyond the visible part of the plant, ready to absorb every drop of rain that falls. Creosotes are the most ubiquitous evergreen shrubs in our deserts. They normally grow 20 to 30 feet apart in the wild, and they are prettiest at the 30-foot spacing, which allows room for a scattering of other plants in between.

A creosote landscape is fairly easy to have. Just find a good piece of creosote desert near you, imitate the layout and plant palette, and then let it come right up to your house. It looks good all year with virtually no maintenance. Average heights of all the desert shrubs in this landscape range from 1 to 6 feet, and nearly everything is aromatic. The colors are mostly silvery, with plenty of lime green and dark green for contrast.

In California chaparral, the evergreen shrubs are crowded together with no bare soil between them. Viewed up close, coastal sage-scrub—soft chaparral—is a waist- to shoulder-high tangle of stems, leaves, and flowers, while inland the evergreen—hard—chaparral often grows well over your head.

One of the most important evergreen shrubs in chaparral is ceanothus, also called California lilac. It is a beautiful evergreen shrub that covers itself with blue or white flowers early every spring. A mass of ceanothus can turn an entire hillside smoky or vivid blue with lush blooms. California gardeners should be ecstatic about them—these shrubs are not only gorgeous in the spring, but they stay green and fresh-looking all through a long rainless summer. They do, however, get root rot when planted next to a lawn or typical California landscape that gets watered more than once every three weeks in the summer. The solution is obvious: Plant them with other California natives—and get the added bonus of lower water bills. There is at least one variety suitable for every coastal and chaparral area of southern California.

OPPOSITE: Planted to provide privacy, these huge, freshly salvaged creosotes at the Lehmann home courtyard in Paradise Valley, Arizona, designed by Christy Ten Eyck, will thicken up in a couple of years. BELOW: Evergreen shrubs that also blossom give structure to a flower garden. In this portion of the native garden at Quail Botanical Gardens in Encinitas, California, two kinds of ceanothus—*Ceanothus cuneatus* var. *fascicularis* and the white form of *C. thyrsiflorus* called 'Snow Flurry'—bloom profusely with coast sunflower, giant coreopsis, and black sage.

42 *Common Name*	Blue manzanita, bigberry manzanita
Latin Name	*Arctostaphylos glauca*
Native Habitat	Dry slopes, chaparral below 4,700 feet from Contra Costa County to desert mountains to Baja California
Regions of Use	1, 2, 3
Soil	Dry, decomposed granite, sand, sandstone, low organic content, well drained
Water	None to once a month–drip irrigation only
Sun or Shade	◗ ○
Height × Width	Maximum: 25 feet × 20 feet. Usual: 8 feet × 8 feet
Protective Mechanisms	None
Leaves or Stems	Evergreen, pale blue, smooth or velvety
Ornamental Value	Dark red to chocolate trunks, white to pink flowers in early spring
Other Value	Flowers used by bees, fruits eaten by birds and coyotes, cover
Related Species	Refugio manzanita (*A. refugioensis*)

Blue manzanita is the most common southern California manzanita. Its beautiful, dark red, smooth trunks turn chocolate brown and peel in the summer, revealing orange-red bark underneath, which then gradually darkens. Then the cycle is repeated. This large shrub needs no supplemental watering at all in the summer and requires very good drainage during the winter. It's happiest planted on a slope. If you're looking for a small leafy tree to accompany fremontia, ceanothus, and other southern California natives that appreciate summer dryness, blue manzanita, pruned up to show off its trunks, is the perfect choice. In a garden with once-a-month summer watering (drip irrigation only; sprinklers cause a leaf fungus), choose **Refugio manzanita** (1, 2, 3). While it's rare in the wild, growing only around sandstone outcrops in Refugio Pass in the Santa Ynez Mountains in Santa Barbara County, it's fairly easy to find in nurseries. It makes a handsome 12-foot shrub, and under some conditions its new leaves are a lovely red.

··

43 *Common Name*	Desert holly
Latin Name	*Atriplex hymenelytra*
Native Habitat	On slopes, washes, and shrubland below 2,000 feet (mostly below 1,000 feet) in Colorado, Mojave, and Sonoran deserts
Regions of Use	3, 4, 5, 6
Soil	Dry, decomposed granite, sand, gypsum, low organic content, well drained
Water	None to once a month in summer
Sun or Shade	○
Height × Width	Maximum: 3 feet × 3 feet. Usual: 18 inches × 2 feet
Protective Mechanisms	Aromatic oils discourage some browsers
Leaves or Stems	Silver, evergreen, rarely drought-deciduous; firm, downy
Ornamental Value	Silvery foliage, golden papery seed clusters on females
Other Value	Fruits for songbirds, browse, holiday decorations

Desert holly has large, soft leaves and a compact shape that makes it ideal for small gardens. Its silvery leaves contrast well with plants bearing dark green or yellow-green foliage, but it also looks good with all the other pale blue, gray, or silvery-leaved plants. This plant is for the warm deserts only. It doesn't have a lot of cold tolerance, and it really hates being both cold *and* wet, as can happen in most of southern California. On the other hand, if this evergreen gets too dry, it can drop its leaves. It will, however, give a warning–the leaves will start turning *pink*. Water right away and they will remain evergreen and not drop. Although masses of desert holly look great as a ground cover in a courtyard or commercial setting, this dense look is foreign to a desert setting. There, scatter desert holly among an open mixture of succulent accents and flowers. This imitates how bursage is used, but looks more elegant.

44 *Common Name*	Red barberry
Latin Name	*Berberis haematocarpa (Mahonia haematocarpa)*
Native Habitat	Between 3,000 and 7,200 feet in Chihuahuan, Sonoran, and eastern Mojave deserts
Regions of Use	2, 3, 4, 6, 7
Soil	Dry, decomposed granite, sand, limestone, low organic content, well drained
Water	None (where native) to twice a month
Sun or Shade	◑ ○
Height × Width	Maximum: 12 feet × 15 feet. Usual: 6 feet × 8 feet
Protective Mechanisms	Prickles on leaves
Leaves or Stems	Evergreen, gray-green, hollylike
Ornamental Value	Fragrant yellow flowers, red berries, purple fall color
Other Value	Flowers used by butterflies and bees, fruits eaten by birds and mammals, cover for many small desert creatures, roots and bark have medicinal properties, yellow dye from stems
Related Species	Nevin's barberry (*B. nevinii* or *M. nevinii*); agarito, algerita (*B. trifoliata*)

You may be familiar with Oregon grape holly (*B. aquifolium*) and creeping mahonia (*B. a.* var. *repens*)–species that are native to cooler parts of the West. For Southwest gardens, instead use these native small-leaved barberries. They can withstand sun, heat, and drought. Also, they have deliciously fragrant flowers and showy red fruit. **Red barberry** is found in foothills and mountains from Texas to California, while **agarito** (4, 7) is a Chihuahuan plant. **Nevin's barberry** (1, 2, 3), limited to chaparral or washes in southwestern California, is considered endangered but is available at nurseries. Use one barberry as a large accent, or mass several in a hedge. Companion plants are sugarbush, littleleaf sumac, Apache-plume, Mormon tea, yuccas, and cacti. Fremontia, California scrub oak, manzanita, and ceanothus can be added in California.

45 *Common Name*	Woolly butterflybush
Latin Name	*Buddleia marrubiifolia*
Native Habitat	Limestone arroyos and canyons from 1,800 to 3,800 feet in Chihuahuan Desert in Texas and Mexico
Regions of Use	3, 5, 6
Soil	Dry, decomposed granite, sand, limestone, low organic content, well drained
Water	Once a month
Sun or Shade	◑ ○
Height × Width	Maximum: 5 feet × 6 feet. Usual: 3 feet × 4 feet
Protective Mechanisms	None
Leaves or Stems	Silver, evergreen, fuzzy
Ornamental Value	Silvery foliage, small orange balls of flowers after rain
Other Value	Flowers used by hummingbirds, butterflies, and bees; browse for sheep, goat, and deer

Many gardeners use the Asian buddleias to attract butterflies. In the deserts of the arid Southwest this doesn't work very well because the plants shrivel up in the heat of summer. **Woolly butterflybush** is in the same family but is well acclimated to the warm deserts. It will occasionally get frozen in Las Vegas, El Paso, and Las Cruces, so it's best to use it in a patio pot in those locales. The flowers are orange and yellow, rather like a lantana flower, but smaller and arranged in a sphere. With a little extra water in spring and fall, woolly butterflybush blooms profusely, but too much water drowns it. Use it wherever you want a very soft shrub. It can get quite big on its own, but you can keep it small if you wish by first making it into a ball the size you want and then pick-pruning. Contrast its softness with a crisp-edged succulent. I love it silhouetted against either adobe or limestone. Chuparosa, ocotillo, globe mallow, and California poppy will accentuate the orange in its flowers.

46 *Common Name*	Santa Barbara ceanothus
Latin Name	*Ceanothus impressus* var. *impressus*
Native Habitat	Chaparral and coastal bluffs below 1,500 feet in Santa Barbara and San Luis Obispo counties
Regions of Use	1, 2
Soil	Dry, decomposed granite, sand, low organic content, well drained
Water	None to once a month
Sun or Shade	◑ ○
Height × Width	Maximum: 10 feet × 8 feet. Usual: 5 feet × 6 feet
Protective Mechanisms	None
Leaves or Stems	Evergreen, dark green, small and round
Ornamental Value	Blue flowers, not fragrant
Other Value	Flowers used by butterflies, honey plant for bees, larval plant for butterflies, browse, cover
Related Species	White lilac (*C. verrucosus*), greenbark ceanothus (*C. spinosus*), and many other species and hybrids

Ceanothus that grow along the coast are used to mist-laden breezes. **Santa Barbara ceanothus** is naturally shorter and denser than many ceanothus. It has an outstanding blue color and has been used in many of the popular hybrids, such as 'Concha'. These hybrids have been chosen for their intensely blue flowers, but even more importantly for being able to withstand extra irrigation. That's why they cannot be naturalized in southern California. Use them in your garden like large flowers, expect them to die young, and replace them every 5 to 10 years. **White lilac** (1, 2, 3) has showy white flowers. It is stiff, most often 8 feet tall, and blooms very early. Use it with Torrey pine, laurel-leaf sumac, black sage, coast sunflower, and Mojave yucca. Once it's established, stop watering it in the summer. **Greenbark ceanothus** (1, 2, 3) can form a tree 20 feet tall, and its lime green bark is attractive all year. It's a little less sensitive than many ceanothus to overwatering in heavy loam soils.

47 *Common Name*	Chaparral whitethorn
Latin Name	*Ceanothus leucodermis*
Native Habitat	Chaparral, southern oak woodland, interior valleys below 6,000 feet from Sierra Nevada foothills to Baja California
Regions of Use	1, 2, 3
Soil	Dry, decomposed granite, sand, sandstone, low organic content, well drained
Water	None to once a month
Sun or Shade	◑ ○
Height × Width	Maximum: 12 feet × 12 feet. Usual: 6 feet × 6 feet
Protective Mechanisms	Small spines on branches
Leaves or Stems	Evergreen
Ornamental Value	Pastel blue, pink, or white fragrant flowers in early spring; smooth white or palest green branches
Other Value	Flowers used by butterflies and bees, fruits for songbirds and game birds, browse, cover, larval plant for butterflies
Related Species	Woollyleaf ceanothus (*C. tomentosus* var. *olivaceus*)

One of the best ceanothus for inland gardens is **chaparral whitethorn**. Take care not to *over*water it. Once a month in the summer is plenty, and be sure the roots get a chance to dry out between waterings. The specimen we saw at Quail Botanical Gardens in San Diego looked enchantingly misty with its pale blue profusion of flowers. Use chaparral whitethorn with fremontia, blue manzanita, and other chaparral plants. **Woollyleaf ceanothus** (1, 2, 3), a large shrub with woolly dark green leaves that might be silvery on the undersides, has flowers that range from a lovely bright shade of blue to palest pastel blue. It grows in chaparral from the Redlands and the Santa Ana Mountains south to Baja California below 3,500 feet. Use it in full sun with blue-eyed grass, purple needlegrass, lemonadeberry, Cleveland sage, and spring perennial morning glory.

48	Common Name	San Diego summer holly
	Latin Name	*Comarostaphylis diversifolia* ssp. *diversifolia*
	Native Habitat	RARE, coastal chaparral in sandy soils below 1,500 feet, from Santa Barbara to Baja California
	Regions of Use	1, 2, 3
	Soil	Dry, decomposed granite, sand, sandstone, low organic content, well drained
	Water	None to once a month
	Sun or Shade	◑ ◐ ○
	Height × Width	Maximum: 20 feet × 20 feet. Usual: 20 feet × 20 feet
	Protective Mechanisms	None
	Leaves or Stems	Evergreen, leathery, glossy
	Ornamental Value	White flowers, red berries from midsummer to winter, red-brown peeling bark
	Other Value	Flowers used by butterflies and bees, fruits eaten by songbirds
	Related Species	Channel Island summer holly (*C. d.* ssp. *planifolia*)

Summer hollies are most often small, multitrunked trees and are prized for their beautifully smooth exfoliating bark. The soft red berries are eye-catching and will attract summer songbirds to your garden. **San Diego summer holly** grows with Vine Hill manzanita (*Arctostaphylos densiflora*), woollyleaf ceanothus, toyon, lemonadeberry, and, where a little more moisture is available, fuchsia flowering current. If you mass it for a thicket effect, it will get 6 to 10 feet tall, but a specimen planted in full sun will always grow to about 20 feet tall. **Channel Island summer holly** (1, 2, 3), found on Santa Rosa, Santa Cruz, and Santa Catalina islands, is the one more frequently found in nurseries. It requires more water than the San Diego summer holly, and some gardeners recommend watering it as much as once a week. You can tell the two apart, because the San Diego summer holly has loose clusters of fruit and leaves that curl under at the margins. The Channel Island summer holly has flat leaves and red berries lined up in rows.

49	Common Name	Littleleaf cordia
	Latin Name	*Cordia parvifolia*
	Native Habitat	Creosote scrub in Sonoran Desert and Baja California
	Regions of Use	2, 3, 5, 6
	Soil	Dry, decomposed granite, sand, low organic content, well drained
	Water	None to once a month
	Sun or Shade	○
	Height × Width	Maximum: 12 feet × 12 feet. Usual: 6 feet × 8 feet
	Protective Mechanisms	None
	Leaves or Stems	Evergreen
	Ornamental Value	White flowers, black bark
	Other Value	Flowers used by butterflies and bees, fruits eaten by birds and mammals

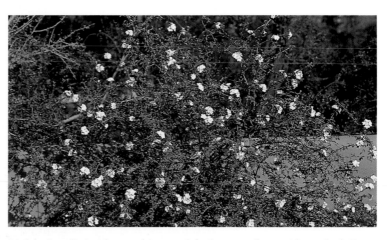

Littleleaf cordia is either a multistemmed shrub or a small tree with gray bark. Stems coming up from the base are so long and straight that the Seri Indians find them useful for dislodging high-growing saguaro fruits. The overall effect is never dense, however, not even in early spring when the branches are covered with pure white 2-inch flowers and last year's dark green leaves have been exchanged for fresh bright green ones. Because its branches are so prominent and airy, littleleaf cordia looks best silhouetted against a smooth wall with no other shrubs around it. Cover its feet with decomposed granite or paving stones, and plant only very low-growing flowers. For an all-white scene, use blackfoot daisy or white zinnia. California poppy blooms at the same time, and a mixture of white, pale yellow, and gold poppies would look breathtaking underneath.

50	*Common Name*	Tree poppy

Latin Name — *Dendromecon rigida*

Native Habitat — Dry slopes, chaparral between 1,000 and 3,000 feet from northern coastal ranges to Baja California

Regions of Use — 1, 2, 3, 5

Soil — Dry, decomposed granite, sand, low organic content, well drained

Water — None to once a month in summer

Sun or Shade — ○

Height × Width — Maximum: 18 feet × 18 feet. Usual: 10 feet × 8 feet

Protective Mechanisms — None

Leaves or Stems — Evergreen, gray, firm and narrow

Ornamental Value — Yellow flowers, white shredding bark

Other Value — Flowers used by bees, cover

Related Species — Channel Island tree poppy (*D. hartfordii*)

Tree poppy has 2- to 3-inch satiny, golden flowers that cover the plant in spring but then continue to display a few blooms nearly all year. It is shrubby when young, but it grows into a small multistemmed tree. The trunks are very pale—some are almost white—and the bark is thin and shredding and very pretty. The leaves are narrow, almost willowlike, and a bright, fresh green. **Channel Island tree poppies** (1, 2) have pale bluish leaves, especially those from Santa Catalina and San Clemente islands. A tree poppy has a deep, carrot-shaped taproot that goes straight down for 3 to 5 feet and makes it very sensitive to irrigation. Your tree poppy will build a tolerance to regular watering if you alternately deep-water the roots with a hose and then let the top few inches of soil dry out. Combine tree poppies with fremontia—the two produce golden blooms at the same time—and for contrasting blue, use Cleveland sage, black sage, chaparral whitethorn, and woolly bluecurls, with wild Canterbury bells.

- -

51	*Common Name*	Hopbush, chapoliztle, switch sorrel, casol

Latin Name — *Dodonaea viscosa*

Native Habitat — Canyons and grassland between 2,000 and 5,000 feet in Sonoran Desert from Verde River south into Mexico

Regions of Use — 2, 3, 5, 6

Soil — Dry, decomposed granite, sand, clay loam, low organic content, well drained

Water — Once or twice a month in dry seasons

Sun or Shade — ◑ ○

Height × Width — Maximum: 12 feet × 8 feet. Usual: 6 feet × 6 feet

Protective Mechanisms — Saponin in leaves discourages most browsers, causes dermatitis on some humans

Leaves or Stems — Evergreen, lime green, aromatic, sticky

Ornamental Value — Rosy papery fruits

Other Value — Flowers used by bees, fruits eaten by game birds, cover for nesting

In a warm desert city where winter temperatures don't fall below the mid-20s, **hopbush** is a good choice for screening. Use it instead of oleanders to frame a pool or patio; it requires less water and less pruning. Its large, bright yellow-green leaves match the lime green trunks of paloverde, and its rosy fruits give color for a long time. For a more interesting hedge, don't plant shrubs in a neat row. Stagger a couple of creosotes, and then mix jojoba and hopbush in a gentle irregular curve. Contrasted with the dark green of creosote and the pale leaves of jojoba, the hopbush will stand out and look especially lush. Hopbush can also be used as a specimen shrub. For example, just one unpruned, openly branched hopbush next to the house could soften and balance a tiny front garden consisting of an ocotillo and a few other desert plants. This would be much less work than a foundation planting, and also much prettier. Two warnings: The purple variety is from New Zealand and is less cold- and drought-hardy. And, all hopbushes are susceptible to Texas root rot if overwatered.

52	
Common Name	Apache-plume, ponil
Latin Name	*Fallugia paradoxa*
Native Habitat	Arroyos, Joshua tree or pinyon woodlands between 3,000 and 8,000 feet in Chihuahuan and Mojave deserts
Regions of Use	1, 2, 3, 4, 5, 6, 7
Soil	Dry, decomposed granite, sand, clay loam, limestone, low organic content, well drained
Water	None to once a month in dry seasons
Sun or Shade	○
Height × Width	Maximum: 6 feet × 6 feet. Usual: 4 feet × 4 feet
Protective Mechanisms	None
Leaves or Stems	Evergreen or winter-deciduous, dark green, tiny
Ornamental Value	White roselike flowers, pink plumed fruits
Other Value	Flowers used by butterflies and bees, browse for mule deer, cover for pack-rat middens

Apache-plume is loved chiefly for its feathery seeds. Colors range from palest peach to a good strong pink. The flowers appear after rains and the seeds ripen quickly, so there are frequently both flowers and pink plumes decorating this shrub. In the Chihuahuan Desert, combine it with littleleaf sumac, creosote, New Mexico agave, banana yucca, ocotillo, turpentinebush, Arizona cottontop, plume tiquilia, chocolate daisy, skeletonleaf goldeneye, and blackfoot daisy. In the Mojave Desert, use it with Joshua tree, creosote, banana yucca, Mojave yucca, Mormon tea, snakeweed (*Gutierrezia sarothrae*), rabbitbrush (*Chrysothamnus nauseosus*), globe mallow, brittlebush, and desert marigold. Two other desert plants of the rose family–cowania (cliff rose) and purshia (antelope bush)–are similar to Apache-plume and sometimes form hybrids with it and each other, producing cream to yellow flowers and aromatic foliage that smells like attar of roses crossed with quinine.

53	
Common Name	California fremontia, flannelbush, California slippery elm
Latin Name	*Fremontodendron californicum* ssp. *californicum*
Native Habitat	Chaparral and oak/pine woodland between 1,300 and 6,000 feet in California, central Arizona, and Baja California
Regions of Use	1, 2, 3
Soil	Dry, decomposed granite, sand, low organic content, well drained
Water	None or once a month, likes to be dry in summer
Sun or Shade	◑ ○
Height × Width	Maximum: 25 feet × 30 feet, with 16-inch trunk. Usual: 12 feet × 15 feet
Protective Mechanisms	Hairs on leaves, stems, and capsules cause skin irritation
Leaves	Evergreen, pale velvet on undersides
Ornamental Value	1- to 2-inch golden flowers in spring
Other Value	Nesting for songbirds, browse for cattle
Related Species	Mexican fremontia (*F. mexicanum*)

When fremontia covers itself with large golden flowers in the spring, it is one of the world's truly spectacular plants. It can be used as a large evergreen shrub, pruned into a small multi-trunked tree, or–in the small garden–trained on a lattice. **California fremontia** flowers profusely and all at once, making it extremely showy when viewed from a distance. **Mexican fremontia (1, 2, 3)** is more treelike in stature; it has showy 3-inch flowers that fade from gold to orange and are spaced out over a two- to three-week period. This fremontia is native within 15 miles of the ocean in Orange, San Diego, and southwest Imperial counties and Baja California. Most fremontias sold at nurseries are hybrids between the two. All grow very quickly, often blooming the first season after planting. Once established, they do best without any watering in the summer–they're very susceptible to root rot. Good companion plants that also do not require summer water are ceanothus, manzanita, tree poppy, Our Lord's candle, and other California chaparral shrubs and flowers.

54 *Common Name*	Toyon, hollywood
Latin Name	*Heteromeles arbutifolia*
Native Habitat	Chaparral and oak woodland below 4,000 feet in California and Baja California
Regions of Use	1, 2, 3
Soil	Semidry, decomposed granite, sand, clay loam, rich to low organic content, well drained
Water	None to once a month
Sun or Shade	◑ ○
Height × Width	Maximum: 24 feet × 10 feet. Usual: 8 to 15 feet × 8 feet
Protective Mechanisms	Toothed edges on leaves
Leaves or Stems	Evergreen, dark green
Ornamental Value	White flowers in summer, red to orange (sometimes yellow) berries in winter
Other Value	Flowers used by bees, fruits eaten by waxwings and robins, cover

The city of Hollywood was named after **toyon**, because once upon a time it was a chaparral community. Toyon was one of the dominant shrubs, along with live oak, California scrub oak, Engelmann oak (*Quercus engelmannii*), coffeeberry, redberry, snowberry, chamise, and many other evergreens. Toyon adapts readily to all types of California gardens because it will tolerate richer soils and more moisture than so many other chaparral plants. In dry chaparral, it is an 8-foot shrub, but in a garden or a more protected site, it makes a 15-foot multitrunked tree. It can be trimmed into a hedge, but it flowers only on second-year growth, so severe and regular pruning prevents the formation of the berries. A few branches pruned for Christmas decorations won't hurt, and light thinning can be done annually. The red berries are dry and somewhat mealy—made for long shelf life rather than juicy succulence. Birds that live in a garden year-round will depend on them during the winter. In early spring, after the berries have fermented, migrating waxwings and robins, in particular, will have a party on your toyon.

55 *Common Name*	Desert lavender
Latin Name	*Hyptis emoryi*
Native Habitat	Washes, canyons, and creosote bush scrub below 5,000 feet in Colorado, southern Mojave, and Sonoran deserts
Regions of Use	2, 3, 4, 5, 6
Soil	Dry, sandy or gravelly, low organic content, well drained
Water	None to once a month
Sun or Shade	○
Height × Width	Maximum: 12 feet × 15 feet. Usual: 8 feet × 8 feet
Protective Mechanisms	Aromatic oils discourage some browsers
Leaves or Stems	Evergreen, silver, velvety, aromatic
Ornamental Value	Lavender flowers, minty fragrance in spring
Other Value	Flowers used by hummingbirds, butterflies, and bees (good honey); fruits eaten by songbirds and game birds, browsed by bighorn sheep, cover, seeds eaten as a kind of chia

Desert lavender is best used as a specimen shrub, preferably near a walk, window, or sitting area, where you can enjoy its minty fresh leaves and flowers. It does get big, so plant it at least 6 feet away. For an elegant, civilized shape, once a year give it an airy pruning from the inside, leaving the tips of the branches soft and natural. This lends gracefulness to the straight stems and ensures that there will be plenty of flowers every year. If its form has gotten out of hand, the plant can be cut to the ground to start anew. From well-established roots, it can regain its former height in just two years. Companion plants that look great with it and like all the same conditions are whitethorn acacia, desert agave, ocotillo, Mojave yucca, and creosote. Either smoketree, with its dark blue flowers and pale branches, or silver-trunked ironwood would echo the pale foliage and lavender flowers.

56 *Common Name*	Bladderpod
Latin Name	*Isomeris arborea*
Native Habitat	Desert washes and coastal bluffs below 4,000 feet in Colorado and Mojave deserts and southwestern California and Channel Islands
Regions of Use	1, 2, 3, 4, 5, 6
Soil	Dry, decomposed granite, sand, low organic content, well drained
Water	None to once a month
Sun or Shade	○
Height × Width	Maximum: 6 feet × 8 feet. Usual: 4 feet × 5 feet
Protective Mechanisms	None
Leaves or Stems	Evergreen, yellow-green or gray, aromatic
Ornamental Value	Yellow flowers almost all year but especially in spring
Other Value	Flowers used by hummingbirds

Bladderpod is a prime evergreen shrub for the Colorado Desert. It survives on its own there, so it needs just a little pruning and irrigation to look wonderful all year in your garden. With irrigation, it is almost everblooming–a point that resident hummingbirds will not miss. Plant it in front of the house or around the patio with ironwood or smoketree for height, and creosote and desert lavender for additional evergreen shrubs. At their feet plant low-growing flowers such as birdcage primrose, desert marigold, Borrego aster, and ephemerals for an easy-care, attractive, and colorful landscape. To make your garden a hummingbird heaven, add globe mallow, ocotillo, desert willow, and chuparosa. In San Diego, the plant palette could include the leafy evergreens jojoba and lemonadeberry; several succulents such as Mojave yucca, Mormon tea, Our Lord's candle, prickly pear, and Shaw's agave; and dudleya for a low ground cover.

57 *Common Name*	Creosote bush, hediondilla, governadora, guamis
Latin Name	*Larrea tridentata* (*L. divaricata* ssp. *tridentata*)
Native Habitat	Flats, washes, dry slopes, below 5,000 feet in Mojave, Colorado, Sonoran, and Chihuahuan deserts
Regions of Use	4, 5, 6, 7
Soil	Dry, decomposed granite, sand, clay loam, limestone, low organic content, well drained
Water	None to once a month in hot weather
Sun or Shade	◑ ○
Height × Width	Maximum: 10 feet × 10 feet. Usual: 6 feet × 6 feet
Protective Mechanisms	Aromatic oils discourage some browsers and, extremely rarely, cause dermatitis on some humans
Leaves or Stems	Evergreen, dark olive green, aromatic
Ornamental Value	Yellow flowers, fragrance of leaves when humidity is high
Other Value	Soil stabilization, shelter for desert tortoise, seeds eaten by desert animals, cover for Gambel and scaled quail

Creosote bush is the primary evergreen shrub in most desert landscapes. It is very difficult to grow from seed, but it has recently become available in large quantities from Mountain States Wholesale Nursery in Glendale, Arizona. With irrigation, these nursery-propagated plants grow fairly quickly. Sometimes nurseries get an opportunity to dig and box up mature wild creosotes 8 feet tall before they get destroyed by construction. These are called salvaged creosotes. If you are building in the desert, you will definitely want to salvage your own. For a natural screen, reserve 20 to 40 feet and mass creosote bushes in a random pattern 4 to 10 feet apart. Pick-prune them, so that their naturally graceful shape is allowed to emerge. They can touch each other, but they will need some irrigation if planted that close. Although creosote is not native to the southern California canyons and interior valleys, it grows quite well there. Since it can survive fire, it's possible that it could naturalize and become a pest there.

58 *Common Name*	Boquillas silverleaf, purple ceniza, cenizo
Latin Name	*Leucophyllum candidum*
Native Habitat	Flats and limestone hills below 4,000 feet in Chihuahuan Desert
Regions of Use	1, 2, 3, 5, 6
Soil	Dry, decomposed granite, sand, limestone, low organic content, well drained
Water	None to once a month
Sun or Shade	○
Height × Width	Maximum: 6 feet × 6 feet. Usual: 3 feet × 4 feet
Protective Mechanisms	None
Leaves or Stems	Evergreen, silvery white, velvety
Ornamental Value	Deep purple flowers after rain, especially in fall
Other Value	Flowers used by butterflies and bees, browse for sheep, larval plant for butterflies
Related Species	Texas ranger (*L. frutescens*), Big Bend silverleaf (*L. minus*), Chihuahuan sage (*L. laevigatum*), Sierra cenizo (*L. revolutum*)

Boquillas silverleaf, a naturally short, dense, silvery shrub, is sold under the cultivar names 'Silver Cloud', selected for its royal purple flowers, and 'Thunder Cloud', selected for dwarfness. It is not winter-hardy in El Paso, Las Cruces, or Las Vegas and is even iffy in Tucson. However, **Big Bend silverleaf** (1, 2, 3, 4, 5, 6, 7), another dwarf cenizo, is hardier. It also has silvery velvet leaves, and its flowers are an indescribable silvery violet-blue. The tallest, most cold-hardy, and most irrigation-tolerant of the cenizos is **Texas ranger** (1, 2, 3, 4, 5, 6, 7). Its leaves are either silver or green, and its flowers range from white to pale pink to lavender. Also available are two Mexican cenizos: **Chihuahuan sage** (1, 2, 3, 5, 6), with tiny green leaves and purple flowers; and **Sierra cenizo** (1, 2, 3, 5, 6), sold as 'Sierra Magic Mix', a sophisticated mix of pale to extremely vivid dark purple flowers. All cenizos defoliate and are susceptible to root rot if subjected to damp soil.

59 *Common Name*	Baja birdbush, Baja California birdbush, palo blanco
Latin Name	*Ornithostaphylos oppositifolia*
Native Habitat	RARE, chaparral below 4,000 feet in San Diego County and Baja California
Regions of Use	1, 2, 3
Soil	Dry, sand, sandstone, low organic content, well drained
Water	None to once a month in summer
Sun or Shade	○
Height × Width	Maximum: 12 feet × 10 feet. Usual: 8 feet × 8 feet
Protective Mechanisms	None
Leaves or Stems	Evergreen, dark green, leathery
Ornamental Value	White stems with coppery red bark, attracts birds
Other Value	Flowers used by bees, fruits eaten by birds and coyotes

Baja birdbush is so rare in San Diego County that it is scarcely native to the United States at all, and it is virtually unheard of in the nursery trade. This is sad, because it has lovely white trunks, and it's very healthy and easy to grow. It was first brought into cultivation at Rancho Santa Ana Botanic Garden in Claremont in 1963. The many white to palest green stems of a young plant turn into a multitrunked small tree. If the tops are damaged (burned, frozen, browsed, or cut), the large burl root resprouts. The leaves are dark green and gracefully narrow. The flowers are clusters of tiny white bells. The fruits are not colorful, but the birds they attract are. Baja birdbush looks better in the summer if given a small amount of irrigation, but like almost all southern California chaparral plants, it is extremely sensitive to being overwatered. Some attractive companion plants that like the same conditions of care are Shaw's agave, toyon, lemonadeberry, tree poppy, coastal sagebrush, California buckwheat, coast sunflower, San Miguel sage, coast red monkeyflower, and chalk dudleya.

60		
Common Name	Catalina cherry	
Latin Name	*Prunus ilicifolia* ssp. *lyonii*	
Native Habitat	Chaparral and woodland below 2,000 feet on Channel Islands and in Baja California	
Regions of Use	1, 2, 3	
Soil	Moist to dry, decomposed granite, sand, sandstone, clay loam, high to low organic content, well drained	
Water	Once or twice a month	
Sun or Shade	◑ ○	
Height × Width	Maximum: 45 feet × 15 feet. Usual: 15 feet × 10 feet	
Protective Mechanisms	Spines on edges of leaves	
Leaves or Stems	Evergreen	
Ornamental Value	White spring flowers, blue-black fruits	
Other Value	Flowers used by bees, fruits eaten by songbirds and game birds, cover for nesting birds	
Related Species	Hollyleaf cherry, islay (*P. ilicifolia* ssp. *ilicifolia*)	

Catalina cherry from the Channel Islands is usually a small glossy-leaved tree; old specimens have spreading branches like coast live oak. Its juicy fruit is great for attracting songbirds, but it can stain the surfaces of a patio or driveway and can be slippery under foot. Catalina cherry has been in cultivation for so long that most of the ones for sale are really hybrids with **hollyleaf cherry**. Hollyleaf cherry (1, 2, 3, 4, 5) is shorter, has red cherries, takes more shade and drought, and is resistant to oak root fungus. In chaparral, from Napa County to Baja California, it is a spiny 5-foot shrub, but in rich soil along streams or in a garden it might get 8 feet tall and 12 feet wide. It will withstand the dryness of the deserts, given sufficient irrigation, but it looks inappropriate alongside true desert plants. It grows quickly. In fact, its roots grow so quickly that they tend to encircle the inside of a nursery container, so be sure to straighten them out or prune them before planting. Use hollyleaf cherry as background shrubbery to attract songbirds.

61		
Common Name	California scrub oak	
Latin Name	*Quercus berberidifolia* (*Q. dumosa* misapplied)	
Native Habitat	Dry north-facing slopes and chaparral below 5,000 feet from North Coast Ranges to Baja California	
Regions of Use	1, 2, 3	
Soil	Dry, decomposed granite, sand, clay loam, low organic content, well drained	
Water	None to once a month	
Sun or Shade	◑ ○	
Height × Width	Maximum: 15 feet × 12 feet. Usual: 8 feet × 8 feet	
Protective Mechanisms	Spines on leaves	
Leaves or Stems	Evergreen, dark green, shiny	
Ornamental Value	Texture	
Other Value	Soil stabilization, acorns eaten by birds, browse, cover	
Related Species	Nuttall's scrub oak (*Q. dumosa*)	

The Basques call their dwarf evergreen oak *chabarra*. The Spanish adapted the word as *chaparro*, and coined *chaparral* to mean "the place where the dwarf evergreen oaks grow." Now California chaparral is divided into many kinds of chaparral such as coastal sagescrub (soft chaparral), and evergreen (hard) chaparrals: chamise chaparral, ceanothus chaparral, manzanita chaparral, scrub oak chaparral, redshanks chaparral, montane chaparral, island chaparral, and desert chaparral. **California scrub oak** is a member of more than half of these chaparrals. In cultivation, it makes a handsome evergreen shrub with dark shiny leaves. It can be conventionally hedged, but my preference is always for more natural pruning. In Los Angeles, use California scrub oak with toyon, chamise, snowberry, laurel-leaf sumac, coffeeberry, and California buckwheat. Farther inland, use it with western redbud, fremontia, sugarbush, tree poppy, creeping sage, purple needlegrass, Cleveland penstemon, and pipestem clematis. The RARE **Nuttall's scrub oak** (1) grows only in sand or sandstone along the south coast and in Baja California.

62	*Common Name*	Coffeeberry
	Latin Name	*Rhamnus californica* ssp. *californica*
	Native Habitat	Along the coast or in ravines, usually below 3,500 feet in California
	Regions of Use	1, 2, 3
	Soil	Medium-dry, decomposed granite, sand, sandstone, high or low organic content, well drained
	Water	Once or twice a month
	Sun or Shade	◑ ◑ ○
	Height × Width	Maximum: 15 feet × 15 feet. Usual: 8 feet × 8 feet
	Protective Mechanisms	None
	Leaves or Stems	Evergreen, dark green, glossy
	Ornamental Value	Creamy flowers in spring, dark red fruits on female plants
	Other Value	Flowers used by bees, fruits eaten by birds, browse, cover

Coffeeberry is a very handsome, very healthy shrub that has been sadly underused by the gardening public. It has large shiny leaves and big berries that stay red for a long time before they ripen to juicy black, and are quickly devoured by native birds. If coffeeberry doesn't get either coastal fog or rich soil and afternoon shade, it will need regular monthly irrigation in the summer. If you live on clay loam, be very careful not to overwater, as good drainage is essential. Use coffeeberry in combination with coast live oak, creeping snowberry, fuchsia flowering currant, evergreen currant, coffeeberry fern, onion lily, and island alumroot. It can be used as a tree, shrub, hedge, or even a 2- to 3-foot ground cover. There are a number of northern California cultivars available, most of them having been chosen for dwarf characteristics. If you are growing coffeeberry to attract birds, be sure to get a female. If no coffeeberries are still growing wild near you, you might need to plant a male as well to ensure pollination.

63	*Common Name*	Lemonadeberry
	Latin Name	*Rhus integrifolia*
	Native Habitat	North-facing slopes in canyons, ocean bluffs, coastal sagescrub, and chaparral below 2,500 feet from Santa Barbara to Baja California
	Regions of Use	1, 2, 3
	Soil	Dry, decomposed granite, sand, clay loam, low organic content, well drained
	Water	None to four times a month, well drained
	Sun or Shade	◑ ◑ ○
	Height × Width	Maximum: 30 feet × 25 feet. Usual: 6 feet × 10 feet
	Protective Mechanisms	None
	Leaves or Stems	Evergreen, dark green, shiny, aromatic
	Ornamental Value	White-coated fruit in clusters in early spring
	Other Value	Soil stabilization, flowers used by butterflies, early fruits eaten by birds and mammals, cover for nesting songbirds
	Related Species	Laurel-leaf sumac (*Malosma laurina*, formerly *R. laurina*)

For hedging or background screening, **lemonadeberry** can't be beat for rugged dependability. In its native habitat, it doesn't need supplemental water in the summer, even though it tolerates more irrigation than most chaparral plants. It makes a fine hedge, but there are lots of more exciting ways to use it. If you live with an ocean view, use lemonadeberry in mass plantings as a waist-high ground cover. Farther inland, lemonadeberry gets much taller and easily makes a 25-foot tree. For screening, instead of lining several shrubs up in a row, plant scattered clumps of lemonadeberry along with coffeeberry, laurel-leaf sumac, and a coastal ceanothus. In a mixed screen like this, don't prune the shrubs into manmade shapes, but allow them to grow as they like. **Laurel-leaf sumac** (1, 2, 3) grows with lemonadeberry on the coast, but it also grows as far inland as Riverside, where it is found with sugarbush. It differs from the sumacs in that it has aromatic leaves and white berries. It gets frost damage when temperatures fall below 25 degrees F.

64 Common Name	Littleleaf sumac, agritos
Latin Name	*Rhus microphylla*
Native Habitat	Washes, dry slopes, gypsum flats between 1,100 and 6,400 feet in Chihuahuan Desert and between 3,500 and 6,000 feet in southeastern Sonoran Desert
Regions of Use	1, 2, 3, 4, 5, 6, 7
Soil	Dry, decomposed granite, sand, limestone, low organic content, well drained
Water	None to once a month
Sun or Shade	◑ ◐ ○
Height × Width	Maximum: 25 feet × 40 feet. Usual: 8 feet × 10 feet
Protective Mechanisms	None
Leaves or Stems	Evergreen or drought- or cold-deciduous, dark green; red, orange, and purple fall color
Ornamental Value	White flowers in spring, orange fruits in early summer
Other Value	Flowers used by butterflies and bees, fruits eaten by quail, browse for mule and Sonora deer

Littleleaf sumac is a huge shrub with tiny leaves. In a home landscape, it can be kept much smaller and used for screening, but it can also easily be pruned into a small multitrunked tree. Its trunks are twisty and smooth when young, gradually getting darker as they age. It is evergreen at low elevations or in mild winters, but at higher elevations it is usually deciduous. If there are sufficient frosts in autumn, the fall color is quite spectacular. The April flowers are profuse but small, in little clusters flushed with pale peach undertones. A more brilliant show is provided in June by the red to orange berries, which attract birds and chipmunks. The berries appear in 2- to 4-inch clusters and last for several weeks. Many people steep these fruits in water to make a tartly sweet, lemony drink. Littleleaf sumac grows rather slowly on its own, but it responds readily to drip irrigation, just as long as it has excellent drainage and isn't overwatered.

65 Common Name	Sugarbush
Latin Name	*Rhus ovata*
Native Habitat	Chaparral below 4,000 feet in southern California, Baja California, and Santa Cruz and Santa Catalina islands and chaparral in central Arizona between 3,000 and 5,000 feet
Regions of Use	1, 2, 3, 4, 5, 6, 7
Soil	Dry, decomposed granite, sand, clay loam, low organic content, well drained
Water	None to once a month
Sun or Shade	◑ ◐ ○
Height × Width	Maximum: 30 feet × 25 feet. Usual: 15 feet × 20 feet
Protective Mechanisms	None
Leaves or Stems	Evergreen, dark and glossy, large
Ornamental Value	Red and cream flowers in spring, red fruits with white fuzz
Other Value	Flowers used by butterflies and bees, fruits eaten by birds, cover for nesting birds

Sugarbush can be used very much like lemonadeberry, but it is more drought-tolerant and also more cold-hardy. Where the two species meet, they often hybridize. Most people prefer sugarbush to lemonadeberry because it has such large glossy leaves and because its flowers are so pretty. The flowers start out as a cluster of red buds. Then, a few at a time, they burst into small cream-colored blossoms, visually combining the reds and creams and keeping the plant in bloom for weeks. The berries form shortly afterward; they're bright red, but they are so frosted with white hairs that they also show as clusters of red and cream. Sugarbush is very important for southern California gardens, but it shouldn't be ignored in desert gardens—not those on the desert floor, but those up in the cooler foothills. With just an occasional watering, sugarbush can be used in desert courtyards below the elevations where it is found naturally. Old tree-sized specimens of sugarbush have a wonderfully shaggy bark.

66	
Common Name	Jojoba, goatnut
Latin Name	*Simmondsia chinensis*
Native Habitat	Dry slopes, washes between 1,000 and 5,000 feet in Sonoran Desert and in Riverside, San Diego, and Imperial counties
Regions of Use	1, 2, 3, 5, 6
Soil	Dry, decomposed granite, sand, clay loam, low organic content, well drained
Water	None to once a month
Sun or Shade	○
Height × Width	Maximum: 10 feet × 12 feet. Usual: 6 feet × 6 feet
Protective Mechanisms	None
Leaves or Stems	Evergreen, pale, muted yellow-green or pale blue-green
Ornamental Value	Texture, color, green nuts on female plants
Other Value	Oily green nuts eaten by squirrels and many other animals, used to make shampoo, browse for deer and livestock, cover

Jojoba grows in the foothills around Tucson, Phoenix, and San Diego. Some plants have leaves that are a pale khaki color, and some have a pale bluish cast. Jojoba's shape is distinctive, even from a distance, because its leaves are held upright to avoid direct rays from the sun at the hottest part of the day. It always appears healthy, even where it gets reflected heat and wind, making it useful as parking lot medians or along streets. It can be used as a hedge, massed into a soft shrubbery, or used as a specimen. It gets much taller in California than in Arizona, where even 7 feet tall is quite unusual. Because it combines the softness of chaparral plants with a desert color, it blends well with both. In Arizona, use it with creosote bush, saguaro, bursage, and a host of succulents. In eastern California, mix it with Joshua tree, blue grama, banana yucca, bladderpod, and lots of ephemeral wildflowers. Or, for a softer look, combine it with fremontia, blue manzanita, chaparral whitethorn, sugarbush, and California buckwheat. Jojoba is easily available because it is grown as a commercial crop.

67	
Common Name	California bay, pepperwood, Oregon myrtle
Latin Name	*Umbellularia californica*
Native Habitat	Canyons, valleys, chaparral below 5,000 feet from eastern slopes of Laguna Mountains in San Diego County north to Oregon
Regions of Use	1, 2, 3
Soil	Dry to moist, decomposed granite, sand, clay loam, high or low organic content, well drained
Water	Once or twice a month
Sun or Shade	◐ ◑ ○
Height × Width	Maximum: 80 feet × 30 feet. Usual: 30 feet × 25 feet
Protective Mechanisms	Aromatic oils in leaves discourage some browsers, are toxic to some humans if more than two to four are eaten
Leaves or Stems	Evergreen, large, glossy leaves, aromatic of camphor
Ornamental Value	Aromatic leaves, fragrant greenish flowers in winter
Other Value	Flowers used by butterflies, fruits eaten by birds, cover, may be used sparingly in cooking or for medicinal tea

The versatile **California bay** can be a large, stately, single-trunked tree that spreads out at the base into a large burl or, on an ocean-facing bluff, a 1- to 2-foot ground cover. On poor soil in southern California, it will most likely be a many-stemmed shrub about 15 feet tall, while 30 feet is about average in a garden. The leaves vary; 'Claremont' is a selection with particularly wide, dark, glossy leaves. Western redbud, coffeeberry, and coast live oak are some of its companion plants. On a large property, you can strategically place several California bays to provide tall screening. For most homeowners, a single specimen is best. Place it in a courtyard where you often sit and can enjoy its scents. If you prune it up like a tree, plant California strawberry underneath in the shadiest portion, and use evergreen currant, creeping snowberry, coffeeberry fern, or island alumroot where sun shines for a few hours during the day. If space is tight, California bay can be grown in a big patio pot.

4 SUNNY GROUND COVERS

BELOW: Creeping cultivars of manzanita and black sage combine with a mass planting of silvery-leaved red buckwheat (*Eriogonum grande* var. *rubescens*)—not yet in bloom—and tufts of pale blue-leaved elymus 'Canyon Prince', in the Manzanita Section opposite the demonstration garden at Santa Barbara Botanic Garden. ABOVE RIGHT: In the foothills of the Sonoran Desert, bursage is the "glue" that visually holds the desert together. In the Lower Colorado Desert, white bursage serves the same purpose. RIGHT: Baccharis 'Twin Peaks' and a taller form of coyote brush are the main ground covers on this large sunny hillside garden in Malibu designed by Paul Nota.

ALL COASTAL SAGESCRUB IS ESSENTIALLY A MIXTURE OF SHRUBBY GROUND COVERS, A low sea washing around the reef of evergreen chaparral. Although normally 3 to 5 feet tall, specimens that are especially short and attractive are continually sought by nurseries as ground cover material; as a result, many of the ones you find there are much shorter than those normally seen in nature. Whacking back both shrubs and grasses just prior to new growth also helps keep them short.

The grassy ground covers go dormant and turn the color of golden straw during the hottest, driest part of the year. The shrubby ones are often drought-deciduous–that is, they will lose their leaves unless watered once or twice a month in the summer. There is some evidence that augmenting rainfall with 5 to 10 inches of water in the winter helps chaparral shrubs hold on to their leaves during the summer.

In the deserts of the Southwest, low shrubs are more drought-tolerant than grasses, which are more often found in the higher Chihuahuan Desert or on flat areas in the foothills. These ground covers are mostly knee-high, and they do not completely cover the ground. Up in the foothills, with tree yuccas and saguaros, they grow in irregularly shaped clumps and the earth shows through in patches. Down on the creosote flats, the ground covers may not grow close enough together to touch. An aerial view shows them evenly polka-dotted across an expanse of desert pavement.

In both cases, from the human perspective, they appear massed, and their texture softens the crisp sculptural forms of yuccas, cacti, ocotillo, and desert trees. These ground covers are the visual element sorely missing in those popular gravel landscapes.

68	Common Name	Bursage
	Latin Name	*Ambrosia deltoidea (Franseria deltoidea)*
	Native Habitat	Plains and mesas between 1,000 and 3,000 feet in Sonoran Desert
	Regions of Use	6
	Soil	Dry, decomposed granite, sand, clay, low organic content, well drained
	Water	None to once a month
	Sun or Shade	◐ ○
	Height × Width	Maximum: 3 feet × 3 feet. Usual: 2 feet × 2 feet
	Protective Mechanisms	Spines on dry seed cases
	Leaves or Stems	Evergreen or drought-deciduous, pale gray-green
	Ornamental Value	Softening effect among succulents
	Other Value	Browse for desert bighorn and wild burro
	Related Species	White bursage, burrobush (*A. dumosa*); and others

Many people think that a landscape composed of saguaro, creosote bush, and other succulent accents, all correctly spaced and with smooth decomposed granite underneath, looks like the Sonoran Desert. This is not true. It's too harsh, too bare, and too tan; it lacks the greenness and softness of the true desert. The missing ingredient is **bursage**, a nondescript little shrub that went virtually unnoticed until Phil Hebets, a landscape architect in Phoenix, made a survey of several intact bits of Sonoran Desert for a revegetation project. He discovered that there are almost always 25 bursage for every 400 square feet—one for each 16 square feet, or every 4 feet, if planted on a grid. But, of course, that would look quite ridiculous, because they are never evenly spaced in nature. Plant bursage in drifts and clumps. If you live near Las Vegas or Palm Springs, use **white bursage** (4, 5) instead for the same effect.

69	Common Name	Coastal sagebrush
	Latin Name	*Artemisia californica*
	Native Habitat	Coastal scrub, chaparral and dry foothills below 2,500 feet in drier parts of central and southern California and Baja California
	Regions of Use	1, 2, 3, 4, 5
	Soil	Dry, decomposed granite, sand, clay loam, low organic content, well drained
	Water	None to twice a month
	Sun or Shade	◐ ○
	Height × Width	Maximum: 5 feet × 5 feet. Usual: 3 feet × 3 feet
	Protective Mechanisms	Aromatic oils discourage some browsers
	Leaves or Stems	Evergreen, silver, aromatic
	Ornamental Value	Feathery, silvery texture
	Other Value	Fruits eaten by birds, browse, cover, larval plant for butterflies

One of the great pleasures of coastal sagescrub is the combined scents of **coastal sagebrush** and the sweet, tangy native salvias. In a small garden, you can use one of the coastal sagebrush cultivars such as 'Montara' along with San Miguel mountain sage or a black sage cultivar to make a shorter, more refined version of this habitat. Coastal sagebrush can also be part of your herb garden; it makes an elegant garnish for a roast and is lovely in dried arrangements. For a ground cover, coastal sagebrush can be planted in masses. 'Canyon Gray', a knee-high, spreading cultivar, can get 10 feet across; plant it as much as 6 feet apart and you'll get solid cover fairly rapidly. Don't worry if it looks rough for a week or so in late spring; it's just dropping old leaves and growing new ones. For a revegetation project, use a local selection instead of one of the less drought-resistant cultivars.

70	
Common Name	Coyote brush
Latin Name	*Baccharis pilularis*
Native Habitat	Coastal bluffs to oak woodland mostly below 2,500 feet from Oregon to Mexico
Regions of Use	1, 2, 3
Soil	Dry, decomposed granite, sand, clay loam, low organic content, well drained
Water	None to twice a month
Sun or Shade	◑ ◐ ○
Height × Width	Maximum: 10 feet × 8 feet. Usual: 2¹/₂ feet × 5 feet
Protective Mechanisms	None
Leaves or Stems	Evergreen, warm green
Ornamental Value	Bright color, fine texture
Other Value	Cover
Related Species	Desert broom (*B. sarothroides*)

Some of the cultivars of **coyote brush** can be maintained below knee height. Although these prostrate selections are far more drought-resistant than most ground covers for southern California, they really can't go all summer without water and remain in tip-top condition. They all use far less water than a lawn, however, and their grass-green color blends in pleasantly with a lush landscape. With age, a large spread of coyote brush develops gentle mounds and waves. 'Centennial' (3, 4, 5, 6, 7) is even more drought-resistant because it is a hybrid with **desert broom** (4), a pioneer species that is native to washes in the Mojave, Sonoran, and Lower Colorado deserts. Desert broom—a tall shrub—is seldom used in landscapes because its seeds come up everywhere. In only 20 years, it has become a nuisance in El Paso arroyos. Only around Las Vegas, where soils are saline and particularly difficult, is it viewed as a valuable landscape plant in its own right.

71	
Common Name	Blue grama
Latin Name	*Bouteloua gracilis*
Native Habitat	Mostly short-grass prairie and pinyon/juniper woodland in western half of North America, between 1,000 and 8,000 feet
Regions of Use	1, 2, 3, 4, 5, 6, 7
Soil	Dry, decomposed granite, sand, clay, limestone, low organic content, well drained
Water	Once a month to once a week
Sun or Shade	○
Height × Width	Maximum: 2 feet when in flower. Usual: 5 to 9 inches
Protective Mechanisms	None
Leaves or Stems	Blue-green, dormant (not green) in drought or cold
Ornamental Value	Turf
Other Value	Erosion control, seeds eaten by songbirds and game birds, browse, larval plant for butterflies
Related Species	Black grama (*B. eriopoda*), sideoats grama (*B. curtipendula*)

Blue grama is probably the most drought-resistant lawn grass on the market; buffalograss (*Buchloe dactyloides*) needs a little more water, and curly mesquite (*Hilaria belangeri*) is not yet available. Blue grama's blades are very narrow, giving it a fine, soft texture. If grown 4 to 6 inches tall, it needs fewer mowings and less water because the roots are shaded. For the short and smooth look, blue grama takes about half to a third of the water Kentucky bluegrass requires. **Black grama** (4, 6, 7), native with Joshua tree, saguaro, and palmilla, is equally short and even more drought-resistant. **Sideoats grama** (1, 2, 3, 4, 6, 7) is twice as tall as the other two and makes a very pretty knee-high ground cover with rosy winter color. All can be used as accents or pot plants.

72 Common Name	Damianita
Latin Name	*Chrysactinia mexicana*
Native Habitat	Rocky slopes in Trans Pecos below 7,000 feet in eastern Chihuahuan Desert to Veracruz
Regions of Use	3, 4, 5, 6, 7
Soil	Dry, decomposed granite, sand, limestone, low organic content, well drained
Water	None to twice a month
Sun or Shade	◖ ◗ ○
Height × Width	Maximum: 4 feet × 4 feet. Usual: 2 feet × 2 feet
Protective Mechanisms	Aromatic oils discourage some browsers
Leaves or Stems	Evergreen, dark olive green, aromatic
Ornamental Value	Yellow flowers
Other Value	Flowers used by butterflies, tea can cause miscarriage
Related Species	Shrubby dogweed (*Thymophylla acerosa,* formerly *Dyssodia acerosa*)

Damianita is a small, self-contained, naturally dense and rounded evergreen shrub—making it a big favorite with most conventional landscapers. At least once a year, after a good rain, it will cover itself with 1-inch golden yellow daisies. Another bonus is that deer don't much like its pungent dark green needles. Use it as a tall ground cover, a flower, or a low hedge. **Shrubby dogweed** (3, 4, 5, 6, 7) will give you almost exactly the same look, but it's even shorter and more drought-resistant. It is also aromatic, sometimes likened to marigolds, although some people will tell you it's more reminiscent of turpentine. Its flowers are smaller than damianita's but just as copious and bright. You can use it totally without water in El Paso, Las Cruces, or Las Vegas, or in the Sonoran Desert where the elevation is over 3,500 feet. In that case, leave 3 to 4 feet between each shrub.

73 Common Name	Gregg dalea, trailing indigobush
Latin Name	*Dalea greggii*
Native Habitat	On rocky hillsides between 2,000 and 4,500 feet in Chihuahuan Desert
Regions of Use	1, 2, 3, 4, 5, 6, 7
Soil	Dry, decomposed granite, sand, clay loam, limestone, low organic content, well drained
Water	None to twice a month in summer
Sun or Shade	◖ ○
Height × Width	Maximum: 2 feet × 10 feet. Usual: 1 foot × 6 feet
Protective Mechanisms	Wiry stems discourage browsers
Leaves	Silver, evergreen or cold-deciduous
Ornamental Value	Purple flowers from spring to fall, fragrant
Other Value	Erosion control, flowers used by bees and butterflies, larval plant for butterflies

Pale, silvery green stems and tiny leaves make Gregg dalea (*DAY lee uh*) handsome even when it isn't dotted with lavender flowers. This popular trailing ground cover is great for erosion control because its stems take root wherever they touch the ground. With irrigation it spreads about 2 feet a year. It cascades gracefully over retaining walls, planter boxes, or large patio pots. Because it is a Chihuahuan plant, it must have some water in the summer (not too much), and it must have excellent drainage in a wet winter. After a hard freeze, it becomes a tangle of silvery stems. These bare stems are considered attractive in their own right by many, and they help keep the roots warm. If you cut them off, fresh new growth as abundant as before will start as soon as the weather warms up. At temperatures below the teens, Gregg dalea is only sporadically root-hardy and takes several years to recover.

74 Common Name	Arizona cottontop
Latin Name	*Digitaria californica* (formerly *Trichachne californica*)
Native Habitat	Rocky hills and grasslands between 1,000 and 6,000 feet in Sonoran and Chihuahuan deserts to Gulf of Mexico
Regions of Use	4, 5, 6, 7
Soil	Dry, decomposed granite, sand, low organic content, well drained
Water	None to twice a month
Sun or Shade	○
Height × Width	Maximum: 4 feet × 5 feet. Usual: 2 feet × 2 feet
Protective Mechanisms	None
Leaves or Stems	Almost evergreen, dormant in winter, dark blue-green
Ornamental Value	White plumelike flowers after rains in fall
Other Value	Forage in Spring

When in bloom or seed, **Arizona cottontop** is as showy as any garden flower. The cottony spikes top a profusion of wiry stems to create a bouquet of white that is dazzling when backlit. Since it is nearly evergreen, it makes a fine ground cover. Heavy watering will make it lush but tall. To keep it short, apply just enough water to keep it green during the summer. When the leaves turn brown or gray, cut them back and wait for new growth. Arizona cottontop is pretty enough to stand alone as an accent, or it can be scattered among large rocks along with agave, cholla, ocotillo, palmilla, and other desert succulents for its softening effect.

. . . .

75 Common Name	Turpentinebush, turpentinebrush, larchleaf goldenweed
Latin Name	*Ericameria laricifolia* (*Haplopappus laricifolius*)
Native Habitat	From pinyon/juniper woodland to creosote scrub on mesas, slopes, and canyons between 2,000 and 6,000 feet in Chihuahuan, Sonoran, and eastern Mojave deserts
Regions of Use	3, 4, 6, 7
Soil	Dry, decomposed granite, sand, clay loam, limestone, low organic content, well drained
Water	None to twice a month
Sun or Shade	◑ ○
Height × Width	Maximum: 3 feet × 4 feet in the wild; 6 feet × 4 feet with irrigation. Usual: 1 feet × 2 feet
Protective Mechanisms	Aromatic oils in leaves and rubber in stems discourage some browsers
Leaves or Stems	Evergreen, dark olive green, aromatic
Ornamental Value	Golden flowers in fall, scented foliage
Other Value	Flowers used by butterflies and bees, cover

Turpentinebush is a beautiful natural ground cover in desert foothills around El Paso, Phoenix, Tucson, and Las Vegas. About knee-high, it is scattered thickly among the taller, more widely spaced desert shrubs and trees. In El Paso, interplant it with plume tiquilia, skeletonleaf goldeneye, and feather dalea beneath little-leaf sumac, ocotillo, and tree yuccas. In the Sonoran Desert, use it under foothill paloverde and saguaro with California buckwheat and pink fairyduster. Around Las Vegas, combine it with New Mexico feathergrass (*Stipa neomexicana*), desert marigold, Apache-plume, Mormon tea, globe mallow, California buckwheat, and brittlebush under Joshua tree, buckhorn cholla, and catclaw acacia. With regular irrigation, it tends to quickly form a narrow, 6-foot-high shrub, suitable for hedging.

76 *Common Name*	California buckwheat
Latin Name	*Eriogonum fasciculatum*
Native Habitat	Coastal sagescrub, chaparral, creosote scrub, washes, and dry rocky slopes between 200 and 7,000 feet from Santa Barbara to Baja California and east to the Mojave (below 4,500 feet), Colorado, and Sonoran deserts
Regions of Use	1, 2, 3, 4, 5, 6, 7
Soil	Dry, decomposed granite, sand, clay loam, low organic content, well drained
Water	None to once a month
Sun or Shade	◐ ◑ ○
Height × Width	Maximum: 5 feet × 7 feet. Usual: 18 inches × 3 feet
Protective Mechanisms	None
Leaves	Evergreen, sometimes drought-deciduous
Ornamental Value	Pink to white flowers in spring and after fall rains, turning copper and russet as they mature in autumn; slightly fragrant
Other Value	Nectar for hummingbirds and butterflies, honey, nesting, seeds eaten by songbirds and game birds

California buckwheat is typically knee-high in the deserts and 5 feet tall in chaparral. It is not a creeping plant, but its horizontal branches and sheer quantity give it a ground-cover appearance. In a suburban garden, mass it for an informal shrubbery, mix it with lots of other native low-growing shrubs, or use it as a flower. It is dependably good-looking, fast, and easy to grow. If it gets too big or flops over, prune it and cut back on the water and fertilizer. There are very short selections from *E. f.* ssp. *fasciculatum* (coastal) and *E. f.* ssp. *foliolosum* (canyon) available for the southern California crowd, but no selections are available yet for *E. f.* ssp. *polifolium* (desert).

....

77 *Common Name*	Oniongrass
Latin Name	*Melica imperfecta*
Native Habitat	Dry rocky hillsides, chaparral, and woodland below 4,500 feet in southern ranges, Mojave Desert, and Baja California
Regions of Use	1, 2, 3, 4
Soil	Dry, decomposed granite, sand, low organic content, well drained
Water	None to twice a month
Sun or Shade	◐ ◑ ○
Height × Width	Maximum: 4 feet × 4 feet. Usual: 18 inches × 2 feet
Protective Mechanisms	None
Leaves or Stems	Bright green, slender, dormant in summer
Ornamental Value	Texture, lacy flowers in spring
Other Value	Erosion control, bee flowers, birdseed, browse

Although **oniongrass** is quite drought-tolerant, its fresh, bright green leaves give this bunch grass a very lush look, contributing the color and texture of a beautiful lawn. In a knee-high mass planting that is cut just once a year, it is a lovely sight, something like cool, gently moving water. It cannot, however, be mowed to produce a smooth turf because it grows in bunches and doesn't spread from the roots. Use it as an accent in full sun or partial shade on the edge of chaparral plantings, or even with creosote and succulents. It lends softness to a flower bed. In a garden setting, cut back oniongrass in summer after it has gone dormant and birds have finished eating the seeds or they have shattered. It will green up again after fall rains in October or November.

78 *Common Name*	Deergrass
Latin Name	*Muhlenbergia rigens*
Native Habitat	Canyons, chaparral, woodlands between 2,500 and 7,000 feet in southern California coastal ranges, and in Mojave and Chihuahuan deserts
Regions of Use	1, 2, 3, 4, 5, 6, 7
Soil	Dry, decomposed granite, sand, clay loam, limestone, low organic content, well drained
Water	None to twice a month
Sun or Shade	○
Height × Width	Maximum: 5 feet × 5 feet. Usual: 3 feet × 4 feet
Protective Mechanisms	None
Leaves or Stems	Blue-green, khaki when dormant because too dry or too cold
Ornamental Value	Texture, spiked flowers in late summer or fall
Other Value	Erosion control, bee flowers, birdseed, browse
Related Species	Bull muhly (*M. emersleyi*), bush muhly (*M. porteri*)

Even when dormant, **deergrass** remains upright, well shaped, and handsomely colored–khaki with faint undertones of green. It's rugged for a grass, and even in desert gardens it needs only a little irrigation. When planted as a ground cover, it looks a bit formal; the separate clumps of grass always stand out as individuals and never quite get together to form one mass. For a less formal look, use one or more as an accent along with agave, sotol, and a profusion of native flowers. There are many *Muhlenbergia* grasses, and all are pretty. The Chihuahuan **bull muhly** (1, 2, 3, 4, 5, 6, 7) has large fluffy flower-and-seed heads that turn from lavender to silver every fall above a soft gray-green leafy base. Its cultural requirements are the same as for deergrass. **Bush muhly** (1, 2, 3, 4, 5, 6, 7) is so drought-tolerant that it can form a sea of misty pink among creosotes.

....

79 *Common Name*	Nodding needlegrass
Latin Name	*Nassella cernua* (formerly *Stipa cernua*)
Native Habitat	Chaparral, coastal sagescrub, and dry woodland below 4,500 feet from northern to Baja California
Regions of Use	1, 2, 3
Soil	Dry, decomposed granite, sand, clay loam, low organic content, well drained
Water	None to once a month
Sun or Shade	○
Height × Width	Maximum: 4 feet × 5 feet. Usual: 2 feet × 3 feet
Protective Mechanisms	Long, thin needles on seeds discourage grazers
Leaves or Stems	Extremely narrow, pale green, dormant in summer
Ornamental Value	Soft, graceful texture
Other Value	Erosion control, grazed by deer and rabbits when not in seed
Related Species	Foothill needlegrass (*N. lepida*), purple needlegrass (*N. pulchra*)

Any one of these needlegrasses is capable of making either a pure stand of softly waving ground cover or a single ornamental accent. **Nodding needlegrass** is a luscious pale green. **Purple needlegrass** (1, 2, 3) has broader, dark green leaves and misty pink flowers in early spring. **Foothill needlegrass** (1, 2, 3) has delicate, open flower clusters and tolerates some shade. These are cool-season grasses–green in fall and winter, flowering and making seed in the spring, and golden in the summer. Back before the Spanish missions, all three–along with deergrass, littleseed muhly (*Muhlenbergia microsperma*), and, to a lesser degree, oniongrass and elymus–dominated southern California grasslands. They were soon obliterated by cattle herds and were replaced by the nonnative annual grasses seen today.

80	
Common Name	Mariola
Latin Name	*Parthenium incanum*
Native Habitat	Dry plains and mesas below 6,500 feet in Chihuahuan and Sonoran deserts and around Lake Mead
Regions of Use	4, 5, 6, 7
Soil	Dry, decomposed granite, sand, low organic content, well drained
Water	None to once a month in hot weather
Sun or Shade	○
Height × Width	Maximum: 3 feet × 4 feet. Usual: 2 feet × 2 feet
Protective Mechanisms	Rubber in stems discourages some browsers
Leaves or Stems	Gray-white, velvety, aromatic, drought- and cold-deciduous
Ornamental Value	Silvery leaves
Other Value	Fruits eaten by birds and other animals, cover
Related Species	Guayule, rubber plant (*P. argentatum*)

A rancher might not be too happy to see **mariola** on his spread; that's a dead giveaway that the land has been overgrazed. From a landscaping point of view, however, this silvery, knee-high shrub is a pretty sight. It often loses its leaves in the summer, but with a little irrigation it stays silvery until a cold snap knocks the leaves off. **Guayule** (4, 5, 6, 7) (pronounced y-OOL-ee) is shorter—only about 1 foot tall—and even prettier. It is native to the Trans Pecos area of Texas and is winter-hardy down to 0 degrees F. Guayule used to be more widespread until it was harvested for rubber during World War II. The two plants are reported to interbreed where they are found growing together. Use either one in a desert garden as easy-care silvery foliage.

81	
Common Name	San Miguel mountain sage
Latin Name	*Salvia munzii*
Native Habitat	RARE, coastal sagescrub and chaparral below 2,500 feet in San Diego and Baja California
Regions of Use	1, 2, 3
Soil	Dry, decomposed granite, low organic content, well drained
Water	None to once a month
Sun or Shade	○
Height × Width	Maximum: 7 feet high. Usual: 2 feet × 3 feet
Protective Mechanisms	Aromatic oils discourage some browsers
Leaves or Stems	Silver-green, aromatic, drought-deciduous
Ornamental Value	Clear blue flowers, spicy fragrance
Other Value	Soil stabilization; flowers used by hummingbirds, butterflies, and honeybees
Related Species	Black sage (*S. mellifera*), purple sage (*S. leucophylla*), white sage (*S. apiana*)

San Miguel Mountain sage, **purple sage** (1, 2, 3) and the more common **black sage** (1, 2, 3) and **white sage** (1, 2, 3, 5) are important components of coastal sagescrub. They are usually waist-high, spreading, and semishrubby. All but white sage have blue to purple flowers clustered in bunches up the stems; white sage has white leaves and flowers and an intense fragrance. On sunny days both the flowers and leaves of these sages release a sweet, invigorating pungency. Cultivars are selected to be low, spreading ground covers. They can be massed in front of taller shrubs or arranged to flank an entrance. One can be an attractive addition to a flower garden, but cut it back pretty severely once a year to keep it small.

5 SHADY GROUND COVERS

DESERT AND CHAPARRAL ARE NOT PRIME HABITATS FOR SHADY GROUND COVERS. A desert offers very little shade, and chaparral tends to be too dense. Houses cast shade, however, and those shady outdoor spots are particularly valued in a hot climate. Any homeowner who would like to be able to sit outside in the shade under a tree with a bit of green underneath is going to need at least one shady ground cover.

Most gardeners think that a shady ground cover should be low, smooth, evergreen, and all one kind of plant–in other words, as much like a conventional lawn as possible. Nature finds this concept utterly boring. Some of nature's ground covers grow in pure patches, but most are mixed in with other ground covers, and many are knee-high or even taller. You can fight nature, but it is much easier to change your views. Thinking of an area for shady ground covers as a flower garden in the shade is on the right track.

Most of the shady, flowering ground covers profiled here grow natively in oak woodlands that abut desert and chaparral. Although requiring irrigation, they are still drought-tolerant by normal gardening standards. Where plants should look photogenic all year and form a thick

Multicolored Douglas iris and pink alumroot (*Heuchera maxima* hybrids), along with nonnative flowers, enliven the intimate garden around the entrance patio at Jeff Powers's home in Laguna Beach, California. The contrast of upright and spreading leaves in different shades of green provides interest on those rare occasions when no flowers are in bloom.

cover, plan to water once a week. In southern California, there are five ground covers that might require no supplemental water: San Diego dudleya, common snowberry, fuchsia flowering currant, elymus, and hummingbird sage.

Maximum widths are usually not given for shady ground covers since they might eventually spread to cover hundreds of square feet. To start a solid cover of one species, place the new plants 1 to 5 feet apart. The shrubby ground covers should always be at least 3 feet apart. For a shady flower garden, place clumps of several of the taller ground covers in a pleasing pattern and then fill in with the ground-hugging ones.

82 *Common Name*	Red columbine
Latin Name	*Aquilegia formosa*
Native Habitat	Streambanks and seeps in chaparral and woodland below 11,000 feet from Alaska to Baja California and Mojave Desert
Regions of Use	1, 2, 3
Soil	Moist, decomposed granite, sand, clay loam, high to low organic content, well drained
Water	Once a week
Sun or Shade	● ◑ ◐
Height × Width	Maximum: 5 feet high when in bloom. Usual: 2 feet × 2 feet
Protective Mechanisms	None
Leaves or Stems	Almost evergreen, pale bluish green
Ornamental Value	Red flowers in spring (summer and fall if moist enough)
Other Value	Flowers used by hummingbirds
Related Species	Yellow columbine (*A. chrysantha*)

Red columbine is an airy perennial with fancy leaves and nodding, long-spurred flowers that hummingbirds love. Heat and drought can force it into dormancy, and poor drainage can kill it. Plant a few among Douglas iris, island alumroot, onion lily, and coffeeberry fern, and then let it scatter its seed around wherever it wants to go; you can't have too much of this delicately leaved ground cover. Encourage its spread by simply cutting off the stalks and shaking out the seed wherever you want more. When the stalks turn brown, the seed is prime. **Yellow columbine** (1, 2, 3, 4, 5, 6, 7) is native to seeps in canyons in the Sonoran and Chihuahuan deserts. You'll find it, along with maidenhair fern, tucked into limestone crevices. You can grow it with the red columbine, but don't be surprised when the two hybridize to produce pastel shades of pink and peach.

83 *Common Name*	Starleaf Mexican orange, zorillo
Latin Name	*Choisya dumosa*
Native Habitat	On shady mountain slopes and canyon sides between 3,900 and 6,500 feet in Chihuahuan Desert
Regions of Use	1, 2, 3, 4, 6, 7
Soil	Dry, decomposed granite, sand, limestone, low organic content, well drained
Water	Once or twice a month
Sun or Shade	● ◑ ◐
Height × Width	Maximum: 6 feet high. Usual: 18 inches × 3 feet
Protective Mechanisms	Aromatic oils discourage some browsers
Leaves or Stems	Evergreen or dormant in winter, orange-scented
Ornamental Value	White fragrant flowers after rain, fancy leaves
Other Value	Flowers used by butterflies, foliage rarely eaten by deer, fruits eaten by songbirds
Related Species	Starleaf Mexican orange (*C. arizonica* and *C. mollis*)—extremely similar species in Chihuahuan Arizona

Starleaf Mexican orange is happy in lots of locales: as a knee-high ground cover under a tree, in an herb garden, or even in a patio pot. The foliage is dark green and lacy with the firm texture of juniper needles. Brush against it and the pungent aroma of oranges is released. The 1-inch flowers, white with golden stamens and shell pink buds, are profuse and sweetly scented. Starleaf Mexican orange grows naturally as a shady ground cover under Texas madrone (*Arbutus texana*) with bull muhly and New Mexico agave in sunny spots nearby. In Arizona, I've seen it under silverleaf oak (*Quercus hypoleucoides*), deerbrush (*Ceanothus integerrimus*), and Pringle manzanita (*Arctostaphylos pringlei*) with shrubby dogweed as the adjacent sunny ground cover. In a courtyard, use starleaf Mexican orange beneath a desert willow, along with bamboo muhly and Mexican plumbago.

84	Common Name	Santa Catalina dudleya
	Latin Name	*Dudleya hassei*
	Native Habitat	Rocks and cliffs below 1,200 feet on Santa Catalina Island
	Regions of Use	1, 2, 3
	Soil	Dry, granite, decomposed granite, sandstone, sand, low organic content, well drained
	Water	None to once a month
	Sun or Shade	◐ ◑ ○
	Height × Width	Maximum: 6 inches high. Usual: 4 inches × 2 feet, 1 foot in flower
	Protective Mechanisms	None
	Leaves or Stems	Evergreen, fleshy, covered with white powder
	Ornamental Value	White flowers, texture
	Other Value	Flowers used by bees
	Related Species	Chalk dudleya (*D. pulverulenta* ssp. *pulverulenta*), Arizona dudleya (*D. p.* ssp. *arizonica*), San Diego dudleya (*D. edulis*)

Santa Catalina dudleya stays very low; it won't get over a foot high even when its white flowers sit atop their slender stems. It prefers half shade but can tolerate reflected heat from a building or pavement. While this dudleya is the shortest, as well as the best spreading, other dudleyas also make good low ground covers, especially in coastal sagescrub and nearby chaparral. San Diego dudleya (1, 2, 3) gets about 8 inches tall and tolerates more sun and cold. Chalk dudleya (1, 2, 3), still more drought-resistant but more of a small accent, looks as though its fleshy fingers have been coated with chalk dust. A smaller version called Arizona dudleya (1, 2, 3, 4) is usable in Las Vegas. These and many other dudleyas—one even native to the Sonoran Desert—can be tucked into stone walls or steps or used in a planter box or patio pot. Flower colors may be red, yellow, orange, pink, or white.

85	Common Name	California fescue
	Latin Name	*Festuca californica*
	Native Habitat	Open forests and chaparral below 5,500 feet in northern California and San Bernadino Mountains
	Regions of Use	1, 2, 3
	Soil	Moist to dry, decomposed granite, sand, clay loam, low to high organic content, well drained
	Water	Once or twice a month
	Sun or Shade	◐ ◑
	Height × Width	Maximum: 4 feet × 5 feet. Usual: 2 feet × 3 feet
	Protective Mechanisms	None
	Leaves or Stems	Pale bluish green, dormant when dry or cold
	Ornamental Value	Soft texture, spring flowers and seeds
	Other Value	Flowers used by bees, seeds eaten by songbirds and game birds

To use California fescue as a massed ground cover in a southern California garden, plan to water twice a month. If watering only once a month, plant it as an accent or a perennial flower. Whether green or dormant, it has a softening effect in a garden, moving delicately and gracefully in even the slightest breeze. Three ideas we observed in southern California gardens are to showcase California fescue as a vertical accent half under a huge rock with its roots tapping into the damp, cool soil beneath; on the edge of a path just as it winds out of the sunshine and into a shady garden; and as the focal point in a bright spot of dappled shade, mixed with fuchsia flowering currant, pitcher sage, bracken, and Douglas iris.

86 *Common Name*	California strawberry	
Latin Name	*Fragaria vesca*	
Native Habitat	Under forest trees below 6,000 feet in the Peninsular Ranges and Baja California north to the Cascade Ranges, eastern North America, and Europe	
Regions of Use	1, 2, 3	
Soil	Moist, decomposed granite, sand, clay loam, rich to low organic content, well drained	
Water	Once or twice a month	
Sun or Shade	● ◑	
Height × Width	Usual: 3 inches high	
Protective Mechanisms	None	
Leaves or Stems	Evergreen	
Ornamental Value	White flowers, strawberries	
Other Value	Strawberries eaten by songbirds, game birds, and humans	
Related Species	Beach strawberry (*F. chiloensis*)	

At first glance, **California strawberry** seems to be an ideal shady ground cover—it's extremely low-growing, evergreen, reasonably drought-resistant, and able to thrive even under trees that cast lots of shade, such as California bay. It also produces small but extremely flavorful strawberries. The drawback is that it doesn't live very long, usually somewhere between 5 and 15 years. Too much water hastens its demise, so use it under a drought-resistant native tree such as netleaf hackberry or western red bud. For a charming, old-fashioned look, plant it along the edges of a stone patio that's been set in sand and let it wander among the pavers. **Beach strawberry** (1, 2, 3) is twice as tall and tolerant of more sun, but it is so fussy about having perfect drainage that it is unsuitable for irrigated gardens. Use it with fremontia and ceanothus, or in deep sand under a Torrey pine.

. . . .

87 *Common Name*	Island alumroot	
Latin Name	*Heuchera maxima*	
Native Habitat	RARE, cliffs in canyons below 1,500 feet in northern Channel Islands	
Regions of Use	1, 2, 3	
Soil	Moist, decomposed granite, sand, clay loam, low organic content, well drained	
Water	Once or twice a month	
Sun or Shade	● ◑	
Height × Width	Usual: 1 foot × 2 feet (leaves), 3 feet in flower	
Protective Mechanisms	None	
Leaves or Stems	Evergreen; round, ruffled leaves 6 inches across	
Ornamental Value	White flowers in spring, airy woodland effect	
Other Value	Flowers used by butterflies and bees	
Related Species	Arizona coralbells (*H. sanguinea*)	

Drifts of **island alumroot** are abundant in southern California gardens during late March and early April. Once established, it can survive in the dry shade under an old coast live oak, but it will look better with irrigation. Use pure masses of it, or mix in a number of other shady flowers and ground covers such as creeping snowberry, fuchsia flowering currant, Douglas iris, and creeping sage. With twice-a-month irrigation, you can use it under fernleaf Catalina ironwood, summer holly, or Catalina cherry, mixed with coffeeberry fern, elymus, any of the wild currants, red columbine, meadow rue (*Thalictrum polycarpum*), Douglas iris, red buckwheat, Mexican evening primrose, and autumn sage. We saw one gorgeous 15-year-old plant in a shaded patio pot that got watered once a week. **Arizona coralbells** (1, 2) is smaller, with pink to carmine flowers. It requires more constant moisture. It has been crossed with island alumroot to make hybrid alumroots of varying shades of pink and moisture needs.

88	
Common Name	Douglas iris
Latin Name	*Iris douglasiana*
Native Habitat	Coastal prairie and mixed evergreen forest below 3,000 feet from Santa Barbara to Oregon
Regions of Use	1, 2, 3
Soil	Moist, decomposed granite, sand, clay loam, high to low organic content, well drained
Water	Once or twice a month
Sun or Shade	● ◐ ◑ ○
Height × Width	Maximum: 3 feet × 2 feet. Usual: 18 inches × 2 feet
Protective Mechanisms	Bitter leaves discourage grazers and browsers
Leaves	Evergreen if irrigated in summer
Ornamental Value	3-inch flowers in white, cream, purple, blue, lavender, or rose; long season in spring
Other Value	Flowers used by hummingbirds and bees

Douglas iris is one of the prettiest of California's native flowers and one of the easiest to grow. It thrives in southern California in both canyon and coastal landscapes with just one or two deep waterings per month during the dry season. Give it some shade and it needs even less irrigation. It naturally hybridizes with other irises in its northern range, inspiring breeders to develop a wide range of colors of their own. One series of 4-inch-flowered irises, called Pacific Coast hybrids, comes in all the above-mentioned lovely hues, plus yellow and peach, but these plants are less drought-resistant. Douglas iris can be used in many situations—as a ground cover under coastal live oaks, or interplanted with other shade-loving perennial flowers, making a lovely ground cover substitute. It combines well with red columbine, island alumroot, creeping snowberry (the canyon snowberry is too tall), evergreen currant, and coffeeberry fern.

....

89	
Common Name	Elymus, giant wild rye
Latin Name	*Leymus condensatus*
Native Habitat	Coastal sagescrub, chaparral, scrub oak woodland, and Joshua tree woodland below 4,500 feet from central western California to Mexico
Regions of Use	1, 2, 3, 4, 6
Soil	Dry to moist, decomposed granite, sand, clay loam, low to rich organic content, well drained
Water	None to twice a month
Sun or Shade	● ◐ ◑ ○
Height × Width	Maximum: 12 feet × 8 feet, counting bloom stalk. Usual: 30 inches × 6 feet, leaves only
Protective Mechanisms	None
Leaves or Stems	Pale blue-green, turning tan (dormant) in drought or cold
Ornamental Value	Blue foliage, feathery flowers in summer
Other Value	Browse all year for elk, pronghorn, and deer; seeds eaten by many animals

Elymus (ee LYE mus) is a bunch grass that forms a clump so tidy and well mannered that the most fastidious gardener would use it in a flower garden. Plus, it grows in shade as well as in sun. Use its wide blue leaves as a bold accent among delicate-leaved red columbine or dark, glossy-leaved evergreen currant. They'll contrast as beautifully as agave or yucca—but with no spines or saw-toothed edges. In most gardens, we saw the handsome cultivar 'Canyon Prince'. To keep it green in the summer, plan to water some, even in the shade. This selection is very handy for some parts of southern California, but a more drought-resistant selection would be a boon for the deserts or for revegetation schemes. A solid planting of elymus as a tall ground cover is striking. Cut it back to the ground when you want all fresh foliage.

90	Common Name	Bamboo muhly
	Latin Name	*Muhlenbergia dumosa*
	Native Habitat	Rocky canyon slopes and valleys at low altitudes in Sonoran Desert
	Regions of Use	1, 2, 3, 4, 5, 6, 7
	Soil	Dry, decomposed granite, sand, clay loam, low organic content, well drained
	Water	Once or twice a month
	Sun or Shade	● ◑ ◐ ○
	Height × Width	Maximum: 10 feet × 10 feet. Usual: 5 feet × 6 feet
	Protective Mechanisms	None
	Leaves or Stems	Pale green to khaki, dormant when dry or cold
	Ornamental Value	Delicate flowers in early spring
	Other Value	Browse, seeds eaten by birds and small mammals

Bamboo muhly (MEW lee) is an unusual grass. For one thing, it tolerates shade. For another, its leaves and stems are a pale, golden khaki all year–never all green. The stems get woody and need to be removed once a year. The flowers and seed heads resemble asparagus foliage, and this delicate mist lasts for months. Bamboo muhly can be massed under a tree. Or use it as an accent–a spineless alternative to sotol or yucca. One clump I'm very fond of is planted by the front door of Ron and Maureen Gass's house in Phoenix. The color is so unusual that it deserves to be played up. Jojoba best echoes it, but the seedpods of hopbush are also good, while the trunks of foothill paloverde bring out its tawniness. The dark greens of creosote bush, Mormon tea, and sugarbush provides stark contrast. Starleaf Mexican orange, Mexican evening primrose, and Mexican plumbago make handsome ground covers around it in the shade, but in sunny spots plant penstemons, desert marigold, phacelia, and verbena.

....

91	Common Name	Mexican evening primrose
	Latin Name	*Oenothera speciosa*
	Native Habitat	Mostly a native of the southern Great Plains, infrequent in Chihuahuan Desert grasslands
	Regions of Use	1, 2, 3, 4, 5, 6, 7
	Soil	Dry, decomposed granite, sand, clay loam, limestone, low to high organic content, well drained
	Water	Twice a month or more
	Sun or Shade	● ◑ ◐ ○
	Height × Width	Maximum: 20 inches high. Usual: 6 to 12 inches high
	Protective Mechanisms	None
	Leaves or Stems	Evergreen or dormant in summer
	Ornamental Value	2-inch pink (white) flowers in daytime, in spring
	Other Value	Seeds eaten by numerous animals

Mexican evening primrose has the potential to be a conventional low-growing ground cover in deep shade with summer irrigation to prevent summer dormancy. It produces few flowers there, however. Plant it in semi-shade to enjoy two months of pale to deeper pink flowers every spring. Full-sun locations require heavy irrigation or coastal mists. Plants from northern stock tend to be white and open up in the evening, while this selection is pink and opens in the morning. Mexican evening primrose is sold throughout the Southwest as *O. berlandieri*. In fact, it is *O. speciosa* var. *childsii*–so called because it was introduced by John Lewis Childs in 1892 from specimens gathered along the Gulf Coast in Texas and adjacent Mexico. It has naturalized in disturbed places below 1,500 feet between Los Angeles and Santa Barbara.

92	
Common Name	Coffeeberry fern
Latin Name	*Pellaea andromedifolia*
Native Habitat	Rocky slopes between 100 and 6,000 feet from North Coast Ranges to Baja California and Channel Islands
Regions of Use	1, 2, 3
Soil	Medium dry, decomposed granite, sand, sandstone, high or low organic content, well drained
Water	Once or twice a month
Sun or Shade	● ◐ ◑
Height × Width	Maximum: 3 feet high. Usual: 2 feet × 2 feet
Protective Mechanisms	None
Leaves or Stems	Almost evergreen, thick, shiny
Ornamental Value	Texture
Other Value	No information

In the wild, **coffeeberry fern** does not actually grow under coffeeberry shrubs. Its roots can colonize but are pretty slow doing it, so don't expect to make an extensive ground cover like western bracken fern. Instead, mix it with a number of other shady ground covers and flowers to resemble a forest floor. Creeping snowberry, fuchsia flowering currant, evergreen currant, island alumroot, and onion lily look good growing with it, and they all share the same requirements for moisture and good drainage. Coffeeberry fern loves to grow in crevices in rock faces, such as an unmortared stone wall or some boulders in your garden, as long as there's plenty of shade. If there's a rocky pocket deep enough to fill with soil, tuck in a young fern and water it carefully until its roots find permanent moisture. If you can't find a planting pocket, tuck spore-laden leaves above where you hope the ferns will eventually grow. The spores will scatter into tiny crevices, and in two to three years you just might have ferns.

93	
Common Name	Mexican plumbago
Latin Name	*Plumbago scandens*
Native Habitat	Canyons and oak woodlands between 2,500 and 4,000 feet in Pinal and Pima counties in Arizona, in Rio Grande Plains and Trans Pecos, Texas, and in Florida and tropical America
Regions of Use	1, 2, 5, 6
Soil	Moist, decomposed granite, sand, clay loam, low organic content, well drained
Water	Twice a month or more
Sun or Shade	● ◑
Height × Width	Maximum: 3 feet × 4 feet. Usual: 2 feet × 3 feet
Protective Mechanisms	Roots and leaves cause dermatitis on some humans
Leaves or Stems	Leaves scarce and reddish purple in winter
Ornamental Value	White or pale blue flowers in spring and fall
Other Value	Flowers used by butterflies and bees

Mexican plumbago is similar to the familiar South African plumbago, but it's more drought-resistant and only half as tall. Each plant is a self-contained, low-growing shrub with arching, almost horizontal branches. Planted 2 to 3 feet apart, Mexican plumbago makes a high ground cover or a low mass of shrubbery. It blooms heavily in the spring and again in the fall. Reflected afternoon summer sun is hard on it, but dappled shade allows it to flower steadily all summer as well. At the onset of cold weather, its bright green leaves turn shades of wine red and purple. Half of them will drop, but the rest will stay on all winter. Companion plants for Mexican plumbago are bamboo muhly, autumn sage, and starleaf Mexican orange. Mexican evening primrose likes the same conditions, but it would overpower the plumbago.

94	Common Name	Western bracken fern
	Latin Name	*Pteridium aquilinum* var. *pubescens*
	Native Habitat	Seeps, from coastal sagescrub to Davis Mountains in Texas
	Regions of Use	1, 2, 3
	Soil	Dry, decomposed granite, sand, low organic content, well drained
	Water	Once or twice a month or more
	Sun or Shade	● ◑ ◐
	Height × Width	Maximum: 4 feet high. Usual: 2 feet × 3 feet
	Protective Mechanisms	Chemical property in leaves toxic to some browsers
	Leaves or Stems	Dormant in winter or when severely drought-stressed
	Ornamental Value	Texture
	Other Value	Soil stabilization

In southern California, a lush garden is often at odds with the need to conserve water. **Western bracken fern** is an attractive solution to that problem–it looks like it needs lots of water, but it does very well on moderate irrigation. Water it too often and the bracken will get quite aggressive; too little and it will go dormant, but only after sending out signals of distress for a couple of weeks, giving you plenty of time to rescue it. In a shady garden watered only once a month, you can maintain a tiny patch of bracken or even just one plant in a shallow swale where it gets runoff from rains. Combine western bracken fern with big rocks, coffeeberry fern, Douglas iris, and California fescue, and enjoy it with a clear conscience.

....

95	Common Name	Fuchsia flowering currant
	Latin Name	*Ribes speciosum*
	Native Habitat	Coastal sagescrub and chaparral below 1,500 feet from Santa Clara to Baja California
	Regions of Use	1, 2, 3
	Soil	Dry, decomposed granite, sand, clay loam, low to some organic content, well drained
	Water	None to twice a month
	Sun or Shade	● ◑
	Height × Width	Maximum: 10 feet high. Usual: 4 feet × 7 feet
	Protective Mechanisms	Spines
	Leaves or Stems	Glossy, dark green, dormant in winter
	Ornamental Value	Red fuchsialike flowers in early spring, red spiny gooseberries in late spring
	Other Value	Flowers used by hummingbirds, fruits eaten by songbirds

Use **fuchsia flowering currant** as a backdrop in a difficult, shady spot with masses of evergreen currant or hummingbird sage at its feet. Fuchsia flowering currant and many other native deciduous currants grow as understory dotted beneath coastal live oaks, toyon, and other tall chaparral shrubs. There are at least six other native flowering currants available in nurseries with very fragrant blooms in shades of yellow, pendulous pale pink, red, white, and cerise. The fruits, called currants or gooseberries, ripen from pink or orange to wine red, purple, and black. All can be combined with fuchsia flowering currant to make a shady flower bed or bird thicket. Other shady companion plants are bracken, snowberry, elymus, California strawberry, and Douglas iris.

96	
Common Name	Evergreen currant, Catalina currant
Latin Name	*Ribes viburnifolium*
Native Habitat	Chaparral below 1,000 feet on Santa Catalina Island and in Baja California, RARE in western San Diego County
Regions of Use	1, 2, 3
Soil	Moist, decomposed granite, sand, clay loam, high or low organic content, well drained
Water	Once or twice a month
Sun or Shade	● ◑
Height × Width	Maximum: 6 feet high. Usual: 3 feet × 6 feet
Protective Mechanisms	None
Leaves or Stems	Evergreen, dark green, glossy, aromatic
Ornamental Value	Glossy leaves, rosy flowers in early spring
Other Value	Flowers used by bees, fruits eaten by birds, cover

Evergreen currant was once very prevalent on mainland California. It received more than 20 inches of rain a year and the summers were cool and misted by fog—of course, this was the late Pleistocene Epoch. Back then it used to grow under summer holly, Torrey pine, and coffeeberry, with coffeeberry fern and perhaps giant coreopsis. It can still be used with these plants, and it doesn't need a mist system to keep it happy. Just put it in shady spots and water it once or twice a month. It sprawls like a conventional ground cover, and an annual pruning easily maintains it at knee height. For a mix of spring-flowering ground cover, combine it with island alumroot, red columbine, and meadow rue (*Thalic trum polycarpum*).

....

97	
Common Name	Hummingbird sage, pitcher sage
Latin Name	*Salvia spathacea*
Native Habitat	Oak woodland, chaparral, coastal sagescrub below 2,500 feet from Solano County to Orange County
Regions of Use	1, 2, 3
Soil	Dry, decomposed granite, sand, clay loam, rich or low organic content, well drained
Water	None to twice a month
Sun or Shade	● ◑ ◐
Height × Width	Maximum: 3 feet high. Usual: 2 feet
Protective Mechanisms	Aromatic oils discourage some browsers
Leaves or Stems	Evergreen if watered or dormant in summer, aromatic
Ornamental Value	Red flowers in spring, minty fragrance
Other Value	Flowers used by hummingbirds, butterflies and bees; seeds rich in protein
Related Species	Creeping sage (*S. sonomensis*)

Hummingbird sage goes perfectly under a coast live oak or an old shade-casting blue manzanita. There, it can be naturalized in large clumps with other dry, shade-loving flowers in front of a drift of another hummingbird favorite—fuchsia flowering currant. Under western sycamore and other trees more accepting of irrigation, hummingbird sage can form an evergreen ground cover over a large area and be mowed once a year to keep it from getting woody. Too much shade combined with too much moisture can cause powdery mildew. **Creeping sage** (1, 2, 3) forms a mat of blue-green leaves with blue flowers and lives in very similar places. It likes shade and moisture but insists on absolutely perfect drainage, so use it in small areas or combine it with less-fussy but nonaggressive shady ground covers such as red columbine, California strawberry, island alumroot, Douglas iris, or coffeeberry fern.

98 *Common Name*	Canyon snowberry, common snowberry
Latin Name	*Symphoricarpos albus* var. *laevigatus* (*S. rivularis*)
Native Habitat	Woods, streambanks, north-facing slopes below 3,600 feet from southwestern California to Alaska
Regions of Use	1, 2, 3
Soil	Dry, decomposed granite, sand, clay loam, low to some organic content, well drained
Water	None to once a month or more
Sun or Shade	● ◐
Height × Width	Maximum: 6 feet high. Usual: 2 feet × 5 feet
Protective Mechanisms	Fruits toxic to some mammals, possibly to humans
Leaves or Stems	Spring green, small and round, dormant in winter
Ornamental Value	Clusters of dry white berries in fall and winter
Other Value	Erosion control, fruits eaten by birds, cover, browse
Related Species	Creeping snowberry (*S. mollis*)

Canyon snowberry is excellent for holding a steep shady bank or as a carefree waist-high ground cover under an ancient spreading coast live oak. Once established, it can naturalize. Place plants 3 feet apart, or, if you're willing to be patient, plant just one–it can eventually form an extensive thicket under toyon, scrub oak, and other tall woody chaparral species. In a more controlled garden setting, choose the shorter **creeping snowberry** (1, 2, 3). Also thicket-forming and good for erosion control, it can be easily maintained at knee height or even a little lower. Its porcelain white berries are much larger and showier. It will look best if you water it once or twice a month during the summer. Flowers on both species are pink bells, but they are so tiny that they often go unnoticed.

6 PERENNIAL FLOWERS

PERENNIAL FLOWERS ARE A JOY AND, FOR MANY PEOPLE, THE MOST EXCITING PART OF gardening. Instead of installing a conventional English-style flower bed, in the Southwest it's much easier to use perennial flowers as a substitute for a ground cover or to weave them among the permanent evergreens in your garden. These bright spots of color come and go with different seasons. A relaxed attitude will allow them to be serendipities in your garden. A rigid attitude will cause frustration.

In southern California and the Southwest, most perennial flowers are actually shrubs, many of which are evergreen. The basic definition of a perennial flower is a flower that lives longer than a year before it dies. Three to five years is average. Some species might live only one and a half years—especially with water and fertilizer, which, interestingly, seem to shorten their lives. Another few species can live as long as 50 years or more.

Perennial flowers usually spend one season of the year dormant. Where winters are cold, as in the northeastern United States, heavy frosts knock perennial flowers back to the roots. During the winter, they might maintain a rosette of green leaves at the base of the plant,

ABOVE: White stars of fleabane daisy (*Erigeron* ssp.)—an annual—plus two perennials (red Eaton's penstemon and desert marigold) and a flowering shrub (pretty dalea) replace a ground cover of bursage here at the entrance of the Frieder Garden designed by Christy Ten Eyck in Phoenix. ABOVE RIGHT: September is not a prime blooming season for the Los Angeles area, but the long-lasting flowers of California buckwheat and St. Catherine's lace are still held high in Andy and Cheryl Charles's garden in Beverly Glen, designed by Paul Nota.

or they might completely disappear. When spring arrives, they send up fresh new stems and leaves. But in southern California and the Southwest, where winters are relatively warm, many perennial flowers continue to grow and even bloom during December, January, and February. A summer drought might cause them to lose their leaves, but it rarely kills the stems. When the stems live longer than a year, they start getting woody, and the perennial flowers are then classified by botanists as shrubs. Even the little 9-inch-tall dwarf white zinnia is called a shrub.

Without being killed to the roots every year, however, some perennials might get larger than desirable. Pruning is allowed, as is pulling out the whole plant if there is a seedling to take its place. There are no rights and wrongs here. Follow your instincts, and if a perennial flower dies, buy another one.

99	Common Name	Desert marigold
	Latin Name	*Baileya multiradiata*
	Native Habitat	Roadsides, washes, and mesas below 5,000 feet in Chihuahuan, Sonoran, and Mojave deserts
	Regions of Use	2, 3, 4, 5, 6, 7
	Soil	Dry, decomposed granite, sand, low organic content, well drained
	Water	None to once a month
	Sun or Shade	◖ ○
	Height × Width	Maximum: 20 inches × 20 inches. Usual: 1 foot × 1 foot
	Protective Mechanisms	None
	Leaves or Stems	Evergreen, pale blue-green
	Ornamental Value	Yellow daisies almost all year
	Other Value	Flowers used by butterflies, seeds important for small mammals, toxic to livestock except horses, rabbits love new growth
	Other Species	Dune marigold (*B. pleniradiata*)

Desert marigold is short, neat, everblooming, and easily the most dependable and useful of the desert flowers. It can be the mainstay of a flower bed or the unifying color in a patch of existing or revegetated desert. Individual plants live an average of only two years. To maintain a constant supply of flowers, let the seed ripen and scatter naturally into decomposed granite or desert pavement. The multilayered daisies make good cut flowers, and the pale blue-gray foliage is attractive even on those rare occasions when no flowers are in bloom. **Dune marigold** (2, 3, 4, 5, 6) is so similar that it is sometimes classified as a variety. It's found in the Colorado Desert above 200 feet, and everywhere else desert marigold grows except for the Chihuahuan Desert.

....

100	Common Name	Chocolate daisy
	Latin Name	*Berlandiera lyrata*
	Native Habitat	Roadsides and mesas below 5,000 feet in Chihuahuan Desert and the extreme southwestern part of the Midwest
	Regions of Use	1, 2, 3, 4, 5, 6, 7
	Soil	Dry, decomposed granite, sand, clay loam, limestone, low organic content, well drained
	Water	None to twice a month
	Sun or Shade	◖ ○
	Height × Width	Maximum: 4 feet × 3 feet. Usual: 1 foot × 1 foot
	Protective Mechanisms	None
	Leaves or Stems	Evergreen
	Ornamental Value	Yellow daisies almost all year, chocolate fragrance
	Other Value	Flowers used by butterflies

Chocolate daisy really does smell like chocolate; its aroma assails you from a distance of 10 to 20 feet, not just when you bury your nose in one. Another endearing feature is the leafy green border that surrounds each maroon center after the petals drop, giving chocolate daisy another common name–brooch flower. Chocolate daisy requires irrigation to bloom all year. Use several in a flower garden or by a walkway or near a patio where the scents can be enjoyed by everyone who walks past. You can also enjoy one for years in a deep 12-inch patio pot. Flowers that like similar conditions are blackfoot daisy, mesa greggia, desert marigold, autumn sage, damianita, skeletonleaf goldeneye, and dwarf white zinnia.

101 *Common Name*	Pink fairyduster, mesquitillo
Latin Name	*Calliandra eriophylla*
Native Habitat	Hillsides between 2,000 and 5,000 feet in Sonoran and Colorado deserts and on the Rio Grande Plains in Texas
Regions of Use	2, 3, 5, 6
Soil	Dry, decomposed granite, sand, low organic content, well drained
Water	None to once a month
Sun or Shade	○
Height × Width	Maximum: 4 feet × 6 feet. Usual: 2 feet × 3 feet
Protective Mechanisms	None
Leaves or Stems	Evergreen or drought- or cold-deciduous, tiny leaflets
Ornamental Value	Fluffy pink flowers after rain
Other Value	Erosion control, flowers used by butterflies and bees, fruits eaten by quail and other birds, browsed by deer

North of Phoenix, there are large hilly lots covered with saguaro, turpentine weed, and a gorgeous shrub called **pink fairyduster**. Its fluffy pink flowers stand out magnificently against the soft earth-colored homes. In the wild, it is about knee-high, kept well pruned by deer and drought. In a garden, it grows larger, and it will need pruning about once a year to clean out dead wood and to shape it into something either airy and sculptural or compact and rounded. In the decomposed granite around the feet of your pink fairyduster, plant Parry's penstemons, white zinnias, and blackfoot daisies. For naturalizing, plant pink fairydusters 3 to 8 feet apart along with California buckwheat, brittlebush, desert marigold, and globe mallow, and lots of stones to resemble a rocky desert hillside. The red fairyduster (*C. californica*), called **Baja fairyduster** because it is native to Baja California, also thrives in sparsely irrigated gardens.

102 *Common Name*	Giant coreopsis
Latin Name	*Coreopsis gigantea*
Native Habitat	Sea bluffs and coastal dunes below 150 feet from San Luis Obispo to Los Angeles County and adjacent Channel Islands
Regions of Use	1, 2, 3
Soil	Dry, decomposed granite, sand, low organic content, well drained
Water	None
Sun or Shade	◐ ◑ ○
Height × Width	Maximum: 10 feet × 3 feet. Usual: 3 feet × 2 feet
Protective Mechanisms	None
Leaves or Stems	Bright green, ferny but succulent, dormant in summer
Ornamental Value	Yellow daisies in spring, fleshy trunk
Other Value	Flowers used by butterflies and bees, seeds eaten by birds
Related Species	Sea dahlia (*C. maritima*)

Giant coreopsis is sometimes called tree coreopsis because of its soft, spongy "trunk," which can get over 6 feet tall and 4 inches in diameter. This is a fun plant to use; it not only looks exotic, it looks improbable. During the last Ice Age, it had a more extensive range, along with other relict plants such as Channel Island tree poppy and Torrey pine. More common companion plants are toyon, chamise, and lemonadeberry, which are good for hiding its leafless trunk in the summer. Fremontia would be effective for this also, as the two bloom yellow together in spring and both hate summer water. **Sea dahlia** (1, 2, 3), another Ice Age relict, is RARE and can be found only along sea bluffs in San Diego County and Baja California. It has fleshy hollow stems but no trunk, and it dies back to the roots in the summer. With summer irrigation, it might die altogether. But no matter; it grows quickly and reseeds easily, producing a wealth of gold flowers every spring.

103	*Common Name*	Pretty dalea, bush dalea
	Latin Name	*Dalea pulchra*
	Native Habitat	Rocky hillsides between 2,500 and 5,000 feet in Southern Arizona
	Regions of Use	2, 3, 5, 6
	Soil	Dry, decomposed granite, sand, low organic content, well drained
	Water	None to once a month
	Sun or Shade	○
	Height × Width	Maximum: 5 feet × 5 feet. Usual: 3 feet × 3 feet
	Protective Mechanisms	None
	Leaves or Stems	Silver, evergreen or cold- or drought-deciduous
	Ornamental Value	Purple flowers in early spring
	Other Value	Flowers used by butterflies and bumblebees
	Related Species	Feather dalea (*D. formosa*), silver dalea (*D. bicolor* var. *argyraea*), black dalea (*D. frutescens*)

Fact is, it is impossible to find an unattractive shrubby dalea. **Pretty dalea** (DAY lee uh) blooms earliest in the spring and looks wonderful in a sea of short wildflowers. It and **silver dalea** (2, 3, 5, 6) have silvery leaves; the leaves on the other shrubby daleas are grayish green. **Feather dalea** (2, 3, 4, 5, 6, 7) is, I think, even prettier than pretty dalea; it has feathery plumes in addition to rosy flowers. **Black dalea** (2, 3, 4, 5, 6, 7) is the dependable fall bloomer; the others tend to flower in either spring or fall—or both. Shrubby daleas can sustain a severe pruning once a year. Immediately after blooming in spring or fall is usually the best time. These daleas are easily used as large flowers in a garden setting along with cenizo, brittlebush, and globe mallow against a backdrop of large creosotes or smooth walls.

104	*Common Name*	Coast sunflower
	Latin Name	*Encelia californica*
	Native Habitat	Coastal sagescrub and chaparral up to 30 miles inland below 2,000 feet from Santa Barbara County to San Diego, Santa Catalina, San Clemente, and Santa Cruz islands
	Regions of Use	1, 2, 3, 4, 6
	Soil	Dry, decomposed granite, sand, low organic content, well drained
	Water	None to once a month
	Sun or Shade	◐ ○
	Height × Width	Maximum: 5 feet × 5 feet. Usual: 2 feet × 2 feet
	Protective Mechanisms	None
	Leaves or Stems	Evergreen
	Ornamental Value	Large yellow daisies in spring
	Other Value	Erosion control, flowers used by butterflies and bees, seeds eaten by songbirds and game birds

Coast sunflower grows quickly from seed; adapts to almost any sunny, well drained condition; and rewards the efforts of children and black-thumb gardeners. It produces quantities of flowers suitable for cutting for many weeks in the spring and needs only an occasional watering during the summer to keep its leaves looking acceptable. In late fall, cut it back to the ground so it can get all new fresh growth. Use it in a flower garden with monkeyflower, various salvias and buckwheats, evergreen lupine, penstemons, woolly bluecurls, and Matilija poppy. For a spectacular easy-care display in early spring, plant it with Santa Barbara or greenbark ceanothus and golden-flowered fremontia and tree poppy.

105 *Common Name*	Brittlebush, incienso
Latin Name	*Encelia farinosa*
Native Habitat	South-facing hillsides and maritime desert scrub below 3,000 feet in Sonoran, Colorado, and Mojave deserts to San Diego County and Baja California
Regions of Use	1, 2, 3, 4, 5, 6
Soil	Dry, decomposed granite, sand, low organic content, well drained
Water	None to once a month
Sun or Shade	○
Height × Width	Maximum: 6 feet × 6 feet. Usual: 2 feet × 3 feet
Protective Mechanisms	Aromatic oils discourage some browsers
Leaves or Stems	Silver, aromatic, evergreen or drought-deciduous
Ornamental Value	Yellow daisies in winter and spring
Other Value	Flowers used by butterflies and bees, seeds eaten by songbirds and game birds, browsed by chuckwalla, dried branches burned as incense

Brittlebush rarely looks its best in municipal plantings. First it gets overwatered and turns leggy. Then it is usually cut back just before it's ready to bloom. Despite this negative reputation, it is actually enormously easy to grow, either from seed or from nursery stock. Plant brittlebush where it will get reflected winter heat from the street, the driveway, the patio, or a south-facing wall. Water it once or twice to get it established, and then *leave it alone.* Its silvery leaves will look good all winter, and in early spring it will bloom for two to four weeks along with globe mallow, chuparosa, bladderpod, sand verbena, Parry's penstemon, and Goodding's verbena. Although it is called a shrub, brittlebush is rather short-lived, and most plants die back in summer without irrigation. Many gardeners cut brittlebush to the ground after flowering, knowing it will green up again with irrigation, and some pull it out by the roots if there are plenty of seedlings to replace it.

....

106 *Common Name*	Panamint daisy, sunray
Latin Name	*Enceliopsis covillei* (formerly *E. argophylla*)
Native Habitat	RARE, rocky slopes and desert washes below 4,000 feet in Mojave Desert
Regions of Use	3, 4, 5, 6
Soil	Dry, decomposed granite, sand, gypsum okay, low organic content, well drained
Water	Once a month
Sun or Shade	◑ ○
Height × Width	Maximum: 4 feet × 3 feet. Usual: 2 feet × 2 feet
Protective Mechanisms	None
Leaves or Stems	Silver, felty, evergreen or drought-deciduous
Ornamental Value	4- to 6-inch yellow daisies in spring
Other Value	Flowers used by butterflies and bees

Panamint daisy grows on the western slopes of the Panamint Mountains and in washes around Lake Mead. It is very impressive-looking. Its leaves are soft and silvery, with downy hairs, and are several inches long and wide—huge by desert standards. The hand-sized golden yellow daisies are atop long, straight stems. We saw it growing with creosote and atriplex in a wash with ephemeral wildflowers—*Mentzelia tricuspis, Lepidium fremontii,* malacothrix, chaenactis, and phacelia. In Las Vegas, we saw one specimen in a garden next to a clump of Santa Rita prickly pear. Other garden plants flowering at the same time were western redbud, beavertail, Parry's penstemon, Dorri sage, pink fairyduster, brittlebush, and globe mallow.

107 *Common Name*	Zauschneria, California fuchsia
Latin Name	*Epilobium canum* ssp. *mexicanum* (formerly *Zauschneria californica* ssp. *californica* and *Z. c.* ssp. *mexicana*)
Native Habitat	Dry slopes below 2,000 feet from Baja California to Monterey County, California
Regions of Use	1, 2, 3
Soil	Dry, decomposed granite, sand, clay loam, low organic content, well drained
Water	None to once a month
Sun or Shade	◐ ◑ ○
Height × Width	Maximum: 18 inches × 4 feet. Usual: 1 foot × 4 feet
Protective Mechanisms	None
Leaves or Stems	Gray-green, finely textured, dormant in winter
Ornamental Value	Orange-red flowers from August to October
Other Value	Erosion control, flowers used by hummingbirds and butterflies

Zauschneria (zosh NER ee uh) is as important to the fall California garden as ceanothus is to the spring garden. At a time when most plants are gasping through the last rigors of summer, zauschneria starts to bloom, producing showy cascades of tubular red to orange flowers. This timing is no accident–the hummingbirds have come to town, and zauschneria is their staple food source. Most gardeners tuck zauschneria into a few niches alongside a path or patio or in front of shrubs, and then let it wander. It spreads underground and is often used as a ground cover to stabilize steep banks. Zauschneria dies back to the ground in winter, so a tidy mulch is necessary to keep its space looking attractive while it is dormant. To control zauschneria's wandering habit, plant it in a big, well-drained pot. Cultivars have been selected for silvery foliage, pale pink flowers, red flowers, especially profuse blooms, and other attributes.

....

108 *Common Name*	Seaside daisy
Latin Name	*Erigeron glaucus*
Native Habitat	Coastal bluffs, dunes, and beaches below 65 feet from Oregon to Santa Barbara Channel Islands
Regions of Use	1, 2, 3
Soil	Moist, decomposed granite, sand, clay loam, high or low organic content, well drained
Water	Twice a month to once a week
Sun or Shade	◑ ○
Height × Width	Maximum: 2 feet × 3 feet. Usual: 1 foot × 2 feet
Protective Mechanisms	None
Leaves or Stems	Blue-green leaves, fuzzy, sometimes sticky, dormant in winter
Ornamental Value	Lavender (blue, white) daisies in spring and summer
Other Value	Flowers used by butterflies and bees

Seaside daisy blooms mostly in the spring, but where it gets coastal mists or irrigation, it can bloom on well into the summer. Be careful not to overwater, however, and make sure it has excellent drainage to withstand winter rains. Its thick, fleshy roots grow outward to make a bigger clump each year, but they can turn to mush if the soil gets saturated. Growing wild on the Channel Islands, seaside daisy is found with giant coreopsis, woody morning glory, coast red monkeyflower, dudleya, Catalina silverlace, island snapdragon, and St. Catherine's lace. These mostly silvery-leaved companion plants have yellow, pink, and red flowers and nicely complement the lavender of seaside daisy. Seaside daisy could also serve as a ground cover under desert willow. Several cultivars are available.

109	Common Name	Sulphur flower, sulphur buckwheat
	Latin Name	*Eriogonum umbellatum* var. *subaridum*
	Native Habitat	Sagebrush shrublands above 4,000 feet in Mojave Desert and surrounding canyon lands near Los Angeles
	Regions of Use	1, 2, 3, 4
	Soil	Dry, decomposed granite, sand, clay loam, low organic content, well drained
	Water	Once or twice a month
	Sun or Shade	◖ ○
	Height × Width	Maximum: 2 feet × 4 feet. Usual: 1 foot × 2 feet
	Protective Mechanisms	None
	Leaves or Stems	Silver, fuzzy, evergreen or drought- or cold-deciduous
	Ornamental Value	Yellow flowers in summer (spring, fall)
	Other Value	Flowers used by butterflies and bees, fruits eaten by birds
	Related Species	St. Catherine's lace (*E. giganteum*)

Sulphur flower is typical of the shrubby buckwheats. There are a multitude of species throughout the West, and all are invaluable landscape plants. Most are long-lived, under 2 feet high, and slightly broader than they are tall. They have showy flat-topped clusters of white, pink, rose, or yellow flowers that bloom in summer or early fall and change to coral and rust as they turn to seed. Most have fuzzy, silvery leaves, at least on the undersides. **California buckwheat** (1, 2, 3, 4, 5, 6, 7) is treated in the chapter on sunny ground covers, but it also works in a flower garden. Silvery-leaved **St. Catherine's lace** (1, 2, 3) is probably the most unusual. Like giant coreopsis, it can reach 10 feet in height, and its trunk can get up to 12 inches in diameter. Lacy clusters of pastel pink, white, or rose flowers are as huge as serving plates. A young plant puts its energy into growing a taproot the first year, so when setting one out, make sure any roots circling in the nursery pot are broken off and then directed downward.

110	Common Name	Catalina silverlace
	Latin Name	*Eriophyllum nevinii*
	Native Habitat	RARE, coastal bluffs below 100 feet on Channel Islands near Santa Barbara, threatened by goats
	Regions of Use	1, 2, 3
	Soil	Moist to dry, decomposed granite, sand, clay loam, low organic content, well drained
	Water	None to once a month
	Sun or Shade	◖ ○
	Height × Width	Maximum: 4 feet × 5 feet. Usual: 3 feet × 4 feet
	Protective Mechanisms	None
	Leaves or Stems	Silver, downy, large, fancy, evergreen
	Ornamental Value	Yellow flowers in fall
	Other Value	Flowers used by butterflies and bees
	Related Species	Golden yarrow (*E. confertiflorum*)

With its lacy silver leaves, **Catalina silverlace** is striking with or without its deep gold flowers. Give it lots of space, and place it against a smooth wall or a solid backdrop of woody morning glory or evergreens to show its foliage to best advantage. If it starts looking shabby because of drought or cold, or a shorter plant is wanted, trim back the damaged leaves or cut the plant to the ground; it will come back fresh and strong. It grows natively with the other giant Channel Island flowers–giant coreopsis and St. Catherine's lace. Dudleya or seaside daisy would make a good ground cover around it. **Golden yarrow** (1, 2, 3) is not nearly so dramatic, but it's useful for a new garden or where you want erosion control. Easy to grow from seed, it has ferny gray leaves and small clusters of yellow flowers. It is often one of the first plants to reappear in coastal sagescrub after a fire, and it can also be found in old established communities of coast live oak, elymus, and hummingbird sage.

111 Common Name	Corethrogyne, California aster
Latin Name	*Lessingia filaginifolia* var. *filaginifolia* (formerly *Corethrogyne leucophylla*)
Native Habitat	Coastal scrub, oak woodlands, grasslands below 8,500 feet in central, southwestern, and Baja California
Regions of Use	1, 2, 3
Soil	Dry, decomposed granite, sand, clay loam, low organic content, well drained
Water	None to once a month
Sun or Shade	◐ ○
Height × Width	Maximum: 3 feet × 5 feet. Usual: 18 inches × 2 feet
Protective Mechanisms	None
Leaves or Stems	Silver, fuzzy, evergreen, aromatic
Ornamental Value	Lavender flowers in summer and fall
Other Value	Flowers used by butterflies and bees

Corethrogyne (core ee THROG nee) grows mostly in sand dunes or on rocky slopes; clearly, it likes very good drainage. Its lavender flowers and silvery, fuzzy leaves are very attractive, but the main reason to include it in the garden is that it blooms in summer and fall when so many other flowers are retreating from the heat. Good companion flowers that bloom at the same time and can be naturalized with it are zauschneria, sulphur flower, Cleveland sage, and woolly bluecurls. In a lightly irrigated garden, it can be grown with mountain marigold, blackfoot daisy, chocolate daisy, mountain sage, autumn sage, and skeletonleaf or San Diego goldeneye. Corethrogyne is so versatile that it can be part of a very dry look with tree poppy and Our Lord's candle or it can thrive in a garden dominated by coast live oak, ceanothus, and manzanita. Spring flowers that can be planted in the same bed with it are purple needlegrass, blue-eyed grass, California gold poppy, owl's clover, fleabane, and arroyo lupine.

112 Common Name	Evergreen lupine
Latin Name	*Lupinus albifrons* var. *albifrons* (including var. *eminens*)
Native Habitat	Dry hillsides, canyons, coastal sage-scrub below 4,500 feet from Humboldt County to the Northern Channel Islands and Ventura County and from San Diego County to Baja California
Regions of Use	1, 2, 3
Soil	Dry, decomposed granite, sand, clay loam, low organic content, well drained
Water	Once to twice a month
Sun or Shade	○
Height × Width	Maximum: 7 feet × 8 feet when in bloom. Usual: 2 feet × 3 feet as a shrub, 4 feet × 4 feet when in bloom
Protective Mechanisms	None
Leaves or Stems	Evergreen, silver (especially in summer)
Ornamental Value	Lavender to purple flowers for one month in spring, fragrant
Other Value	Flowers used by butterflies and bumblebees

The only garden in which we saw **evergreen lupine** is at Rancho Santa Ana, but it deserves wider popularity. The stems are straight and vase-shaped and are covered about 2 feet up with silky, silvery, star-shaped leaves. When it gets close to 10 years old, a short woody trunk develops. The flowers are like little sunbonnets on long, straight spikes. They bloom from the bottom up, and the lavender flowers turn purple after being fertilized. Their fragrance is sweet but with a certain sharpness—not at all cloying. The seedpods grow fat, turn green, and then dry to tan. Trim off the flowering stalks after they are no longer ornamental. Tests have shown evergreen lupine to be fairly tolerant of heavy soil, summer irrigation, and air pollution, although these factors can shorten its life.

113	Common Name	Blackfoot daisy
	Latin Name	*Melampodium leucanthum*
	Native Habitat	Rocky hillsides, mesas, below 5,000 feet in Chihuahuan Desert, eastern edge of Sonoran Desert, and south-western quarter of Great Plains
	Regions of Use	1, 2, 3, 4, 5, 6, 7
	Soil	Dry, decomposed granite, sand, clay loam, limestone, low organic content, well drained
	Water	None to once a week
	Sun or Shade	◐ ○
	Height × Width	Maximum: 18 inches × 4 feet. Usual: 6 inches × 1 foot
	Protective Mechanisms	None
	Leaves or Stems	Silver, evergreen
	Ornamental Value	White 1-inch daisies, fragrant
	Other Value	Flowers used by butterflies

Blackfoot daisy seems to be at home in any kind of soil in a flower garden—thin limestone, sandy, slightly acid, even rich—just as long as it is well drained. Its size and life expectancy depend directly on how well you treat it. It behaves as though it has the potential to produce a finite number of flowers, which can appear all in one year or spread themselves out over two or three years. It is immensely useful in dry gardens, because it doesn't grow too tall, blooms all summer, and remains green as long as it stays alive. Also, it tolerates being planted 1 to 2 feet apart to make a white honey-scented carpet. In a desert landscape, tuck its roots under rocks to increase its drought resistance. When planting a whole landscape, save blackfoot daisy for the very end of the job; its stems are very fragile, and if they get damaged, the newly planted roots will never resprout.

....

114	Common Name	Monkeyflower
	Latin Name	*Mimulus aurantiacus* (includes coast red monkeyflower [*M. puniceus*] and southern bush monkeyflower [*M. longiflorus*])
	Native Habitat	Coastal sagescrub, chaparral, rocky slopes, open forests, below 5,000 feet in nondesert California
	Regions of Use	1, 2, 3
	Soil	Dry, decomposed granite, sand, clay loam, low organic content, well drained
	Water	None to once a month ('Capistrano Collection' hybrids twice a month)
	Sun or Shade	◑ ◐ ○
	Height × Width	Maximum: 5 feet × 5 feet. Usual: 2 feet × 2 feet
	Protective Mechanisms	None
	Leaves or Stems	Evergreen
	Ornamental Value	Orange, red, or yellow flowers in spring and fall
	Other Value	Flowers used by hummingbirds, butterflies, and bees

All too often gardeners get attracted to **monkeyflower**, use it with their nonnative plants, water to meet the needs of those nonnatives, and drown the monkeyflower. Instead, team monkeyflower with equally drought-tolerant natives. I've seen it in late March blooming with black sage, Mojave yucca, and coast sunflower in a coastal sagescrub garden. I've also seen it in a refined flower garden in September with sulphur flower, seaside daisy, and California fescue. It takes a break from blooming in the summer, but it stays green. Its color and growth habit are perfect for a 14-inch terra-cotta pot and also work well when tucked between stones in a retaining wall. To keep monkeyflower small and full of flowers, cut it back by one-third every winter. Don't confuse it with another native—scarlet monkeyflower (*M. cardinalis*), which grows by or in springs and streams in our western mountains.

115	Common Name	Mesa greggia
	Latin Name	*Nerisyrenia camporum*
	Native Habitat	Roadsides, arroyos, hills, plains below 4,000 feet in eastern Chihuahuan Desert
	Regions of Use	1, 2, 3, 5, 6
	Soil	Dry, decomposed granite, sand, limestone, low organic content, well drained
	Water	None to twice a month
	Sun or Shade	◑ ○
	Height × Width	Maximum: 2 feet × 2 feet. Usual: 9 inches × 1 foot
	Protective Mechanisms	None
	Leaves or Stems	Evergreen, silver, fuzzy
	Ornamental Value	White to pink or lavender flowers from March to November and sometimes in winter, fragrant
	Other Value	Flowers used by butterflies and bees, larval plant for white butterflies, browsed by black-tailed deer

Mesa greggia is a lot like blackfoot daisy in that it makes a short fragrant mound of everblooming flowers and is tolerant of a wide range of well-drained soils. The half-inch flowers start off white and gradually, on successive days, darken to pale pink and then to rose or lavender, producing a very pretty pink-and-white effect at all times. It is somewhat short-lived, so give it a mulch of decomposed granite or desert floor to catch and hold the tiny seeds. Mesa greggia and desert marigold would do well intermingled in a desert garden of ocotillo, yucca, creosote, false agave, candelilla, and other succulents, watered just once or twice a year. Or plant it under a desert willow with blackfoot daisy, chocolate daisy, and Terlingua aster, watered once a month or whenever blooms start to lag.

....

116	Common Name	Fragrant evening primrose
	Latin Name	*Oenothera caespitosa*
	Native Habitat	Stony slopes between 4,000 and 7,500 feet in Chihuahuan, Sonoran, Mojave, and Great Basin deserts
	Regions of Use	1, 2, 3, 4, 5, 6, 7
	Soil	Dry, decomposed granite, sand, limestone, low organic content, well drained
	Water	Once or twice a month
	Sun or Shade	◑ ○
	Height × Width	Maximum: 1 foot × 2 feet. Usual: 8 inches × 1 foot
	Protective Mechanisms	None
	Leaves or Stems	Evergreen rosette, sometimes silky and silvery
	Ornamental Value	White to pale pink flowers in spring (fall), fragrant
	Other Value	Flowers used by hummingbirds, butterflies, and white-lined hawk moths (*Hyles lineata*)
	Related Species	Birdcage primrose (*O. deltoides* ssp. *deltoides*)

Fragrant evening primrose has sweetly scented flowers that open at sunset and stay open in the morning until the sun gets hot. The 3- to 4-inch flowers are white when they first appear but turn pink just before they fold up and fall off. They usually open two evenings in a row. If mulched with 1 to 4 inches of decomposed granite, one watering a month is enough to keep the rosette of fragrant evening primrose green all summer, especially if it receives a little light shade cast by a paloverde or acacia. It blooms at the same time as pretty dalea, Parry's penstemon, brittlebush, and globe mallow. **Birdcage primrose** (1, 2, 3, 4, 5, 6), or dune primrose, looks very similar until it dies, at which point its stems begin to dry up and curl toward the center like a bird cage. It's an ephemeral when it grows in sand dunes in the Colorado Desert, but it can be a short-lived perennial if given summer irrigation.

117 *Common Name*	Eaton's penstemon
Latin Name	*Penstemon eatonii*
Native Habitat	Sagebrush scrub, pinyon/juniper, yellow pine forests between 2,000 and 9,000 feet from San Bernardino Mountains to Mojave and Great Basin deserts
Regions of Use	2, 3, 4, 5, 6, 7
Soil	Dry, decomposed granite, sand, clay loam, low organic content, well drained
Water	Once or twice a month
Sun or Shade	◑◐○
Height × Width	Maximum: 4 feet × 3 feet. Usual: 3 feet × 2 feet
Protective Mechanisms	None
Leaves or Stems	Silver, evergreen rosette
Ornamental Value	Red flowers in spring
Other Value	Flowers used by hummingbirds, larval plant for butterflies
Related Species	Cleveland penstemon (*P. clevelandii*), scarlet bugler (*P. centranthifolius*), cardinal penstemon (*P. cardinalis*), Havard penstemon (*P. havardii*), and superb penstemon (*P. superbus*)

Penstemons are one of our most dependable sources of spring color and hummingbird activity. Native on rocky hillsides, they live five years or more in courtyard gardens if given regular irrigation and excellent drainage. Blooms begin in early spring at the same time as the ephemeral wildflowers. When the stalks turn brown, they can be cut and the ripe seed scattered wherever you'd like more penstemons. Colors range from red and blue to pastels and white. Red-flowered penstemons are found in this entry. **Eaton's penstemon** is the best for Arizona. **Cleveland penstemon** (1, 2, 3, 4, 5, 6, 7) is native to the Lower Colorado Desert, and **scarlet bugler** (1, 2, 3) grows in chaparral and oak woodland in southern California. Red penstemons native to the mountains in the Chihuahuan Desert are **cardinal penstemon** (7), **Havard penstemon** (7), and **superb penstemon** (7). All these penstemons are available in nurseries.

....

118 *Common Name*	Parry's penstemon
Latin Name	*Penstemon parryi*
Native Habitat	North-facing slopes in canyons between 1,500 and 5,000 feet in Sonoran Desert
Regions of Use	1, 2, 3, 4, 5, 6, 7
Soil	Dry, decomposed granite, sand, low organic content, well drained
Water	Once or twice a month
Sun or Shade	◑◐○
Height × Width	Maximum: 4 feet × 3 feet. Usual: 3 feet × 2 feet
Protective Mechanisms	None
Leaves or Stems	Evergreen rosette
Ornamental Value	Rose-pink flowers in spring, faintly fragrant
Other Value	Flowers used by hummingbirds, larval plant for butterflies, browsed by deer
Related Species	Palmer penstemon (*P. palmeri*), foothill penstemon (*P. heterophyllus* ssp. *australis*), Wright penstemon (*P. wrightii*), pink plains penstemon (*P. ambiguus*), and canyon penstemon (*P. pseudospectabilis*)

Parry's penstemon is now a frequent sight in gardens from Santa Barbara to Palm Desert to El Paso, but just a few years ago it was being grown only by native-plant lovers Louis and Lucretia Hamilton of Tucson. They gave seeds to Ron and Maureen Gass of Mountain States Wholesale Nursery, who then raised hundreds of seedlings and personally planted them at the Desert Botanical Garden near downtown Phoenix, hoping to convert the general public. They succeeded. The result is a spectacular display of color every spring. Other pink penstemons are the 6-foot-tall, pale pink, fragrant **Palmer penstemon** (1, 2, 3, 4, 5, 6, 7), native around Las Vegas; and the rose to lavender (sometimes blue) **foothill penstemon** (1, 2, 3), a medium-height penstemon with narrow leaves, native to chaparral in southwestern California. From pale to rosy pink, **Wright penstemon** (7) is endemic to mountains in the Texas Trans Pecos. **Pink plains penstemon** (1, 2, 3, 4, 5, 6, 7) makes magnificent 3-foot-wide pastel pink mounds, but only in deep sand. Rosy-colored **canyon penstemon** (4, 6, 7) grows above 2000 feet, primarily in the Sonoran Desert.

119	Common Name	Royal penstemon
	Latin Name	*Penstemon spectabilis*
	Native Habitat	Coastal sagescrub, chaparral, oak woodland between 300 and 7,500 feet in southwestern California to Mexico
	Regions of Use	1, 2, 3, 4, 5, 6, 7
	Soil	Dry, decomposed granite, sand, low organic content, well drained
	Water	None to twice a month
	Sun or Shade	◑ ◐ ○
	Height × Width	Maximum: 4 feet × 3 feet. Usual: 3 feet × 2 feet
	Protective Mechanisms	None
	Leaves or Stems	Evergreen rosette
	Ornamental Value	Purple-blue flowers in spring
	Other Value	Flowers used by hummingbirds, larval plant for butterflies

Penstemons also come in blues and purples, but these are usually cold-tolerant varieties. One species that will take the heat is **royal penstemon**. Its chief concern is good drainage. An unhappy royal penstemon isn't thirsty–it's drowning; hold back on further irrigation. Royal penstemon can be grown without water in southwestern California along with fremontia, Cleveland penstemon, woolly bluecurls, black sage, pitcher sage, golden yarrow, Our Lord's candle, and foothill needlegrass. In the Lower Colorado Desert, give it periodic light irrigation and grow it under the delicate shade of an ironwood or smoketree along with other garden perennials such as Cleveland penstemon, Borrego aster, and desert marigold. Or sow it with ephemerals in a sunny but irrigated garden among yuccas and cacti.

....

120	Common Name	Matilija poppy, fried-egg flower
	Latin Name	*Romneya coulteri*
	Native Habitat	UNCOMMON, dry washes, canyons below 4,000 feet in Riverside and San Diego counties
	Regions of Use	1, 2, 3, 4
	Soil	Dry, decomposed granite, sand, low organic content, well drained
	Water	Once a month
	Sun or Shade	◑ ◐ ○
	Height × Width	Maximum: 8 feet × 10 feet. Usual: 4 feet × 6 feet
	Protective Mechanisms	None
	Leaves or Stems	Pale blue-green, smooth, evergreen or drought-deciduous
	Ornamental Value	Huge white flowers, yellow centers, May to July, fragrant
	Other Value	Flowers used by butterflies and bees
	Related Species	Matilija poppy (*R. trichocalyx*)

Bart O'Brien

Matilija poppy is enormously attractive and easy to grow–ideal for black-thumb gardeners. It has 6- to 9-inch flowers that bear an uncanny resemblance to fried eggs. With judicious deep watering in late summer, it will stay evergreen, but many gardeners let it go dormant and cut it back so it will get all new fresh growth with fall and winter rain. This slows it down a little, which is good; this is an aggressive plant. Matilija poppy can get huge and shrubby, extending its roots and getting larger each year. It can also seed out aggressively, so in a home garden surround it with pavement or mulch and give it the space you'd allot to a large shrub. To visually anchor a long backyard or driveway, plant Wolf's beargrass in a far corner (its pale blue foliage would match that of the poppy) and scatter Matilija poppies around it. There is another **Matilija poppy** (1, 2, 3), which looks almost the same and grows along the coast from Ventura County to Baja California.

121	Common Name	Cleveland sage
	Latin Name	*Salvia clevelandii*
	Native Habitat	Chaparral, coastal sagescrub in mountains mostly below 3,000 feet from San Diego County to Baja California
	Regions of Use	1, 2, 3, 6
	Soil	Dry, decomposed granite, sand, low organic content, well drained
	Water	None to once a month
	Sun or Shade	◐ ○
	Height × Width	Maximum: 5 feet × 6 feet. Usual: 3 feet × 4 feet
	Protective Mechanisms	Aromatic oils discourage some browsers
	Leaves or Stems	Silver, fuzzy, aromatic, evergreen or dormant in late summer
	Ornamental Value	Blue to purple flowers from April to July, aromatic leaves
	Other Value	Flowers used by hummingbirds, butterflies, and bees; leaves used in cooking and to make herbal tea
	Related Species	Canyon sage (*S. lycioides*)

Cleveland sage is a low-growing, compact shrub with plentiful blue flowers. Its leaves are wonderfully aromatic and can scent an entire garden, especially if kept dry in summer to enhance its pungency. Flowers that like the same conditions and bloom at the same time are woolly bluecurls, corethrogyne, and yellow sulphur flower. Evergreens could be succulents such as Wolf's beargrass, Our Lord's candle, and Mojave yucca, or soft, leafy shrubs such as bladderpod, toyon, sugarbush, chaparral whitethorn, and fremontia. **Canyon sage** (1, 2, 3, 4, 5, 6, 7), native to Chihuahuan Desert hillsides under 8,000 feet, is special because it is shrubby but very short–usually only about a foot tall–and its flowers are sky blue with no trace of lavender. In winter it might be evergreen or, in a severe cold snap, it might lose its leaves. It grows with Apache-plume, autumn sage, desert spoon, sacahuista, lechuguilla, New Mexico feathergrass (*Stipa neomexicana*), and starleaf Mexican orange.

122	Common Name	Dorri sage, desert sage
	Latin Name	*Salvia dorrii*
	Native Habitat	Desert slopes and washes between 2,500 and 6,000 feet in southern Mojave Desert
	Regions of Use	3, 4, 6, 7
	Soil	Dry, decomposed granite, sand, low organic content, well drained
	Water	None to once a month
	Sun or Shade	◐ ◐ ○
	Height × Width	Maximum: 3 feet × 3 feet. Usual: 18 inches × 2 feet
	Protective Mechanisms	Aromatic oils discourage some browsers
	Leaves or Stems	Silver, evergreen or dormant in winter, aromatic
	Ornamental Value	Blue and purple flowers
	Other Value	Flowers used by hummingbirds, butterflies, and bees; leaves used in cooking and to make herbal tea

The soft, smooth, blue-gray leaves of **Dorri sage** are handsome enough, but the two-tone flowers are simply stunning–bright blue with yellow stamens emerging from balls of reddish purple fuzz. The whole color scheme is one of my favorites, and only plume tiquilia has anything similar. Lots of Dorri sage can be naturalized to soften a scene composed of Joshua tree, banana yucca, Mojave yucca, claret-cup cactus, Mormon tea, buckhorn cholla, and creosote bush surrounded with a mulch of desert pavement or decomposed granite. In a small desert garden, place Dorri sage next to a boulder with a tree yucca, a clump of New Mexico feathergrass (*Stipa neomexicana*), and low-growing ephemerals or flowers such as blackfoot daisy. For a softer look in the San Gabriel Mountains in California, combine it with Apache-plume, desert ceanothus (*Ceanothus greggii*), red barberry, coffeeberry, California buckwheat, and blue manzanita. You could also use fremontia, woolly bluecurls, and corethrogyne, along with a clump of deergrass as an accent.

123	Common Name	Autumn sage
	Latin Name	*Salvia greggii*
	Native Habitat	Canyons and rocky mountain slopes between 2,200 and 5,800 feet in Chihuahuan Desert and south-central Texas
	Regions of Use	1, 2, 3, 4, 5, 6, 7
	Soil	Moist, decomposed granite, sand, limestone, high or low organic content, well drained
	Water	Twice a month to once a week
	Sun or Shade	◑ ◐ ○
	Height × Width	Maximum: 6 feet × 5 feet. Usual: 3 feet × 3 feet
	Protective Mechanisms	Aromatic oils discourage some browsers
	Leaves or Stems	Evergreen or dormant in winter, aromatic
	Ornamental Value	Pink, red, or white flowers in spring, summer, or fall
	Other Value	Flowers used by hummingbirds and butterflies
	Related Species	Mountain sage (*S. regla*)

Autumn sage is becoming very popular in southwestern gardens because of its cheerful flowers and mostly evergreen foliage. In its native range, it blooms most profusely in fall after summer rains; with irrigation, it flowers lightly all through the warm season—even as late as December—to feed hummingbirds. Prune it severely once a year to keep it compact, and irrigate it regularly to keep its branches from drying back. It hates the wet/dry fluctuations of clay soil. **Mountain sage** (1, 2, 3, 4, 7) blooms only in autumn. The flowers are large, orange-red rather than pink-red, and plentiful. The leaves are scalloped and glossy. This plant might be more useful for southwestern California gardens than for lowland desert gardens, because it grows with Chihuahuan mountain forms of oak, snowberry, currant, blue-eyed grass, and needlegrass.

....

124	Common Name	Globe mallow, desert mallow, apricot mallow
	Latin Name	*Sphaeralcea ambigua*
	Native Habitat	Disturbed soils and desert washes mostly below 3,500 feet in Mojave, Colorado, and Sonoran deserts
	Regions of Use	1, 2, 3, 4, 5, 6, 7
	Soil	Dry, decomposed granite, sand, low organic content, well drained
	Water	None to once a month
	Sun or Shade	◑ ◐ ○
	Height × Width	Maximum: 3 feet × 3 feet. Usual: 2 feet × 2 feet
	Protective Mechanisms	Silvery hairs on leaves cause irritation if rubbed in eyes
	Leaves or Stems	Gray-green to yellow-green, drought-deciduous
	Ornamental Value	Orange, pink, white, or lavender flowers, mostly in spring
	Other Value	Flowers used by butterflies and bees; browse for deer; larval plant for butterflies; roots made into a tea for eyedrops, sore throat, and diarrhea
	Related Species	Scarlet globe mallow (*S. coccinea*)

Globe mallow is a small shrub that gardeners cut to the ground after flowering to get fresh, compact growth. The translucent petals seem to cup themselves around sunlight, capturing an inner glow. The flowers come in a wide range of pastels along with a few darker shades. A drift of a dozen plants faced randomly about 5 feet apart looks great for gardens that have the room. For smaller areas, use two or three with brittlebush and desert ephemerals for a big show in late March or early April. Globe mallow lives only a few years. When a mother plant seeds out, most of the offspring will be shades of orange ranging from almost red to pumpkin. Another garden-worthy globe mallow is **scarlet globe mallow** (4, 7). This ankle-high flower has glowing cups of Chinese red to golden orange flowers and fuzzy gray-green leaves. As it normally lives among junipers, it requires regular water in low desert gardens, but it can reward you by blooming all summer.

125	
Common Name	Scarlet betony, Texas betony
Latin Name	*Stachys coccinea*
Native Habitat	Rich soil and moist crevices in canyons between 1,500 and 8,000 feet in Chihuahuan and eastern Sonoran deserts
Regions of Use	1, 2, 3, 4, 5, 6, 7
Soil	Moist, decomposed granite, loam, limestone, high organic content, well drained
Water	Once to twice a week or by a watering hole or seep
Sun or Shade	● ◑ ◑ ○
Height × Width	Maximum: 3 feet × 3 feet. Usual: 2 feet × 2 feet
Protective Mechanisms	None
Leaves or Stems	Dark green, velvety, evergreen rosette
Ornamental Value	Red flowers in spring and fall
Other Value	Flowers used by hummingbirds

Scarlet betony really isn't drought-tolerant, but it is such a good hummingbird plant, I couldn't leave it out. It is already popular in conventional gardens that require more watering than native gardens. You can use it in a shady depression where a faucet or a drip irrigation system on a timer releases water for wildlife at dawn and dusk. It can be grown with scarlet monkeyflower (*Mimulus cardinalis*), columbine, and island alumroot–a combination to attract hummingbirds in the spring and, perhaps, again in the fall. A boulder over the roots helps to keep them cool and evenly moist, especially if it shades the plant from the hot afternoon sun. Don't attempt this plant, though, if you don't have time for watering.

....

126	
Common Name	Mountain marigold
Latin Name	*Tagetes lemmonii*
Native Habitat	RARE, mountain canyons between 4,000 and 8,000 feet in Cochise, Santa Cruz, and Pima counties in southeastern Arizona and oak woodlands in Mexico
Regions of Use	1, 2, 3, 5, 6
Soil	Moist, decomposed granite, sand, rich organic content, well drained
Water	Once a month to once a week or more
Sun or Shade	◑ ◐ ○
Height × Width	Maximum: 2 feet × 2 feet. Usual: 18 inches × 18 inches
Protective Mechanisms	Aromatic oils discourage some browsers
Leaves or Stems	Evergreen or dormant in winter, dark green, aromatic
Ornamental Value	Yellow daisies in fall, sometimes to early spring
Other Value	Flowers used by butterflies

Bart O'Brien

Mountain marigold can survive on only one deep watering a month in coastal California, but it requires weekly watering in the deserts. It has fancy, dark green foliage that smells pungent when crushed, and clusters of showy yellow 1-inch daisies that start blooming in September and continue through frost-free winters until the end of March. Some botanists think that the mountain marigold, found in the nursery trade, is really *T. palmeri*, a Mexican shrub from the Sierra Madre. The Arizona marigold is much smaller than the nursery marigold, is rarely woody except at the base, and has greater cold tolerance. It can be grown under the light shade of paloverde, mesquite, and desert willow alongside autumn sage, scarlet betony, deergrass, bull muhly, and red yucca.

127	Common Name	Plume tiquilia, Gregg coldenia, hierba del cenizo
	Latin Name	*Tiquilia greggii* (formerly *Coldenia greggii*)
	Native Habitat	Mountain slopes and flats below 4,200 feet in Chihuahuan Desert
	Regions of Use	4, 6, 7
	Soil	Dry, decomposed granite, sand, limestone, low organic content, well drained
	Water	None to once a month
	Sun or Shade	◐ ○
	Height × Width	Maximum: 18 inches × 3 feet. Usual: 1 foot × 2 feet
	Protective Mechanisms	None
	Leaves or Stems	Silver, evergreen
	Ornamental Value	Magenta flowers in lavender plumy heads after rains in summer and fall
	Other Value	Flowers used by butterflies and bees

Plume tiquilia (tuh KEE lee uh) is one of my favorite plants. I love the combination of tiny velvety gray leaves, 2-inch balls of purple and silver plumes, and magenta flowers that open every evening and stay open during the cool of the morning. It grows all over the foothills of the Franklin Mountains in the suburbs of El Paso, along with other short shrubs such as black dalea, feather dalea, threeleaf sumac (*Rhus trilobata*), littleleaf sumac, skeletonleaf goldeneye, turpentine weed, Apache-plume, and globe mallow. An eye-pleasing mosaic of hard and soft forms might be plume tiquila in combination with creosote and succulents such as lechuguilla, Mormon tea, desert spoon, ocotillo, Torrey yucca, and prickly pear, and a host of colorful flowers, plus several ankle- to knee-high grasses. For a purple-and-gold fall-blooming garden, use plume tiquilia with black dalea, skeletonleaf goldeneye, turpentine weed, and desert marigold.

128	Common Name	Woolly bluecurls, romero
	Latin Name	*Trichostema lanatum*
	Native Habitat	Coastal sagescrub, chaparral below 2,500 feet from Monterey to San Diego counties, often with chamise
	Regions of Use	1, 2, 3
	Soil	Dry, decomposed granite, sand, clay loam, low organic content, well drained
	Water	None to once a month
	Sun or Shade	◐ ○
	Height × Width	Maximum: 5 feet × 5 feet. Usual: 2 feet × 4 feet
	Protective Mechanisms	Aromatic oils discourage some browsers
	Leaves or Stems	Evergreen, minty aromatic
	Ornamental Value	Purple flowers, mostly in spring and summer
	Other Value	Flowers used by hummingbirds and butterflies

Bart O'Brien

The aromatic leaves of **woolly bluecurls** make it an asset to the herb garden, while its long blooming season recommends it for the flower garden. Furthermore, it actively attracts hummingbirds and butterflies. This valuable garden flower is a small, airy shrub with long spikes of flowers that range in color from palest lavender to deep blue-purple. The flowers are covered with short woolly purply hairs, out of which emerge long curling stamens and pistils. Blooms seem to be in evidence almost all year long, especially if spent blossoms are pinched back to prevent them from going to seed. If the plant gets floppy, it can be cut in half or even almost to the base and it will bounce right back. Average life span is about five years—much longer on dry slopes and much shorter in irrigated clay loam. Complementary flowers from spring until fall are royal penstemon, Matilija poppy, St. Catherine's lace, and zauschneria. This is a great flower to plant with ceanothus, fremontia, and manzanita, because it looks good with no supplemental summer water.

129 *Common Name*	Goodding's verbena, Mojave verbena
Latin Name	*Verbena gooddingii*
Native Habitat	Washes and rocky slopes below 6,000 feet from the Rio Grande Plains in Texas into the eastern Sonoran and Mojave deserts
Regions of Use	1, 2, 3, 4, 5, 6, 7
Soil	Dry, decomposed granite, sand, clay, low organic content, well drained
Water	None to once a week
Sun or Shade	◑ ◐ ○
Height × Width	Maximum: 18 inches × 4 feet. Usual: 9 inches × 1 foot
Protective Mechanisms	None
Leaves or Stems	Gray-green velvet, ephemeral or evergreen up to 3 years
Ornamental Value	Pale lavender-blue flowers from February to November, fragrant
Other Value	Flowers used by butterflies and bees
Related Species	Wright's verbena (*V. wrightii*, now lumped with *V. bipinnatifida*)

Verbenas do best in the disturbed ground of new gardens. They're good for erosion control in the winter, and they deliver a long season of flowering the first year while the more long-term plants are still putting down roots. Plant yours in early fall for best results. Leaves and roots will grow all through fall and winter and start blooming in February. Blooming will continue until the verbenas succumb to drought or until they just wear themselves out. They self-sow, so you can treat them like ephemerals in desert landscapes. **Goodding's verbena** is especially handsome because of its pale velvety leaves and its beautiful, almost luminescent flowers. **Wright's verbena** (1, 2, 3, 4, 5, 6, 7), often called desert verbena, is rosy lavender (one strain is pure white) with lacy, dark green leaves. This is the verbena that is so prevalent in the Chihuahuan Desert.

130 *Common Name*	Skeletonleaf goldeneye, resinbush
Latin Name	*Viguiera stenoloba*
Native Habitat	Desert scrub below 6,200 feet in Chihuahuan Desert and Rio Grande Plains
Regions of Use	1, 2, 3, 4, 6, 7
Soil	Dry, decomposed granite, sand, clay loam, limestone, low organic content, well drained
Water	None to twice a month
Sun or Shade	◑ ◐ ○
Height × Width	Maximum: 4 feet × 4 feet. Usual: 2 feet × 3 feet
Protective Mechanisms	Aromatic oils discourage some browsers
Leaves or Stems	Evergreen or winter-deciduous, dark green, ferny with center groove, aromatic
Ornamental Value	Golden flowers any time after rains
Other Value	Flowers used by butterflies, larval plant for butterflies
Related Species	Nevada goldeneye (*V. parishii*, formerly *V. deltoidea*), San Diego goldeneye (*V. laciniata*)

Skeletonleaf goldeneye is a dense, shrubby, yellow daisy, somewhat larger than damianita and more drought-tolerant than mountain marigold. The flowers are most profuse in the fall, but given sufficient moisture they can also be plentiful in spring and summer. Like most shrubby flowers, this one can be whacked in half once a year to make it smaller or thicker. Use it in a flower garden, or naturalize it with plume tiquilia, turpentine weed, feather dalea, Mormon tea, and Spanish bayonet. In washes and foothills around Tucson and Phoenix and west to Riverside, use **Nevada goldeneye** (1, 2, 3, 4, 5, 6). It is shorter and broader (2 feet × 5 feet) and grows well with Dorri sage, California buckwheat, Joshua tree, Mojave yucca, Mormon tea, fremontia, and blue manzanita. **San Diego goldeneye** (1, 2), in that county but also found in Mexico and available in nurseries, RARE, has shiny green leaves.

131 *Common Name*	Borrego aster, Mojave aster
Latin Name	*Xylorhiza orcuttii* (formerly *Machaeranthera orcuttii*)
Native Habitat	Badlands and dry gravelly slopes below 1,000 feet in Colorado Desert
Regions of Use	5, 6
Soil	Dry, decomposed granite, sand, clay, caliche and other difficult soils, low organic content, well drained
Water	None to once a month
Sun or Shade	◑ ○
Height × Width	Maximum: 5 feet × 5 feet. Usual: 2 feet × 3 feet
Protective Mechanisms	None
Leaves or Stems	Evergreen or dormant in winter
Ornamental Value	3-inch lavender flowers in spring, sometimes in fall
Other Value	Flowers used by butterflies
Related Species	Terlingua aster, gyp daisy (*X. wrightii*); desert aster (*X. tortifolia*)

Borrego aster has huge lavender flowers that look more suitable for an English flower garden than for the desert. But it can survive on 2 inches of rain a year in soil so bad most plants won't even try. We saw Borrego aster growing within 2 feet of diminutive silver-leaved desert holly. Also within sight were golden-flowered brittlebush, creosote bush, white bursage, and ocotillo, with smoketree and blue paloverde in the washes. In the garden, give it excellent drainage and be patient while it grows a massive root system. Goodding's verbena, sand verbena, and phacelia bring out its delicate color. **Terlingua aster** (5, 6) grows in the lower Chihuahuan Desert. It also tolerates nasty soils such as gypsum and bentonite clay. **Desert aster** (3, 4, 5, 6, 7), of the Sonoran, Colorado, and Mojave deserts, is very similar. Probably the most cold tolerant of these three perennials, it goes dormant in the winter, giving it a less shrubby look. In the Mojave, it is often found growing with Joshua trees.

132 *Common Name*	Dwarf white zinnia
Latin Name	*Zinnia acerosa*
Native Habitat	Deserts, desert grasslands between 2,500 and 5,000 feet in Chihuahuan and Sonoran deserts
Regions of Use	3, 4, 5, 6, 7
Soil	Dry, decomposed granite, sand, clay loam, limestone, low organic content, well drained
Water	None to once a month
Sun or Shade	◑ ○
Height × Width	Maximum: 6 inches × 18 inches. Usual: 3 inches × 1 foot
Protective Mechanisms	None
Leaves or Stems	Evergreen, sometimes gray-green
Ornamental Value	White flowers that become papery, spring to frost or anytime it rains and temperatures are warm
Other Value	Flowers used by butterflies, bees
Related Species	Plains zinnia (*Z. grandiflora*)

Here is a short, dainty evergreen to grow in front of taller plants. In addition to these virtues, it's nonaggressive and it blooms, too. The foliage of **dwarf white zinnia** makes a mat of tiny blue-green needles. The 1-inch white flowers bloom a long time, and once-a-month watering can extend its bloom time. Instead of dropping, the petals dry out and turn the color of parchment. Dwarf white zinnia can take light shade cast by ironwood or paloverde. Mix it with blackfoot daisy, blue grama, Terlingua aster, Goodding's verbena, and mesa greggia for a lavender and white low-growing ground cover bordering your patio. **Plains zinnia** (1, 2, 3, 4, 6, 7) is bright yellow with bright green needlelike foliage. It takes more cold than its dwarf cousin and can be grown with sideoats grama, black grama, deergrass, penstemons, chocolate daisy, fairyduster, black dalea, blackfoot daisy, sacahuista, and fleabane.

7 EPHEMERALS

EPHEMERALS, THE WILDFLOWERS OF SOUTHERN CALIFORNIA AND THE SOUTHWEST, last only a short time–but what a show they put on! Mostly annuals and bulbs, they bloom and set seed quickly in the spring and then disappear to escape the heat. In frost-free California, they might start blooming as early as December. Expect them by late February in Phoenix and not until mid-April in Las Vegas and El Paso. The season begins with lupines, owl's clover, phacelias, and abronia–all shades of blue, lavender, or purple. Very shortly, they are joined by California gold poppy and primroses. One group of species is followed by another until the few summer annuals finish the show. Dozens of species may be native on any one site, with the highest diversity occurring in the Colorado and Mojave deserts where harsh conditions leave plenty of open ground for the ephemerals to fill.

The Birte Endicott Memorial Wildflower Garden, dedicated in 1993, is maintained by volunteers of Desert Botanical Garden in Phoenix. Public parks, neighborhood parkways, school grounds, and many other open spaces are being converted into wildflower gardens instead of being maintained as lawns. Wild Canterbury bells, desert marigold, Parry's penstemon, brittlebush, and Goodding's verbena bloom, with creosote, saguaro, and Papago Buttes in the background.

Ephemerals are ideal for scattering among the more permanent desert plants or on the sunny edges of chaparral plants. They also enliven patches of grass. Wherever there is bare earth showing, wildflowers can be planted in early to late fall to make a big show in the spring. Ephemerals can also be used in a flower bed planted among perennials and flowering shrubs, as long as they get plenty of sun and no competition. A large selection of seed is available to buy, although some of the wildflowers sold are from other continents and are not well labeled as nonnatives. They usually do well the first year and then dwindle away in subsequent years, but some become pests.

A 1- to 4-inch mulch of decomposed granite works wonderfully well as a planting medium. It provides a multitude of tiny crevices for seeds to fall into to escape summer sun and hungry creatures. Sow seed as generously as you can afford the first fall, and then add species or supplement if self-seeding is not as successful as you had hoped. If you aren't having good luck, it's probably because you are irrigating regularly at the hottest time of year. The wildflower seeds are responding to the moisture, and are then shriveling in the heat. Their survival is based on their staying dry and hidden when humidity is exceptionally low and temperatures are high.

In general, wildflowers do best in an unirrigated landscape. There are good years for wildflowers and bad years, and there are more bad years than good since the timing and amount of rain are crucial and undependable. If rains are scant or oddly timed and your wildflowers are not germinating when you expect them to, water very, *very* lightly for three or four days—preferably when skies are overcast—to trick the wildflowers into thinking they got some rain. If fall rains were good but winter rains have been scarce, one good watering (an inch) in mid- to late February will give the leafy rosettes the boost they need to reach a healthy flowering size.

In chaparral or on grassy desert slopes, sow the seed among existing plant material. Mowing and pruning first will probably be necessary, as fire and grazing animals used to make sure that woody species and old dry vegetation did not shade out the wildflowers or prevent the seed from reaching the soil. Now there is an even more serious problem—the hundreds of weedy and invasive foreign wildflowers and grasses that crowd out our native wildflowers will have to be weeded by hand. Extensive bed preparation can help. Some people till over and over again until the supply of weed seeds is greatly diminished. Others lay plastic over a well-tilled and watered bed for several months and let heat and darkness thwart the growth of new weeds. In the deserts, withholding water decreases the number of weeds so that they can be eliminated by hand without too much trouble.

Herbicide companies often publish booklets with pictures of these weeds to help with identification. Weeds that are especially noxious in chaparral are mustard and wild oats, which supposedly release an herbicide to kill off their competition. Other nuisance weeds are red brome, foxtail fescue, filaree, henbit, shepherd's purse, wild radish, castor bean, Indian tobacco, bromegrass, sweet alyssum, mock strawberry, Spanish broom, lamb's-quarters, and other aggressive, cool-season upstarts. In the deserts, prominent weeds are Russian thistle, Lehmann grass, filaree, prickly lettuce, mustards, yellow rocket, Arabian grass, Mediterranean grass, red brome, buffelgrass, horehound, and tumbleweed.

133	Common Name	Sand verbena
	Latin Name	*Abronia villosa* var. *villosa*
	Native Habitat	Sand dunes, creosote bush scrub below 3,000 feet in Colorado and Mojave deserts
	Regions of Use	2, 3, 4, 5, 6
	Soil	Dry, decomposed granite, sand, clay loam in on a slope, low organic content, well drained
	Water	None to once a month
	Sun or Shade	◑○
	Height × Width	Maximum: 32 inches × 10 feet. Usual: 8 inches × 2 feet
	Protective Mechanisms	Leaves sticky and often covered with sand
	Leaves or Stems	Germinate after fall rain; die in late spring after setting seed
	Ornamental Value	3-inch clusters of pink to purple flowers all spring (rarely white, rarely in fall); fragrant, especially in the evening
	Other Value	Flowers used by butterflies
	Related Species	San Diego sand verbena (*A. villosa* var. *aurita*), narrowleaf sand verbena (*A. angustifolia*)

When temperatures and fall and winter rainfalls are just right, **sand verbena** runs rampant, blanketing vacant lots as well as acres of desert. It is most likely to bloom from the first of March to the first of April, although different climatic conditions, extra rain, or judicious irrigation can extend blooming either earlier or later. Sow seed in early fall just before you expect fall rains. Young seedlings can easily be rearranged between November and January. The seed might not germinate right on cue, so plant seeds of other ephemerals as well. Companion plants for seeding in the desert are bird-cage primrose and desert sunflower (*Geraea canescens*), desert dandelion (*Malacothrix glabrata*), and Arizona lupine. In a garden setting, try wild Canterbury bells, blue-eyes grass, owl's clover, and arroyo lupine. **San Diego sand verbena** (1, 2, 3) grows in coastal sagescrub and chaparral below 5,000 feet. **Narrowleaf sand verbena** (7) is the equivalent for the Chihuahuan Desert. It grows from 1,000 to 4,000 feet from Phoenix and Tucson to El Paso.

134	Common Name	Onion lily
	Latin Name	*Allium hyalinum*
	Native Habitat	Grassland, foothill woodland below 5,000 feet from Eldorado to Kern counties, California
	Regions of Use	1, 2, 3
	Soil	Moist to dry, decomposed granite, sand, clay loam, low to high organic content, well drained
	Water	None to once a month
	Sun or Shade	◑◑○
	Height × Width	Maximum: 1 foot × 2 feet. Usual: 9 inches × 9 inches
	Protective Mechanisms	Onion taste discourages some browsers
	Leaves or Stems	Green, flavored like chives, dormant June to November
	Ornamental Value	White (pink, lavender) flowers in spring
	Other Value	Flowers used by butterflies, bulbs and leaves edible
	Related Species	Desert onion lily (*A. macropetalum*)

The onions we buy at the supermarket are actually lilies. They have many wild cousins growing throughout the world. Native **onion lilies** can be used in cooking and also ornamentally for their deep rose to pastel spring flowers. Plant the tiny bulbs in a scatter pattern. Once a colony has been well established, they'll increase by self-seeding. An old clump that has developed numerous baby bulblets can also be divided. Varieties that are native to moist places tend to be almost evergreen; the ones native to dry spots need to go dormant in the summer. Use onion lily in light shade with accents of Douglas irises under a western redbud or with a scattering of blue-eyed grass in front of the misty blueness of chaparral whitethorn. **Desert onion lily** (4, 6, 7) grows as low as 1,000 feet in the Chihuahuan and Sonoran deserts, and in years when it gets enough rain, it can blanket the desert floor with orchid-pink flowers.

135 Common Name	Purple owl's clover, escobita
Latin Name	*Castilleja exserta* (formerly *Orthocarpus purpurascens*)
Native Habitat	Grasslands between 1,500 and 4,500 feet in southern and eastern California; Sonoran, Mojave, and Colorado deserts
Regions of Use	1, 2, 3, 4, 5, 6
Soil	Dry, decomposed granite, sand, clay loam, low organic content, well drained
Water	None to once a winter
Sun or Shade	◑ ○
Height × Width	Maximum: 18 inches × 2 feet. Usual: 9 inches × 1 foot
Protective Mechanisms	None
Leaves or Stems	Germinates after fall rain; dies in late spring after setting seed
Ornamental Value	Purple flowers in late winter to early spring
Other Value	Flowers used by butterflies and bees, grazed by cattle and sheep

In southern California, **purple owl's clover** usually blooms from mid-February to mid-March. Its bright raspberry flowers appear at the same time as baby-blue-eyes (*Nemophila menziesii*), purple-spotted fivespot (*N. maculata*), and pale yellow creamcups (*Platystemon californicus*). Other companion plants are California gold poppy and blue-eyed grass—especially in a grassland of nodding, purple, and foothill needlegrasses. In Sonoran Desert grasslands of sideoats grama and pink burrograss (*Scleropogon brevifolius*), purple owl's clover grows with mariposa lily (*Calochortus*), blue and purple lupines, orange globe mallow, lavender phacelia, and pure white tackstem (*Calycoseris wrightii*). Sow the seed shallowly in early fall so that it will be ready to take advantage of cool, fall rains. In an irrigated garden, wait until November or early December to sow.

136 Common Name	Fleabane daisy
Latin Name	*Erigeron divergens* (including *E. modestus*)
Native Habitat	Mountain forests to desert scrub between 1,000 and 9,000 feet from the San Gabriel Mountains to western Texas, north to Canada and south to Mexico
Regions of Use	1, 2, 3, 4, 6, 7
Soil	Dry, decomposed granite, sand, clay loam, limestone, low to high organic content, well drained
Water	None to twice a month or more
Sun or Shade	◑ ○
Height × Width	Maximum: 18 inches × 18 inches. Usual: 9 inches × 1 foot
Protective Mechanisms	None
Leaves or Stems	Usually die or go dormant in summer, but might be evergreen 4 years or more
Ornamental Value	Lots of half-inch white daisies
Other Value	Flowers used by butterflies and bees, seeds eaten by songbirds

Fleabane daisy is a fairly flexible plant. In locales where it runs the risk of being killed by drought, it flowers and seeds out quickly. But where conditions are comfortable, it takes a more leisurely approach, flowering and remaining green, like a perennial, for a number of years. Often it doesn't bloom until the second spring, perhaps lying dormant the first summer. It frequently blooms in the Chihuahuan and Sonoran deserts along with California poppy, various phacelias, globe mallow, and brittlebush. In a garden, it would also work well with pretty dalea, chuparosa, Parry's and Eaton's penstemons, Goodding's verbena, and lupines—its airy white daisies lighten and unify any combination of plants. In an irrigated California garden, fleabane daisy is likely to bloom from April until frost, as long as it gets good drainage. Near the coast it might bloom year-round.

137	Common Name	California gold poppy, Mexican gold poppy
	Latin Name	*Eschscholzia californica* (includes subspecies *californica* and *mexicana*)
	Native Habitat	Grassy hillsides or rocky slopes below 6,000 feet from El Paso to the Pacific Ocean
	Regions of Use	1, 2, 3, 4, 5, 6, 7
	Soil	Dry, decomposed granite, sand, low organic content, well drained
	Water	None to once a winter
	Sun or Shade	◑ ○
	Height × Width	Maximum: 1 foot × 2 feet. Usual: 6 inches × 9 inches
	Protective Mechanisms	None
	Leaves or Stems	Pale blue-green, dies or goes dormant after setting seed
	Ornamental Value	Orange to yellow (white, pink, scarlet) flowers
	Other Value	Flowers used by butterflies and bees; seeds eaten by birds

California gold poppy can be used in all the areas covered by this book. The large golden flowers close at night and reopen in the morning, each flower lasting three to four days. As the weather heats up, the blooms get smaller and more deeply orange in the desert, but paler yellow in California. This is a variable species. Over 90 forms have been described. Supposedly, Mexican gold poppy blooms in early to mid-March and is a small re-seeding desert annual. California gold poppy is defined as a larger-flowered chaparral perennial that blooms a month later. Gardeners from El Paso and Phoenix claim the commercial seed is subspecies *californica* and gardeners in California claim the same seed is subspecies *mexicana*. Sow seeds in the fall for spring bloom. Germination takes less than two weeks when moisture is present. The rosettes grow all winter, but they remain very small until close to bloom time. If winter rains have been scarce, give them one good watering in February to bring them up to blooming size. Sow exactly where you want the flowers to grow, because a long taproot makes transplanting difficult.

....

138	Common Name	Arroyo lupine
	Latin Name	*Lupinus succulentus*
	Native Habitat	Open slopes and mesas between 1,500 and 4,500 feet north of Phoenix and in disturbed areas below 2,500 feet in California and Baja California
	Regions of Use	1, 2, 3, 4, 6
	Soil	Dry, decomposed granite, clay loam, low organic content, well drained
	Water	None to once a winter
	Sun or Shade	○
	Height × Width	Maximum: 40 inches. Usual: 1 foot × 1 foot
	Protective Mechanisms	None
	Leaves or Stems	Germinates after fall rain, dies in late spring after setting seed, sometimes biennial
	Ornamental Value	Purple-blue (white, pink) flowers, fragrant
	Other Value	Erosion control, flowers used by butterflies and bees
	Related Species	Arizona lupine (*L. arizonicus*), sand lupine (*L. sparsiflorus*)

There are many attractive lupines in the Southwest, mostly blue, purple, or rose-colored. Sow the seed untreated, or soak it overnight in plain water or in a commercial inoculant containing root bacteria. **Arroyo lupine** is easily available and easily grown, sometimes germinating in a rare summer shower but usually after temperatures have become more moderate. Blooms might start as early as December and continue as late as the first week in April. Its wide leaves and blue flowers combine well with ceanothus and blue-dicks (*Dichelostemma* ssp.) and add character to an existing stand of California poppies. In Phoenix and Tucson, **sand lupine** (6), with its feathery leaves, is better for wildflower plantings in dry gardens. In Yuma and Palm Desert, purply pink **Arizona lupine** (5) works best.

139	*Common Name*	Desert Canterbury bells
	Latin Name	*Phacelia campanularia*
	Native Habitat	Washes below 5,000 feet in Colorado and Mojave deserts
	Regions of Use	1, 2, 3, 4, 5, 6, 7
	Soil	Dry, decomposed granite, sand, clay loam, low organic content, well drained
	Water	None to twice a winter or more
	Sun or Shade	◐ ◑ ○
	Height × Width	Maximum: 2 feet × 2 feet. Usual: 9 inches × 1 foot
	Protective Mechanisms	Aromatic oils discourage some browsers, cause dermatitis on some humans
	Leaves or Stems	Germinates after fall rain, dies in late spring after setting seed
	Ornamental Value	Blue flowers
	Other Value	Flowers used by hummingbirds, butterflies, and bees
	Related Species	Baby blue phacelia (*P. coerulea*), notchleaf phacelia (*P. crenulata*)

The intensely dark, true blue of **desert Canterbury bells** seems to intensify all the colors around it—the lavenders of other phacelias, lupines, Goodding's verbena, and Mojave aster, as well as the yellows and oranges of California gold poppy and globe mallow. Although not native to Arizona's Sonoran Desert, it has been successfully used there in irrigated wildflower plantings and as a spring ground cover under paloverde. It has long been popular in California. The southern population is available in seed catalogs. The northern subspecies (*vasiformis*) grows naturally in drifts under Joshua trees. There are dozens of other attractive phacelias—usually lavender in color—with flowers growing in a crookneck. **Notchleaf phacelia** (6) is common in creosote scrub around Phoenix and Tucson, while **baby blue phacelia (4, 7)** grows near Las Vegas and El Paso.

....

140	*Common Name*	Blue-eyed grass
	Latin Name	*Sisyrinchium bellum*
	Native Habitat	Grassy clearings below 8,000 feet in California and Oregon
	Regions of Use	1, 2, 3, 4
	Soil	Moist to dry, decomposed granite, sand, clay loam, low to high organic content, well drained
	Water	None to once a month
	Sun or Shade	◐ ◑ ○
	Height × Width	Maximum: 2 feet × 2 feet. Usual: 1 foot × 1 foot
	Protective Mechanisms	None
	Leaves or Stems	Green only in spring while flowering
	Ornamental Value	Blue (rarely white) flowers, grassy leaves
	Other Value	Flowers used by butterflies and bees

Blue-eyed grass is a member of the iris family and blooms whenever other irises are blooming in your area. The flowers are a half-inch across and open only when the sun shines on them. This may not sound very showy, but a field of them or a cluster in a blue grama lawn is a very pretty sight. I especially like their blueness under the hot pink of western redbud. Another winning combination is to mix them with the yellow daisies of coast sunflower in a minimeadow of needlegrass. In a semishady area, scatter them among onion lily and Douglas iris. Blue-eyed grass is easy to grow from seed, and seedlings often bloom the first year. Each year, the stems increase until you have a good-sized clump. Ready-made clumps are available in gallon cans and can be divided before you plant them. In Las Vegas, blue-eyed grass can be grown under Torrey mesquite. Water it once a month while it's green, but not after it has gone dormant.

8 VINES

Once established, woody morning glory—in this instance 'Anacapa'—is drought-tolerant in California canyons and along the coast. The one growing at Rancho Santa Ana Botanic Garden in Claremont was planted from a 1-gallon pot just two years before this photograph was taken.

ASK ME WHAT GENIUS IS, AND I'D ANSWER THAT IT IS THE ABILITY TO LOOK AT THE SAME thing everyone else is looking at—and see it in an entirely new way. Take vines, for instance. In the wild, they don't exactly inspire poetry. Wild vines are rarely charming or attractive; they clamber awkwardly and aggressively over shrubs and stumps and on up into trees, often smothering the host tree or shrub in the process. It must have taken someone of rare vision and creativity to figure out that by taming them, they'd look terrific clinging to the outer walls of cottages and castles.

When folks in the Northeast are digging out from under blizzards, people in the Southwest are dining al fresco on their patios. An outdoor "room," or living area, is a common element of many homes in this part of the country. It might be a simple portico, or a walled garden with a paneless window in one wall. It might be an arbored patio, or a courtyard surrounded on three sides by the house, guesthouse, and garage and with an elaborate gate entrance for the fourth wall. In all these cases, a vine is the perfect adornment for such structures. Woody morning glory, pipestems, ropevine, and wild grapes grow the highest, but thicket creeper climbs 8 feet or so—high enough for most walls.

Many homes in the Southwest are built on steep lots. Retaining walls, terracing, huge planters, or walled beds are common. This calls for vines that drape nicely, such as spring morning glory, campo pea, and thicket creeper. Island snapdragon, although shrubby, is also a good choice. Chuparosa, in the accents chapter, is another clambering shrub that can be used successfully as a vine.

141	Common Name	Spring morning glory
	Latin Name	*Calystegia purpurata* ssp. *purpurata*
	Native Habitat	Chaparral and coastal scrub below 1,000 feet from Santa Barbara northward
	Regions of Use	1, 2, 3
	Soil	Moist, decomposed granite, sand, clay loam, high or low organic content, well drained
	Water	Once a month or more
	Sun or Shade	◑ ○
	Height × Width	As high as can grow before dying back each winter
	Protective Mechanisms	None
	Leaves	Blue-green, dormant in winter
	Ornamental Value	White to purple flowers, sometimes striped, open all day
	Other Value	Flowers used by butterflies
	Related Species	Woody morning glory (*C. macrostegia* ssp. *macrostegia*), island morning glory (*C. m.* ssp. *amplissima*)

"Polite and gentle" is an apt description for **spring morning glory**. This vine displays a profusion of pastel pink blooms and pale blue-green leaves, and it is ideal for draping over a low fence or short trellis, clambering over a retaining wall, or hanging over the rim of a planter. You can even let a mass planting cascade down a hillside, but in this setting, it will require some water in the summer to look its best. Cut spring morning glory back in late fall after frost has withered the leaves. For an arbor or pergola, select the faster-growing **woody morning glory** (1, 2, 3). Its stems form slender twisting trunks and branches. Prune it once or twice a year to keep it the size you want. The large pink and white flowers bloom most flamboyantly in the spring but will continue to produce blossoms until frost. **Island morning glory** (1, 2, 3) has trailing stems and can be used as a ground cover.

142	Common Name	Pipestems
	Latin Name	*Clematis lasiantha*
	Native Habitat	Canyons, chaparral, open woodland below 6,000 feet from Baja California to Shasta and Trinity counties
	Regions of Use	1, 2, 3
	Soil	Moist to dry, decomposed granite, sand, clay loam, low organic content, well drained
	Water	None to once a month or more
	Sun or Shade	◐ ◑ ○
	Height × Width	Usual: climbs 15 to 18 feet
	Protective Mechanisms	None
	Leaves or Stems	Dormant in winter
	Ornamental Value	White flowers in spring, pale green plumy seeds
	Other Value	Flowers used by butterflies
	Related Species	Ropevine (*C. pauciflora*)

Use **pipestems** on an arbor, fence, or trellis; it needs some sort of structure to twine around in order to climb. In the wild, it drapes over shrubs and climbs into trees. Starting in early spring, it covers itself with large clusters of small cream to pure white flowers with fancy yellow centers. Then, in fall, the seed heads form plumes that catch the light and are just as attractive as the flowers. Pruning is best done in early spring, when it is easy to tell which stems have made it safely through the winter. **Ropevine** (1, 2, 3) is very similar, but it is a little faster-growing and more drought-resistant, and its seed heads tend to be whiter and showier.

143	*Common Name*	Island snapdragon
	Latin Name	*Galvezia speciosa*
	Native Habitat	Canyons below 3,000 feet on Santa Catalina, San Clemente, and Guadalupe islands
	Regions of Use	1, 2, 3
	Soil	Moist, decomposed granite, sand, clay loam, low organic content, well drained
	Water	Once or twice a month
	Sun or Shade	◐ ◑ ○
	Height × Width	10 feet when climbing, 2 to 3 feet as ground cover
	Protective Mechanisms	None
	Leaves or Stems	Evergreen
	Ornamental Value	Red flowers in spring and whenever warm
	Other Value	Flowers used by hummingbirds

Island snapdragon is evergreen and almost never without flowers. No wonder it has been popular for many years. Because of its sprawling character, it is frequently used as a 3-foot-tall ground cover or low shrub. Unfortunately, its woody evergreen branches have a tendency to lie all over other shrubs and even scale a tree to a height of 10 feet—not very attractive. However, espaliering it on wires or a trellis or fence where you want an evergreen vine works very well. Initially, you will have to tie some of the canes to get them growing in the direction you want. Then prune as you would pyracantha or Lady Banks rose. For a ground cover, use the cultivar 'Firecracker', which has been selected for its low, mounding character and added drought resistance.

144	*Common Name*	Campo pea, pride-of-California
	Latin Name	*Lathyrus splendens*
	Native Habitat	UNCOMMON, chaparral below 3,500 feet from San Diego County to Baja California
	Regions of Use	1, 2, 3
	Soil	Dry, decomposed granite, sand, low organic content, well drained
	Water	None to once a month
	Sun or Shade	◐ ◑ ○
	Height × Width	As high as can climb in one season
	Protective Mechanisms	None
	Leaves or Stems	Dies back to roots each year
	Ornamental Value	Red pea flowers in early spring
	Other Value	Flowers used by hummingbirds and butterflies

When it's in bloom, **campo pea** looks like bright red wisteria. Roy and Ysabel Fetterman, native-plant gardeners in Pasadena, California, let theirs climb over an evergreen shrub beside their driveway. They look forward to its scarlet blossoms every spring but don't notice it the rest of the year. It dies to the ground after drought or frost and starts new growth in late winter. By March, when it blooms, it is already 6 to 10 feet high. Campo pea isn't suitable for a patio pot or as a ground cover, because it blooms only when it is climbing. It climbs by tendrils, so grow it on an arbor, fence, shrub, or tree, or give it the support of a trellis or wires if you want it on a wall. If you want yours to grow on an evergreen shrub, choose Mexican fremontia. These two grow together in the wild and are equally fussy about not wanting any irrigation in the summer.

145 Common Name	Thicket creeper
Latin Name	*Parthenocissus inserta*
Native Habitat	Canyons above 3,000 feet in the Chihuahuan, Sonoran, and Mojave deserts and possibly naturalized rather than native below 3,000 feet in California north to Quebec
Regions of Use	2, 3, 4, 6, 7
Soil	Dry, decomposed granite, sand, clay loam, limestone, low to high organic content, well drained
Water	Once or twice a month
Sun or Shade	◑ ◐ ○
Height × Width	Usual: climbs 8 to 10 feet or sprawls like a ground cover
Protective Mechanisms	None
Leaves or Stems	Dark green, thick, glossy, red to wine fall color, deciduous in winter
Ornamental Value	Fall color, blue fruits with red stems
Other Value	Fruits eaten by birds and mammals

Thicket creeper looks its prettiest after summer has started winding down. First the fruits ripen to a dark blue. The stems are a startling red. Then the leaves turn red, wine, or purple–the brighter colors occurring where the leaves get both hot sun and cold nights. With regular irrigation, thicket creeper can take full sun, even in the desert cities. But it is best used in half sun planted above a retaining wall where it can cascade over. It can also be trained on a trellis, however, and its large, dark, shiny leaflets look unexpectedly lush against adobe or stucco, where the fall color has its most dramatic backdrop.

146 Common Name	Desert wild grape
Latin Name	*Vitis girdiana*
Native Habitat	Streamsides and canyon bottoms below 4,000 feet in southwestern California, Baja California, and Santa Catalina Island
Regions of Use	1, 2, 3, 4, 5, 6, 7
Soil	Moist, decomposed granite, sand, clay loam, low to some organic content, well drained
Water	None to once a month
Sun or Shade	◑ ◐ ○
Height × Width	High, climbing by tendrils
Protective Mechanisms	None
Leaves or Stems	Velvety, pale green, dormant in winter
Ornamental Value	Leaves, occasional clusters of small black grapes
Other Value	Grapes eaten by birds and mammals, host plant for Achemon hawk moth
Related Species	Canyon grape (*V. arizonica*)

Grapevines are healthy and long-lived and can take amazingly dry air as long as their roots get moisture during the summer. Each vine usually forms a single sinewy trunk several inches in diameter. The southwestern wild grapes are much easier to grow and more drought-resistant than cultivated grapes, and their pale velvety leaves are very attractive. **Desert wild grape** has small black grapes. Animals love them—and you will, too, but for a different reason; they are so dry and sparse that they don't stain the patio. **Canyon grape** (1, 2, 3, 4, 5, 6, 7) has sweet, succulent grapes that make excellent jelly. There is a glossy-leaved version of canyon grape found throughout its range from Lake Mead, Arizona, to the Big Bend area in Texas. The most typical companion plant for a grapevine is a cottonwood, but scarlet betony, deergrass, bull muhly, and bamboo muhly would also be good choices.

INDIGENOUS CHARTS

The charts indicate what is indigenous, that is, what evolved natively right in the areas now occupied by these cities. They are a guide for revegetation *so you can convert a conventional landscape or a scraped lot into an envelope garden. They are not a guide for all the plants that can be used in a courtyard garden. For that information, consult the Regions of Use entry in the plant profiles.*

INDIGENOUS TREES

W = native near watercourses, needs water in landscapes, but soil must always be well drained
D = drought-tolerant, only transplants need water to get reestablished
W/D = prefers some water, but can be dry in special situations
EP = El Paso, LC = Las Cruces, T = Tucson, P = Phoenix, Y = Yuma, LV = Las Vegas,
PS = Palm Springs, SD = San Diego, R = Riverside, SB = Santa Barbara, LA = Los Angeles

#	Common Name	EP	LC	T	P	Y	LV	PS	SD	R	SB	LA	Latin Name
1	Whitethorn	D	D	D	W/D		D						*Acacia constricta*
1	Small's huisache												*Acacia farnesiana* var. *smallii*
1	Catclaw acacia	D	D	D	D	D	D	D					*Acacia greggii*
1	Roemer acacia												*Acacia roemeriana*
2	Redshanks								D	D	D		*Adenostoma sparsifolium*
3	Canotia			D	D								*Canotia holacantha*
4	Saguaro			D	D								*Carnegiea gigantea*
5	Granjeno			W/D	W/D								*Celtis pallida*
5	Netleaf hackberry	W/D	W/D	W/D	W/D				D	D			*Celtis reticulata*
6	Blue paloverde			W/D	W/D	W/D		W/D					*Cercidium floridum*
6	Foothill paloverde			D	D								*Cercidium microphyllum*
7	Mexican redbud												*Cercis canadensis* var. *mexicana*
7	Western redbud								D	D	D	D	*Cercis occidentalis*
8	Desert willow	W	W	W	W	W	W	W					*Chilopsis linearis*
9	Ocotillo	D	D	D	D	D	D	D					*Fouquieria splendens*
10	Fragrant ash												*Fraxinus cuspidata*
10	California flowering ash												*Fraxinus dipetala*
11	Goldenball leadtree												*Leucaena retusa*
12	Catalina ironwood												*Lyonothamnus floribundus*
13	Ironwood			D	D	W/D		W/D					*Olneya tesota*
4	Senita												*Pachycereus schottii*
14	Torrey pine								D				*Pinus torreyana*
15	Western sycamore								W	W	W	W	*Platanus racemosa*
16	Fremont cottonwood			W	W	W	W	W	W	W	W	W	*Populus fremontii*
16	Rio Grande cottonwood	W	W										*Populus wislizeni*
17	Honey mesquite	D	D										*Prosopis glandulosa* var. *glandulosa*
17	Torrey mesquite						W/D	W/D					*Prosopis grandulosa* var. *torreyana*
17	Tornillo	W	W	W	W	W	W	W		W			*Prosopis pubescens*
17	Velvet mesquite			W/D	W/D								*Prosopis velutina*
18	Smoketree					W/D		W/D					*Psorothamnus spinosus*
19	Coast live oak								D	W/D	D	D	*Quercus agrifolia*
4	Organpipe cactus												*Stenocereus thurberi*
20	California fan palm							W/D					*Washingtonia filifera*
21	Joshua tree						D						*Yucca brevifolia*
22	Carneros yucca												*Yucca carnerosana*
23	Palmilla	D	D	D	D								*Yucca elata*
22	Spanish bayonet												*Yucca faxoniana*
22	Beaked yucca												*Yucca rostrata*
22	Thompson yucca												*Yucca thompsoniana*
22	Torrey yucca	D											*Yucca torreyi*

INDIGENOUS SUCCULENT ACCENTS

W = native near watercourses, needs water in landscapes, but soil must always be well drained
D = drought-tolerant, only transplants need water to get reestablished
W/D = prefers some water, but can be dry in special situations
EP = El Paso, LC = Las Cruces, T = Tucson, P = Phoenix, Y = Yuma, LV = Las Vegas,
PS = Palm Springs, SD = San Diego, R = Riverside, SB = Santa Barbara, LA = Los Angeles

#	Common Name	EP	LC	T	P	Y	LV	PS	SD	R	SB	LA	Latin Name
24	Desert agave							D					*Agave deserti*
25	Havard agave												*Agave havardiana*
24	Lechuguilla	D	D										*Agave lechuguilla*
25	New Mexico agave	D											*Agave neomexicana*
25	Palmer agave			D									*Agave palmeri*
25	Parry agave												*Agave parryi*
24	Schott's agave			D									*Agave schottii*
26	Shaw's century plant								D				*Agave shawii ssp. shawii*
27	Ajamete			W/D	W/D	W/D		W/D					*Asclepias subulata*
28	Desert spoon	D	D		D								*Dasylirion wheeleri*
29	Claret-cup cactus	D	D	D				D					*Echinocereus triglochidiatus*
30	Mormon tea				D			D	D	D			*Ephedra californica*
30	Running ephedra												*Ephedra coryi*
30	Mormon tea												*Ephedra fasciculata*
30	Mormon tea						D	D					*Ephedra nevadensis*
30	Mormon tea	D	D	D	D	D	D	D					*Ephedra trifurca*
31	Candelilla												*Euphorbia antisyphilitica*
32	California barrel cactus						D	D					*Ferocactus cylindraceus*
32	Coville barrel cactus		D										*Ferocactus emoryi*
32	Fishhook barrel cactus	D	D	D	D								*Ferocactus wislizeni*
33	Texas falseagave												*Hechtia texensis*
34	Red yucca												*Hesperaloe parviflora*
35	Heartleaf jatropha												*Jatropha cardiophylla*
35	Ashy limberbush												*Jatropha cinerea*
35	Limberbush					D							*Jatropha cuneata*
35	Leatherstem	D	D										*Jatropha dioica* var. *graminea*
36	Chuparosa			D	D	D		D					*Justicia californica*
37	Bigelow nolina						D	D					*Nolina bigelovii*
37	Mesa sacahuista												*Nolina erumpens*
37	Wolf's beargrass												*Nolina parryi ssp. wolfii*
37	Texas sacahuista												*Nolina texana*
39	Buckhorn cholla				D		D						*Opuntia acanthocarpa*
38	Beavertail			D		D							*Opuntia basilaris*
39	Teddybear cholla			D	D	D							*Opuntia bigelovii*
39	Jumping cholla			D									*Opuntia fulgida*
39	Tree cholla	D											*Opuntia imbricata*
38	Brownspine prickly pear	D											*Opuntia phaeacantha* var. *major*
38	Santa Rita prickly pear												*Opuntia violacea* var. *santa-rita*
39	Staghorn cholla												*Opuntia versicolor*
40	Banana yucca												*Yucca baccata*
40	Mojave yucca						D	D	D				*Yucca schidigera*
41	Our Lord's candle								D	D	D	D	*Yucca whipplei*

INDIGENOUS LEAFY EVERGREEN SHRUBS

W = native near watercourses, needs water in landscapes, but soil must always be well drained

D = drought-tolerant, only transplants need water to get reestablished

W/D = prefers some water, but can be dry in special situations

EP = El Paso, LC = Las Cruces, T = Tucson, P = Phoenix, Y = Yuma, LV = Las Vegas,
PS = Palm Springs, SD = San Diego, R = Riverside, SB = Santa Barbara, LA = Los Angeles

#	Common Name	EP	LC	T	P	Y	LV	PS	SD	R	SB	LA	Latin Name
2	Chamise								D	D	D	D	Adenostoma fasciculatum
42	Blue manzanita								D	D	D	D	Arctostaphylos glauca
42	Refugio manzanita									D			Arctostaphylos refugioensis
43	Desert holly				D		D						Atriplex hymenelytra
70	Desert broom			W/D	W/D	W/D	W/D	W/D					Baccharis sarothroides
44	Red barberry	D	D			D							Berberis haematocarpa
44	Nevin's barberry									W/D		W/D	Berberis nevinii
44	Agarito	D	D										Berberis trifoliata
45	Woolly butterflybush												Buddleia marrubiifolia
46	Santa Barbara ceanothus										D		Ceanothus impressus var. impressus
47	Chaparral whitethorn								D	D		D	Ceanothus leucodermis
46	Greenbark ceanothus								D	D	D	D	Ceanothus spinosus
47	Woollyleaf ceanothus								D	D		D	Ceanothus tomentosus var. olivaceus
46	White lilac								D				Ceanothus verrucosus
48	San Diego summer holly								D	D	D	D	Comarostaphylis diversifolia spp. diversifolia
48	Channel Island summer holly												Comarostaphylis diversifolia ssp. planifolia
49	Littleleaf cordia												Cordia parvifolia
50	Channel Island tree poppy												Dendromecon harfordii
50	Tree poppy								D	D	D	D	Dendromecon rigida
51	Hopbush			D	W/D								Dodonaea viscosa
52	Apache-plume	D	D				D						Fallugia paradoxa
53	California fremontia								D	D	D	D	Fremontodendron californicum ssp. californicum
53	Mexican fremontia								D				Fremontodendron mexicanum
54	Toyon								D	D	D	D	Heteromeles arbutifolia
55	Desert lavender				W/D		W/D	W/D					Hyptis emoryi
56	Bladderpod					W/D	W/D		D	D		D	Isomeris arborea
57	Creosote bush	D	D	D	D	D	D	D					Larrea tridentata
58	Boquillas silverleaf												Leucophyllum candidum
58	Texas ranger												Leucophyllum frutescens
58	Big Bend silverleaf												Leucophyllum minus
63	Laurel-leaf sumac								D	D	D	D	Malosma laurina
59	Baja birdbush								D				Ornithostaphylos oppositifolia
60	Hollyleaf cherry								D	D	D	D	Prunus ilicifolia ssp. ilicifolia
60	Catalina cherry												Prunus ilicifolia ssp. lyonii
61	California scrub oak								D	D	D	D	Quercus berberidifolia
61	Nuttall's scrub oak								D			D	Quercus dumosa
62	Coffeeberry								D	W/D	D	D	Rhamnus californica ssp. californica
63	Lemonadeberry								D	D	D	D	Rhus integrifolia
64	Littleleaf sumac	D	D										Rhus microphylla
65	Sugarbush			D					D	D	D	D	Rhus ovata
65	Mearn sumac	D	D										Rhus virens var. choriophylla
66	Jojoba				W/D				D	D	D		Simmondsia chinensis
67	California bay								D	W/D	W/D	D	Umbellularia californica

INDIGENOUS SUNNY GROUND COVERS

W = native near watercourses, needs water in landscapes, but soil must always be well drained
D = drought-tolerant, only transplants need water to get reestablished
W/D = prefers some water, but can be dry in special situations
EP = El Paso, LC = Las Cruces, T = Tucson, P = Phoenix, Y = Yuma, LV = Las Vegas,
PS = Palm Springs, SD = San Diego, R = Riverside, SB = Santa Barbara, LA = Los Angeles

#	Common Name	EP	LC	T	P	Y	LV	PS	SD	R	SB	LA	Latin Name
68	Bursage			D	D	D							Ambrosia deltoidea
68	White bursage						D	D		D			Ambrosia dumosa
69	Coastal sagebrush								D	D	D	D	Artemisia californica
70	Coyote brush								D	D	D	D	Baccharis pilularis
71	Side oats grama	D	D	D			D						Bouteloua curtipendula
71	Black grama	D	D	D			D		D				Bouteloua eriopoda
71	Blue grama	D	D	D									Bouteloua gracilis
72	Damianita												Chrysactinia mexicana
73	Gregg dalea	D	D										Dalea greggii
74	Arizona cottontop												Digitaria californica
75	Turpentinebush	D	D	D			D						Ericameria laricifolia
76	California buckwheat			D	D	D	D		D	D	D	D	Eriogonum fasciculatum
77	Oniongrass						W/D		D	D	D	D	Melica imperfecta
78	Bull muhly												Muhlenbergia emersleyi
78	Bush muhly			D	D		D						Muhlenbergia porteri
78	Deergrass								D	D	D	D	Muhlenbergia rigens
79	Nodding needlegrass								D	D		D	Nassella cernua
79	Foothill needlegrass								D	D	D	D	Nassella lepida
79	Purple needlegrass								D	D	D	D	Nassella pulchra
80	Guayule												Parthenium argentatum
80	Mariola	D	D	D			D						Parthenium incanum
81	White sage							W/D	D	D	D	D	Salvia apiana
81	Purple sage										D	D	Salvia leucophylla
81	Black sage								D	D	D	D	Salvia mellifera
81	San Miguel mountain sage								D				Salvia munzii
72	Shrubby dogweed	D	D	D	D		D						Thymophylla acerosa

INDIGENOUS SHADY GROUND COVERS

W = native near watercourses, needs water in landscapes, but soil must always be well drained
D = drought-tolerant, only transplants need water to get reestablished
W/D = prefers some water, but can be dry in special situations
EP = El Paso, LC = Las Cruces, T = Tucson, P = Phoenix, Y = Yuma, LV = Las Vegas,
PS = Palm Springs, SD = San Diego, R = Riverside, SB = Santa Barbara, LA = Los Angeles

#	Common Name	EP	LC	T	P	Y	LV	PS	SD	R	SB	LA	Latin Name
82	Yellow columbine												Aquilegia chrysantha
82	Red columbine								W	W	W	W	Aquilegia formosa
83	Starleaf Mexican orange												Choisya dumosa
84	San Diego dudleya								D	D		D	Dudleya edulis
84	Santa Catalina dudleya												Dudleya hassei
84	Arizona dudleya						D						Dudleya pulverulenta ssp. arizonica
84	Chalk dudleya								D		D	D	Dudleya pulverulenta ssp. pulverulenta

#	Common Name	EP	LC	T	P	Y	LV	PS	SD	R	SB	LA	Latin Name
85	California fescue								D	W/D	D	D	*Festuca californica*
86	Beach strawberry										W/D		*Fragaria chiloensis*
86	California strawberry										W/D		*Fragaria vesca*
87	Island alumroot												*Heuchera maxima*
87	Arizona coralbells												*Heuchera sanguinea*
88	Douglas iris										D		*Iris douglasiana*
89	Elymus						W		W/D	W/D	W/D	W/D	*Leymus condensatus*
90	Bamboo muhly												*Muhlenbergia dumosa*
91	Mexican evening primrose												*Oenothera speciosa*
92	Coffeeberry fern								W/D	W/D	W/D	W/D	*Pellaea andromedifolia*
93	Mexican plumbago												*Plumbago scandens*
94	Western bracken fern								W/D	W/D	W/D	W/D	*Pteridium aquilinum* var. *pubescens*
95	Fuchsia flowering currant								D	D	D	D	*Ribes speciosum*
96	Evergreen currant								D				*Ribes viburnifolium*
97	Creeping sage								D	D	D	D	*Salvia sonomensis*
97	Hummingbird sage								D	W/D	D	W/D	*Salvia spathacea*
98	Canyon snowberry								D	D	D	D	*Symphoricarpos albus* var. *laevigatus*
98	Creeping snowberry								D	D	D	D	*Symphoricarpos mollis*

INDIGENOUS PERENNIAL FLOWERS

W = native near watercourses, needs water in landscapes, but soil must always be well drained
D = drought-tolerant, only transplants need water to get reestablished
W/D = prefers some water, but can be dry in special situations
EP = El Paso, LC = Las Cruces, T = Tucson, P = Phoenix, Y = Yuma, LV = Las Vegas,
PS = Palm Springs, SD = San Diego, R = Riverside, SB = Santa Barbara, LA = Los Angeles

#	Common Name	EP	LC	T	P	Y	LV	PS	SD	R	SB	LA	Latin Name
99	Desert marigold	D	D	D	D		D						*Baileya multiradiata*
99	Dune marigold				D	D							*Baileya pleniradiata*
100	Chocolate daisy												*Berlandiera lyrata*
101	Pink fairyduster			D									*Calliandra eriophylla*
102	Giant coreopsis									D		D	*Coreopsis gigantea*
102	Sea dahlia								D				*Coreopsis maritima*
103	Silver dalea												*Dalea bicolor* var. *argyraea*
103	Feather dalea	D	D										*Dalea formosa*
103	Black dalea	D	D										*Dalea frutescens*
103	Pretty dalea												*Dalea pulchra*
104	Coast sunflower								D		D	D	*Encelia californica*
105	Brittlebush		D	D	D	D	D	D		D			*Encelia farinosa*
106	Panamint daisy						W/D						*Enceliopsis covillei*
107	Zauschneria								D	D	D	D	*Epilobium canum* ssp. *mexicanum*
108	Seaside daisy										D		*Erigeron glaucus*
109	St. Catherine's lace												*Eriogonum giganteum*
109	Sulphur flower						W/D						*Eriogonum umbellatum* var. *subaridum*
110	Golden yarrow								W/D	W/D	W/D	W/D	*Eriophyllum confertiflorum*
110	Catalina silverlace												*Eriophyllum nevinii*
111	Corethrogyne								D	D	D	D	*Lessingia filaginifolia* var. *filaginifolia*
112	Evergreen lupine								D	D	D	D	*Lupinus albifrons* var. *albifrons*
113	Blackfoot daisy	D	D	D									*Melampodium leucanthum*
114	Monkeyflower								D	D	D	D	*Mimulus aurantiacus*

#	Common Name	EP	LC	T	P	Y	LV	PS	SD	R	SB	LA	Latin Name
115	Mesa greggia	D											Nerisyrenia camporum
116	Fragrant evening primrose							D					Oenothera caespitosa
116	Birdcage primrose				W/D	D		D					Oenothera deltoides spp. deltoides
118	Pink plains penstemon	D	D										Penstemon ambiguus
117	Cardinal penstemon												Penstemon cardinalis
117	Scarlet bugler								D	D	D	D	Penstemon centranthifolius
117	Cleveland penstemon												Penstemon clevelandii
117	Eaton's penstemon												Penstemon eatonii
117	Havard penstemon	D											Penstemon havardii
118	Foothill penstemon								D	D	D	D	Penstemon heterophyllus ssp. australis
118	Palmer penstemon						W/D						Penstemon palmeri
118	Parry's penstemon			D									Penstemon parryi
118	Canyon penstemon			W/D	W/D								Penstemon pseudospectabilis
119	Royal penstemon								D	D	D	D	Penstemon spectabilis
117	Superb penstemon												Penstemon superba
118	Wright penstemon												Penstemon wrightii
120	Matilija poppy								D	D			Romneya coulteri
120	Matilija poppy								D			D	Romneya trichocalyx
121	Cleveland sage								D				Salvia clevelandii
121	Canyon sage												Salvia lycioides
122	Dorri sage						W/D						Salvia dorrii
123	Autumn sage												Salvia greggii
123	Mountain sage												Salvia regla
124	Globe mallow			D	D	D	D	W/D					Sphaeralcea ambigua
124	Scarlet globe mallow	D	D										Sphaeralcea coccinea
125	Scarlet betony												Stachys coccinea
126	Mountain marigold												Tagetes lemmonii
127	Plume tiquilia	D	D										Tiquilia greggii
128	Woolly bluecurls								D	D	D	D	Trichostema lanatum
129	Wright's verbena	D	D	D									Verbena bipinnatifida
129	Goodding's verbena			D	D		D						Verbena gooddingii
130	San Diego goldeneye												Viguiera laciniata
130	Nevada goldeneye					W/D	D	W/D		D			Viguiera parishii
130	Skeletonleaf goldeneye	D	D										Viguiera stenoloba
131	Borrego aster												Xylorhiza orcuttii
131	Desert aster												Xylorhiza tortifolia
131	Terlingua aster												Xylorhiza wrightii
132	Dwarf white zinnia	D	D	D	D								Zinnia acerosa
132	Plains zinnia	D	D										Zinnia grandiflora

INDIGENOUS EPHEMERALS

W = native near watercourses, needs water in landscapes, but soil must always be well drained
D = drought-tolerant, only transplants need water to get reestablished
W/D = prefers some water, but can be dry in special situations
EP = El Paso, LC = Las Cruces, T = Tucson, P = Phoenix, Y = Yuma, LV = Las Vegas,
PS = Palm Springs, SD = San Diego, R = Riverside, SB = Santa Barbara, LA = Los Angeles

#	Common Name	EP	LC	T	P	Y	LV	PS	SD	R	SB	LA	Latin Name
133	Narrowleaf sand verbena	D	D										*Abronia angustifolia*
133	San Diego sand verbena								D				*Abronia villosa* var. *aurita*
133	Sand verbena			D	D	D	D	D					*Abronia villosa* var. *villosa*
134	Onion lily												*Allium hyalinum*
134	Desert onion lily	D	D	D	D		D						*Allium macropetalum*
135	Purple owl's clover			D	D	D	D	D	D	D	D	D	*Castilleja exserta (Orthocarpus)*
136	Fleabane daisy	D	D	D	D								*Erigeron divergens*
136	Fleabane daisy	D	D										*Erigeron modestus*
137	California gold poppy	D	D	D	D	D	D	D	D	D	D	D	*Eschscholzia californica*
138	Arizona lupine			D	D		D						*Lupinus arizonicus*
138	Sand lupine			D	D								*Lupinus sparsiflorus*
138	Arroyo lupine								D	D	D	D	*Lupinus succulentus*
139	Desert Canterbury bells							D					*Phacelia campanularia*
139	Baby blue phacelia	D	D				D						*Phacelia coerulea*
139	Notchleaf phacelia			D	D								*Phacelia crenulata*
140	Blue-eyed grass								W/D	W/D	W/D	W/D	*Sisyrinchium bellum*

INDIGENOUS VINES

W = native near watercourses, needs water in landscapes, but soil must always be well drained
D = drought-tolerant, only transplants need water to get reestablished
W/D = prefers some water, but can be dry in special situations
EP = El Paso, LC = Las Cruces, T = Tucson, P = Phoenix, Y = Yuma, LV = Las Vegas,
PS = Palm Springs, SD = San Diego, R = Riverside, SB = Santa Barbara, LA = Los Angeles

#	Common Name	EP	LC	T	P	Y	LV	PS	SD	R	SB	LA	Latin Name
141	Island morning glory												*Calystegia macrostegia* ssp. *amplissima*
141	Woody morning glory								W/D		W/D	W/D	*Calystegia macrostegia* ssp. *macrostegia*
141	Spring morning glory								W/D		W/D	W/D	*Calystegia purpurata* ssp. *purpurata*
142	Pipestems								W/D	W/D	W/D	W/D	*Clematis lasiantha*
142	Ropevine								D	D			*Clematis pauciflora*
143	Island snapdragon												*Galvezia speciosa*
144	Campo pea								D	D	D	D	*Lathyrus splendens*
145	Thicket creeper	W	W	W									*Parthenocissus inserta*
146	Canyon grape	W	W	W									*Vitis arizonica*
146	Desert wild grape						W	W	W	W	W	W	*Vitis girdiana*

FLOWER COLOR CHARTS
The color and time of bloom charts indicate season of bloom and bloom colors, so you can easily develop a garden that is in bloom all year, or that follows a certain color scheme. Because desert flowers are rain-dependent, few are in full bloom for the entire time indicated. In watered gardens, the earliest bloom time is likely to be the most profuse.

COLORS & BLOOM TIMES OF TREES

Y = yellow, usually attractive to bees and butterflies; *OR/R* = orange to red, usually pollinated by hummingbirds; *R/P* = rosy red to pastel pink, another butterfly favorite; *BL/P* = blue to purple (blue flowers sometimes photograph pink, so trust the chart more than a photo); *WH* = white, sometimes creamy or greenish or marked with other colors, but mainly white; *F-M* = February to March, the earliest spring flowers; *A-M* = April to May; *RAIN* = tends to bloom after rains, especially if spring bloom season received no rain at all; *J-JL* = June to July; *A-S* = August to September; *O-N* = October to November
* = bloom is possible, but not certain

#	Common Name	Y	OR/R	R/P	BL/P	WH	F-M	A-M	RAIN	J-JL	A-S	O-N	Latin Name
1	Whitethorn	Y						A-M	RAIN		A*-S*		*Acacia constricta*
1	Small's huisache	Y					J*-M*	A-M		J*-JL	A-S	O-N*	*Acacia farnesiana* var. *smallii*
1	Catclaw acacia					WH		A-M	RAIN	J-JL*	A-S	O*	*Acacia greggii*
1	Roemer acacia					WH		A-M	RAIN				*Acacia roemeriana*
2	Redshanks					WH				J-JL	A		*Adenostoma sparsifolium*
4	Saguaro					WH	M			J			*Carnegiea gigantea*
6	Blue paloverde	Y					M	A-M			A*-S	O*	*Cercidium floridum*
6	Foothill paloverde	Y				WH		A-M					*Cercidium microphyllum*
7	Mexican redbud			R				M			A		*Cercis canadensis* var. *mexicana*
7	Western redbud			P		WH	F-M	A					*Cercis occidentalis*
8	Desert willow			R/P	P	WH		A-M	RAIN	J*-JL	A*		*Chilopsis linearis*
9	Ocotillo		OR/R				M*	A-M		J			*Fouquieria splendens*
10	Fragrant ash					WH		A-M		J			*Fraxinus cuspidata*
10	California flowering ash					WH		A-M					*Fraxinus dipetala*
11	Goldenball leadtree	Y						A-M	RAIN	J-JL			*Leucena retusa*
12	Catalina ironwood					WH		M		J			*Lyonothamnus floribundus*
13	Ironwood			P				M		J			*Olneya tesota*
4	Senita			P				A-M		J-JL	A		*Pachycereus schotii*
16	Fremont cottonwood	Y	OR/R				M	A					*Populus fremontii*
16	Rio Grande cottonwood	Y	OR/R				M	A-M		J-JL			*Populus wislizeni*
17	Honey mesquite	Y					M	A-M	RAIN	J-JL	A		*Prosopis glandulosa* var. *glandulosa*
17	Torrey mesquite	Y					M	A-M		J			*Prosopis glandulosa* var. *torreyana*
17	Tornillo	Y					M			J-JL			*Prosopis pubescens*
17	Velvet mesquite	Y					M	A-M	RAIN	J-JL	A		*Prosopis velutina*
18	Smoketree				BL/P					J-JL			*Psorothamnus spinosus*
4	Organpipe cactus			P	P	WH		M		J-JL			*Stenocereus thurberi*
21	Joshua Tree					WH		A-M					*Yucca brevifolia*
22	Carneros yucca					WH	M	A-M					*Yucca carnerosana*
23	Palmilla					WH	M			J-JL			*Yucca elata*
22	Spanish bayonet					WH	M	A-M		J-JL			*Yucca faxoniana*
22	Beaked yucca					WH	M	A					*Yucca rostrata*
22	Thompson yucca					WH		A-M					*Yucca thompsoniana*
22	Torrey yucca					WH	M	A-M					*Yucca torreyi*

COLORS & BLOOM TIMES OF SUCCULENT ACCENTS

Y = yellow, usually attractive to bees and butterflies; OR/R = orange to red, usually pollinated by hummingbirds; R/P = rosy red to pastel pink, another butterfly favorite; BL/P = blue to purple (blue flowers sometimes photograph pink, so trust the chart more than a photo); WH = white, sometimes creamy or greenish or marked with other colors, but mainly white; F-M = February to March, the earliest spring flowers; A-M = April to May; RAIN = tends to bloom after rains, especially if spring bloom season received no rain at all; J-JL = June to July; A-S = August to September; O-N = October to November * = bloom is possible, but not certain

#	Common Name	Y	OR/R	R/P	BL/P	WH	F-M	A-M	RAIN	J-JL	A-S	O-N	Latin Name
24	Desert agave	Y				WH		M		J-JL			*Agave deserti*
25	Havard agave	Y							RAIN	J-JL			*Agave havardiana*
24	Lechuguilla	Y	OR/R					M	RAIN	J-JL			*Agave lechuguilla*
25	New Mexico agave	Y								J-JL			*Agave neomexicana*
25	Palmer agave	Y								J-JL	A		*Agave palmeri*
25	Parry agave	Y							RAIN	J-JL	A		*Agave parryi*
24	Schott's agave	Y				WH		M	RAIN	J-JL	A-S	O	*Agave schottii*
26	Shaw's century plant	Y					F-M	A-M	RAIN		S	O-N	*Agave shawii*
27	Ajamete	Y				WH		A-M	RAIN	J*-JL	A-S	O-N*	*Asclepias subulata*
28	Desert spoon	Y						A-M	RAIN	J-JL			*Dasylirion wheeleri*
29	Claret-cup cactus		OR/R	R/P			M	A-M		J			*Echinocereus triglochidiatus*
32	California barrel cactus	Y						A-M					*Ferocactus cylindraceus*
32	Coville barrel cactus	Y	R							J-JL	A		*Ferocactus emoryi*
32	Fishhook barrel cactus	Y	OR/R							JL	A-S		*Ferocactus wislizeni*
33	Texas falseagave					WH	F-M	A-M	RAIN				*Hechtia texensis*
34	Red yucca		R				M	A-M	RAIN	J-JL	S*	O*	*Hesperaloe parviflora*
36	Chuparosa		R				M	A-M		J*	S	O*	*Justicia californica*
37	Bigelow nolina					WH		M		J			*Nolina bigelovii*
37	Mesa sacahuista					WH		M	RAIN	J*-JL*			*Nolina erumpens*
37	Wolf's beargrass					WH		M		J			*Nolina parryi* ssp. *wolfii*
37	Texas sacahuista						M	A-M		J-JL			*Nolina texana*
39	Buckhorn cholla	Y	OR/R					M		J			*Opuntia acanthocarpa*
38	Beavertail			R/P			M	A-M		J			*Opuntia basilaris*
39	Teddybear cholla					WH	F-M	A-M					*Opuntia bigelovii*
39	Jumping cholla			R				A-M					*Opuntia fulgida*
39	Tree cholla			R/P			M			J			*Opuntia imbricata*
38	Brownspine prickly pear	Y	OR/R					A-M		J			*Opuntia phaeacantha* var. *major*
38	Santa Rita prickly pear	Y						A-M					*Opuntia santa-rita*
39	Staghorn cholla	Y	OR/R	R/P			M						*Opuntia versicolor*
40	Banana yucca					WH		A-M	RAIN	J*			*Yucca baccata*
40	Mojave yucca			P	P	WH	F-M	A-M	RAIN	J			*Yucca schidigera*
41	Our Lord's candle					WH	F-M	A-M		J			*Yucca whipplei* ssp. *intermedia*

COLORS & BLOOM TIMES OF LEAFY EVERGREEN SHRUBS

Y = yellow, usually attractive to bees and butterflies; OR/R = orange to red, usually pollinated by hummingbirds; R/P = rosy red to pastel pink, another butterfly favorite; BL/P = blue to purple (blue flowers sometimes photograph pink, so trust the chart more than a photo); WH = white, sometimes creamy or greenish or marked with other colors, but mainly white; F-M = February to March, the earliest spring flowers; A-M = April to May; RAIN = tends to bloom after rains, especially if spring bloom season received no rain at all; J-JL = June to July; A-S = August to September; O-N = October to November
* = bloom is possible, but not certain

#	Common Name	Y	OR/R	R/P	BL/P	WH	F-M	A-M	RAIN	J-JL	A-S	O-N	Latin Name
3	Chamise					WH		M	RAIN	J			Adenostoma fasciculatum
42	Blue manzanita					WH	F-M	A					Arctostaphylos glauca
42	Refugio manzanita			P*		WH	F						Arctostaphylos refugioensis
44	Red barberry	Y					M	A-M		J			Berberis haematocarpa
44	Nevin's barberry	Y					M	A					Berberis nevinii
44	Agarito	Y					F-M	A					Berberis trifoliolata
45	Woolly butterflybush		OR				M	A-M*	RAIN	J-JL	A*		Buddleja marrubiifolia
46	Santa Barbara ceanothus				BL/P		M	A					Ceanothus impressus
47	Chaparral whitethorn				BL/P		M	A-M					Ceanothus leucodermis
46	Greenbark ceanothus				BL/P		F-M	A-M					Ceanothus spinosus
47	Woollyleaf ceanothus				BL/P			A-M					Ceanothus tomentosus var. olivaceous
46	White lilac					WH	F-M	A					Ceanothus verrucosus
48	San Diego summer holly					WH		M		J			Comarostaphylis diversifolia
48	Channel Island summer holly					WH	M	A-M					Comarostaphyllis diversifolia ssp. planifolia
49	Littleleaf cordia					WH	F-M	A-M	RAIN	J*-JL	A-S	O-N*	Cordia parvifolia
50	Channel Island tree poppy	Y						A-M		J-JL	A*-S	O-N*	Dendromecon harfordii
50	Tree poppy	Y						A-M		J-JL	A*-S	O-N*	Dendromecon rigida
52	Apache-plume			P		WH		M	RAIN	J*-JL	A-S	O-N*	Fallugia paradoxa
53	California fremontia	Y					M	A-M*		J*			Fremontodendron californicum
53	Mexican fremontia	Y	OR				M	A-M		J			Fremontodendron mexicanum
54	Toyon					WH				J-JL			Heteromeles arbutifolia
55	Desert lavender				BL/P		F-M	A-M					Hyptis emoryi
56	Bladderpod	Y					F-M	A-M		J*-JL	A-S	O-N*	Isomeris arborea
57	Creosote	Y					F-M	A-M	RAIN	J-JL	A		Larrea tridentata
58	Boquillas silverleaf				P						S	O	Leucophyllum candidum
58	Texas ranger			R/P	P	WH	F-M	A-M	RAIN	J-JL	A-S	O-N	Leucophyllum frutescens
58	Big Bend silverleaf				BL/P					J-JL	A-S	O-N	Leucophyllum minus
63	Laurel-leaf sumac					WH		M		J-JL			Malosma laurina
59	Baja birdbush					WH	F-M	A					Ornithostaphylos oppositifolia
60	Hollyleaf cherry					WH		M		J			Prunus ilicifolia ssp. ilicifolia
60	Catalina cherry					WH		M		J			Prunus ilicifolia ssp. lyonii
62	Coffeeberry					WH		A-M		J			Rhamnus californica
63	Lemonadeberry			P*		WH	F-M						Rhus integrifolia
64	Littleleaf sumac					WH	M	A					Rhus microphylla
65	Sugarbush			R		WH	M	A-M					Rhus ovata
65	Mearn sumac					WH					A-S		Rhus virens var. choriophylla

COLORS & BLOOM TIMES OF SUNNY GROUND COVERS

Y = yellow, usually attractive to bees and butterflies; OR/R = orange to red, usually pollinated by hummingbirds; R/P = rosy red to pastel pink, another butterfly favorite; BL/P = blue to purple (blue flowers sometimes photograph pink, so trust the chart more than a photo); WH = white, sometimes creamy or greenish or marked with other colors, but mainly white; F-M = February to March, the earliest spring flowers; A-M = April to May; RAIN = tends to bloom after rains, especially if spring bloom season received no rain at all; J-JL = June to July; A-S = August to September; O-N = October to November * = bloom is possible, but not certain

#	Common Name	Y	OR/R	R/P	BL/P	WH	F-M	A-M	RAIN	J-JL	A-S	O-N	Latin Name
72	Damianita	Y						A-M	RAIN	J-JL	A-S		Chrysactinia mexicana
73	Gregg dalea			P			M	A-M	RAIN	J-JL	A		Dalea greggii
74	Arizona cottontop					WH		A-M		J-JL	A-S	O	Digitaria californica
75	Turpentinebush	Y										O-N	Ericameria laricifolia
76	California buckwheat			R/P		WH	M	A-M	RAIN	J			Eriogonum fasciculatum
79	Purple needlegrass			P	P		M	A-M					Nassella pulchra
81	White sage					WH		A-M		J-JL	A-S		Salvia apiana
81	Purple sage				BL/P			M		J-JL			Salvia leucophylla
81	Black sage				BL/P			A-M					Salvia mellifera
81	San Miguel mountain sage				BL/P		F-M	A					Salvia munzii
72	Shrubby dogweed	Y					M	A-M	RAIN	JL	A-S	O-N	Thymophylla acerosa

COLORS & BLOOM TIMES OF SHADY GROUND COVERS

Y = yellow, usually attractive to bees and butterflies; OR/R = orange to red, usually pollinated by hummingbirds; R/P = rosy red to pastel pink, another butterfly favorite; BL/P = blue to purple (blue flowers sometimes photograph pink, so trust the chart more than a photo); WH = white, sometimes creamy or greenish or marked with other colors, but mainly white; F-M = February to March, the earliest spring flowers; A-M = April to May; RAIN = tends to bloom after rains, especially if spring bloom season received no rain at all; J-JL = June to July; A-S = August to September; O-N = October to November * = bloom is possible, but not certain

#	Common Name	Y	OR/R	R/P	BL/P	WH	F-M	A-M	RAIN	J-JL	A-S	O-N	Latin Name
82	Yellow columbine	Y					M	A-M	RAIN	J-JL	A		Aquilegia chrysantha
82	Red columbine		R				M	A-M	RAIN	J-JL	A		Aquilegia formosa
83	Starleaf Mexican orange					WH		A-M	RAIN	J-JL	A-S		Choisya dumosa
84	San Diego dudleya					WH		M		J			Dudleya edulis
84	Santa Catalina dudleya					WH		A-M		J			Dudleya hassei
84	Arizona dudleya		OR/R					A-M		J-JL		O-N	Dudleya pulverulenta ssp. arizonica
84	Chalk dudleya		R					M		J-JL			Dudleya pulverulenta ssp. pulverulenta
87	Island alumroot					WH	F-M	A					Heuchera maxima
87	Arizona coralbells			R/P			M	A-M		J*-JL	A-S	O*	Heuchera sanguinea
88	Douglas iris				BL/P		M	A-M					Iris douglasiana

#	Common Name	Y	OR/R	R/P	BL/P	WH	F-M	A-M	RAIN	J-JL	A-S	O-N	Latin Name
91	Mexican evening primrose			P		WH	M	A					Oenothera speciosa
93	Mexican plumbago				BL	WH		M		J-JL	A-S		Plumbago scandens
95	Fuchsia flowering currant		R				F-M	A-M					Ribes speciosum
96	Evergreen currant			R			F-M	A					Ribes viburnifolium
97	Creeping sage				BL/P			M		J			Salvia sonomensis
97	Hummingbird sage		R				M	A-M					Salvia spathacea

COLORS & BLOOM TIMES OF PERENNIAL FLOWERS

Y = yellow, usually attractive to bees and butterflies; OR/R = orange to red, usually pollinated by hummingbirds; R/P = rosy red to pastel pink, another butterfly favorite; BL/P = blue to purple (blue flowers sometimes photograph pink, so trust the chart more than a photo); WH = white, sometimes creamy or greenish or marked with other colors, but mainly white; F-M = February to March, the earliest spring flowers; A-M = April to May; RAIN = tends to bloom after rains, especially if spring bloom season received no rain at all; J-JL = June to July; A-S = August to September; O-N = October to November
Bold italics indicate bloom is possible, but not certain

#	Common Name	Y	OR/R	R/P	BL/P	WH	F-M	A-M	RAIN	J-JL	A-S	O-N	Latin Name
99	Desert marigold	Y					F*-M	A-M*	RAIN	J-JL	A-S	O-N*	Baileya multiradiata
99	Dune marigold	Y					M	A-M	RAIN	J		O-N	Baileya pleniradiata
100	Chocolate daisy	Y						A-M	RAIN	J-JL	A-S	O	Berlandiera lyrata
101	Pink fairyduster			P			F-M	A-M	RAIN	J			Calliandra eriophylla
102	Giant coreopsis	Y					M	A-M					Coreopsis gigantea
102	Sea dahlia	Y					M	A-M					Coreopsis maritima
103	Silver dalea			P						JL	A-S		Dalea bicolor var. argyraea
103	Feather dalea			P	P		M	A-M	RAIN	J-JL	A-S		Dalea formosa
103	Black dalea			P						JL	A-S	O	Dalea frutescens
103	Pretty dalea			P			M	A					Dalea pulchra
104	Coast sunflower	Y					F-M	A-M		J			Encelia californica
105	Brittlebush	Y					M	A					Encelia farinosa
106	Panamint daisy	Y						A-M					Enceliopsis covillei
107	Zauschneria		OR/R								A-S	O	Epilobium canum ssp. mexicana
108	Seaside daisy				BL/P	WH		A-M		J-JL	A		Erigeron glaucus
109	St. Catherine's lace			R/P		WH		M		J-JL	A		Eriogonum giganteum
109	Sulphur flower	Y								JL	A		Eriogonum umbellatum
110	Golden yarrow	Y						A-M		J-JL	A		Eriophyllum confertiflorum
110	Catalina silverlace	Y						A-M		J-JL	A		Eriophyllum nevinii
111	Corethrogyne			P	P					JL	A-S	O	Lessingia filaginifolia
112	Evergreen lupine			P	BL/P	WH	M	A-M*		J-JL*			Lupinus albifrons
113	Blackfoot daisy					WH	M	A-M		J-JL*	A*-S	O-N	Melampodium leucanthum
114	Monkeyflower		OR				M	A-M			A-S	O	Mimulus aurantiacus
115	Mesa greggia			P	P	WH	M	A-M		J-JL	A-S	O-N	Nerisyrenia camporum
116	Fragrant evening primrose			P		WH	M	A-M		J-JL*	A*		Oenothera caespitosa
116	Birdcage primrose						M	A-M					Oenothera deltoides
118	Pink plains penstemon			P		WH		M		J-JL	A		Penstemon ambiguus
117	Cardinal penstemon		R					M		J-JL			Penstemon cardinalis
117	Scarlet bugler		R					A-M		J-JL			Penstemon centranthifolius
117	Cleveland penstemon		R				M	A-M					Penstemon clevelandii
117	Eaton's penstemon		R				M	A-M		J-JL			Penstemon eatonii
117	Havard penstemon		R					A-M		J-JL	A-S	O	Penstemon havardii

#	Common Name	Y	OR/R	R/P	BL/P	WH	F-M	A-M	RAIN	J-JL	A-S	O-N	Latin Name
118	Foothill penstemon			P				M		J			P. heterophyllus ssp. australis
118	Palmer penstemon			P				M		J			Penstemon palmeri
118	Parry's penstemon			P			F-M	A					Penstemon parryi
118	Canyon penstemon			R/P			M	A-M					Penstemon pseudospectabilis
119	Royal penstemon				BL/P			A-M		J			Penstemon spectabilis
117	Superb penstemon		R					A-M					Penstemon superbus
118	Wright's penstemon			R/P				A-M		J			Penstemon wrightii
120	Matilija poppy					WH		M		J-JL			Romneya coulteri
120	Matilija poppy					WH		M		J-JL			Romneya trichocalyx
121	Cleveland sage				BL/P		M	A-M		J-JL	A		Salvia clevelandii
121	Canyon sage				BL			A-M			S	O	Salvia lycioides
122	Dorri sage				BL/P		F-M	A					Salvia dorrii
123	Autumn sage			R/P			M	A-M	RAIN		A-S	O-N	Salvia greggii
123	Mountain sage		R								S	O	Salvia regla
124	Globe mallow		OR/R	R/P	P		M	A					Sphaeralcea ambigua
124	Scarlet globe mallow		OR/R					A-M	RAIN	J-JL	A		Sphaeralcea coccinea
125	Scarlet betony		OR/R				M	A-M			S	O	Stachys coccinea
126	Mountain marigold	Y					F*-M*				S	O-N	Tagetes lemmonii
127	Plume tiquilia				BL/P		M*	A-M*	RAIN		A-S	O	Tiquilia greggii
128	Woolly bluecurls				BL/P			M		J-JL	A		Trichostema lanatum
129	Wright verbena			R/P	P	WH*	F-M	A-M		J*-JL	A-S*	O-N	Verbena bipinnatifida
129	Goodding's verbena			P*	BL/P		F-M	A-M		J*-JL	A-S*	O-N	Verbena gooddingi
130	San Diego goldeneye	Y					F-M	A-M		J			Viguiera laciniata
130	Nevada goldeneye	Y					F-M	A-M			S	O	Viguiera parishii
130	Skeletonleaf goldeneye	Y						M	RAIN	J-JL	A-S	O-N	Viguiera stenoloba
131	Borrego aster				BL/P	WH*	M	A		J*			Xylorhiza orcuttii
131	Desert aster				BL/P	WH*	M	A-M				O	Xylorhiza tortifolia
131	Terlingua aster				BL/P		M	A					Xylorhiza wrightii
132	Dwarf white zinnia					WH		A-M			S	O	Zinnia acerosa
132	Plains zinnia	Y						M		J-JL	A-S	O	Zinnia grandiflora

COLORS & BLOOM TIMES OF EPHEMERALS

Y = yellow, usually attractive to bees and butterflies; OR/R = orange to red, usually pollinated by hummingbirds; R/P = rosy red to pastel pink, another butterfly favorite; BL/P = blue to purple (blue flowers sometimes photograph pink, so trust the chart more than a photo); WH = white, sometimes creamy or greenish or marked with other colors, but mainly white; F-M = February to March, the earliest spring flowers; A-M = April to May; RAIN = tends to bloom after rains, especially if spring bloom season received no rain at all; J-JL = June to July; A-S = August to September; O-N = October to November
* = bloom is possible, but not certain

#	Common Name	Y	OR/R	R/P	BL/P	WH	F-M	A-M	RAIN	J-JL	A-S	O-N	Latin Name
133	San Diego sand verbena			R/P	P		M	A-M		J*-JL	A*		Abronia villosa var. aurita
133	Sand verbena			R/P	P	WH*	F-M	A-M*		J-JL*			Abronia villosa var. villosa
133	Narrowleaf sand verbena			R/P	P	WH		M		J-JL			Abronia angustifolia
134	Onion lily			P*		WH	M	A-M		J*			Allium hyalinum
134	Desert onion lily			R/P	P		M	A-M					Allium macropetalum
135	Purple owl's clover			R	P		M	A-M					Castilleja exserta (Orthocarpus)
136	Fleabane daisy					WH	M	A-M		J-JL	A-S	O-N	Erigeron divergens
137	California gold poppy	Y	OR					M		J			Eschscholzia californica ssp. californica

#	Common Name	Y	OR/R	R/P	BL/P	WH	F-M	A-M	RAIN	J-JL	A-S	O-N	Latin Name
137	Mexican gold poppy	Y	OR	R*		WH*	M	A					*Eschscholzia californica* ssp. *mexicana*
138	Arizona lupine			P	P		F-M	A-M					*Lupinus arizonicus*
138	Sand lupine				P		F-M	A-M					*Lupinus sparsiflorus*
138	Arroyo lupine				BL/P		F-M	A*					*Lupinus succulentus*
139	Desert Canterbury bells				BL		F-M	A					*Phacelia campanularia*
139	Baby blue phacelia				BL/P	WH	M	A-M					*Phacelia coerulea*
139	Notchleaf phacelia				BL/P		F-M	A					*Phacelia crenulata*
140	Blue-eyed grass				BL/P	WH*	M	A-M					*Sisyrinchium bellum*

COLORS & BLOOM TIMES OF VINES

Y = yellow, usually attractive to bees and butterflies; OR/R = orange to red, usually pollinated by hummingbirds; R/P = rosy red to pastel pink, another butterfly favorite; BL/P = blue to purple (blue flowers sometimes photograph pink, so trust the chart more than a photo); WH = white, sometimes creamy or greenish or marked with other colors, but mainly white; F-M = February to March, the earliest spring flowers; A-M = April to May; RAIN = tends to bloom after rains, especially if spring bloom season received no rain at all; J-JL = June to July; A-S = August to September; O-N = October to November * = bloom is possible, but not certain

#	Common Name	Y	OR/R	R/P	BL/P	WH	F-M	A-M	RAIN	J-JL	A-S	O-N	Latin Name
141	Island morning glory			P				A-M		J-JL			*Calystegia macrostegia* ssp. *amplissima*
141	Woody morning glory			P				A-M		J*-JL	A-S	O-N*	*Calystegia macrostegia* ssp. *macrostegia*
141	Spring morning glory			P				A					*Calystegia purpurata* ssp. *purpurata*
142	Pipestems					WH	M	A-M		J			*Clematis lasiantha*
142	Ropevine					WH	M	A					*Clematis pauciflora*
143	Island snapdragon		R				F-M	A-M		J*-JL	A-S	O-N*	*Galvezia speciosa*
144	Campo pea		R					M	A-M				*Lathyrus splendens*

DIRECTORY

NURSERIES

Nothing in life is unchanging; and that's certainly true of lists of native plant nurseries. New ones appear all the time, while others change their names or locations, get new phone numbers, or go out of business. This updated list represents a number of excellent sources for plants and information, and should be a big help in getting you started.

R = Retail, W = Wholesale, MO = Mail Order

Amargosa Garden Center   R W MO
5050 North Rainbow Boulevard
Las Vegas, NV 89130
(702) 645-9163

Arid Zone Trees   W
P.O. Box 167
Queen Creek, AZ 85242
(602) 331-4355

Community College of Southern Nevada   R W
Desert Garden Center
6221 West Charleston Boulevard
Las Vegas, NV 89102
(702) 651-5050

Desert Foothills Gardens   W
33840 North Cave Creek Road
Cave Creek, AZ 85331
(602) 488-9455

Desert Survivors   R W
1020 West Starpass
Tucson, AZ 85713
(520) 791-9309

Desert Tree Farm   W
2744 East Utopia
Phoenix, AZ 85050
(602) 569-6604

Desert Tree Nursery   R
2335 East Lone Cactus Road
Phoenix, AZ 85024
(602) 569-1300

Environmental Seed Producers, Inc.   W
605 Bodger Road
Lompoc, CA 93436
(805) 735-8888

Green Oaks Ranch
1237 Green Oaks Road
Vista, CA 92083
(760) 727-0251

Green Thumb Nursery   R
2211 North Mesquite
Las Cruces, NM
(505) 524-0592

Las Pilitas Nursery   R W MO
3232 Las Pilitas Road
Santa Margarita, CA 93453
(805) 438-5992

Living Desert Plant Nursery   R W
47900 Portola Avenue
Palm Desert, CA 92260
(706) 346-5694

Matilija Nursery   R W
8225 Waters Road
Moorpark, CA 93021
(805) 523-8604

Mountain States Wholesale Nursery   W
10020 West Glendale Avenue
Glendale, AZ 85307
(602) 247-8509

Native Sons Nursery   W
379 West El Campo Road
Arroyo Grande, CA 93420
(805) 481-5996

Pearson's Tree Place   R W
6900 Doniphan
Canutillo, TX 79835
(915) 877-3808

Plants for Dry Places   R W MO
25735 Garbani Road
Menifee Valley, CA 92584
(805) 679-6612

Plants of the Southwest   R W MO
Agua Fria
Route 6, Box 11-A
Santa Fe, NM 87501
(505) 438-8888

Plants of the Southwest   R W MO
6670 4th Street NW
Albuquerque, NM
(505) 344-8830

Shady Way Gardens   R
566 West Superstition Boulevard
Apache Junction, AZ 85220

Sierra Vista Growers   R W
2800 New Mexico Highway 28
La Union, NM 88021
(505) 874-2415

Southwestern Native Seeds   R MO
P.O. Box 50503
Tucson, AZ 85703

Starr Nursery   R W
3340 RuthAnn Road
Tucson, AZ 85745
(520) 743-7052

Theodore Payne Foundation   R MO
10459 Tuxford Street
Sun Valley, CA 91352
(818) 768-1802

Tree of Life Nursery   W
33201 Ortega Highway
San Juan Capistrano, CA 92693
(949) 728-0685

Western Sere
1555 North VIP Boulevard
Casa Grande, AZ 85222
(520) 836-8246

Wild Seed, Inc.   R W MO
P.O. Box 27751
Tempe, AZ 85285
(602) 276-3536

Yucca Do Nursery   MO
P.O. Box 655
Waller, TX 77484
(409) 826-4580

INFORMATION RESOURCES

Anza-Borrego Desert State Park
P.O. Box 299
Borrego Springs, CA 92004
(760) 767-5311

Arizona Native Plant Society
P.O. Box 41206
Sun Station
Tucson, AZ 85704

Arizona-Sonora Desert Museum
2021 North Kinney Road
Tucson, AZ 85743
(520) 883-2702

Boyce-Thompson Southwestern Arboretum
P.O. Box AB
Highway 60
Superior, AZ 85273
(520) 689-2811

California Native Plant Society
909 12th Street
Suite 116
Sacramento, CA 95814
(916) 447-2677

Chihuahuan Desert Gardens
Centennial Museum
University of Texas at El Paso
El Paso, TX 79968
(915) 747-5565

Chihuahuan Desert Research Institute
P.O. Box 1334
Alpine, TX 79831
(915) 837-8370
Annual spring native plant sale

Descanso Gardens
1418 Descanso Drive
La Canada, CA 91011
(818) 952-4400

Desert Botanical Garden
1201 North Galvin Parkway
Phoenix, AZ 85008
(602) 941-1225

Desert Demonstration Garden
3701 Alta Drive
Las Vegas, NV 89153
(702) 258-3205

Desert Water Agency Demonstration Gardens
1200 Gene Autry Trail, South
Palm Springs, CA 92264
(760) 323-4971

Ethel M Botanic Garden
2 Cactus Garden Drive
Henderson, NV 89014
(702) 458-8864

Fullerton Arboretum
P.O. Box 34080
Fullerton, CA 92634-9480
(714) 278-3579

Joshua Tree National Monument
74485 National Monument
Twenty-Nine Palms,
CA 92277-3597
(760) 367-5525

Lady Bird Johnson Wildflower Center
2600 FM 973 N
Austin, TX 78725-4201
(512) 292-3600

Living Desert
47900 Portola Avenue
Palm Desert, CA 92260
(760) 346-5694

Mojave Native Plant Society
8180 Placid Street
Las Vegas, NV 89123

Moorten Botanic Garden
1701 South Palm Canyon Drive
Palm Springs, CA 92264
(760) 327-6555

Native Plant Society
of Texas
P.O. Box 891
Georgetown, TX 78627
(512) 238-0695

New Mexico Native Plant
Society
P.O. Box 5917
Santa Fe, NM 87502
(505) 434-3041

New Mexico State
University Botanical Garden
P.O. Box 3Q
Las Cruces, NM 88003-0003
(505) 646-3405

Quail Botanical Gardens
230 Quail Gardens Drive
Encinitas, CA 92024
(760) 436-3036

Rancho Los Alamitos
6400 Bixby Hill Road
Long Beach, CA 90815
(562) 431-3541

Rancho Santa Ana
Botanic Garden
1500 North College Avenue
Claremont, CA 91711
(909) 625-8767

Santa Barbara
Botanic Garden
1212 Mission Canyon Road
Santa Barbara, CA 93105
(805) 682-4726

Texas Agricultural
Extension Service
1030 North Zaragosa Road
El Paso, TX 79907
(915) 859-7725

Texas A & M Experiment
Station
1380 A & M Circle
El Paso, TX 79927
(915) 859-9111

Theodore Payne Foundation
10459 Tuxford
Sun Valley, CA 91352
(818) 768-1802

Tohono Chul Park
7366 North Paseo del Norte
Tucson, AZ 85704
(520) 742-6455

Tucson Botanical Gardens
2150 North Alvernon Way
Tucson, AZ 85712
(520) 326-9255

University of California
Riverside Botanic Gardens
UCR Campus
Riverside, CA 92521
(909) 787-4650

University of Nevada Las
Vegas Arboretum
4505 Maryland Parkway
Las Vegas, NV 89154-1013
(702) 895-3392

LANDSCAPE ARCHITECTS & DESIGNERS

Anybody can stick a plant in the ground. But when the plants are native, it takes a special sensitivity and knowledge to create landscapes that are not only beautiful and low maintenance, but communicate a true sense of place.

Wynn Anderson LD
3015 Piedmont
El Paso, TX 79902
(915) 533-6072

Andre Landscaping LA
10830 North 71st Place
Scottsdale, AZ 85254
(602) 483-8088

Bowden Design Group LA
7100 East Lincoln Drive
Suite D-224
Scottsdale, AZ 85253
(602) 443-0223

Dave Buchanan LD
462 La Mesa Avenue
Encinitas, CA 92024
(760) 942-9254

Ann Christoph LA
31713 Coast Highway
Laguna Beach, CA 92651
(949) 499-3574

Gage Davis Associates LA
7377 East Doubletree Ranch Road
Suite 180
Scottsdale, AZ 85258
(602) 596-1976

Susan Frommer LD
Plants for Dry Places
25735 Garbani Road
Menifee Valley, CA 92584
(909) 679-6612

Guy S. Greene &
Associates LA
P.O. Box 65883
Tucson, AZ 85728
(520) 573-6336

Logan-Simpson Design,
Inc. LA
398 South Mill Avenue
Suite 200
Tempe, AZ 85281
(602) 967-1343

Greg Magee/Naturescapes
LD
P.O. Box 2404
Las Cruces, NM 88004
(505) 525-9424

Steve Martino & Associates
LA
3336 North 32nd
Suite 110
Phoenix, AZ 85018
(602) 957-6150

Paul Nota/Lost West LA
5238 Townsend Avenue
Los Angeles, CA 90041
(323) 258-8214

Judith Phillips LD
1 Sanchez Road
Veguita, NM 87062
(505) 345-6248

Jeff Powers LA
1100 South Coast Highway
#209
Laguna Beach, CA 92651
(949) 494-8131

Greg Rubin LD
1457 North Broadway
Suite D
Escondido, CA 92026
(760) 746-6870

Jana Ruzicka LA
530 Cress
Laguna Beach, CA 92651
(949) 494-8871

Chuck Saladino LA/Cella
Barr and Associates
1771 East Flamingo Road
Las Vegas, NV 89119
(702) 893-7779

Sonoran Desert Designs,
Inc.
31055 North 56th Street
Cave Creek, AZ 85331
(480) 595-6400

Southern Nevada American
Society of Landscape
Architects
UNLV
Box 454018
4505 Maryland Parkway
Las Vegas, NV 89154-4018

Southwick and Associates
LA
2601 North Tenaya Way
Las Vegas, NV 89128
(702) 255-8100

Kay Stewart LA
2171 India Street
Suite A
San Diego, CA 92101
(619) 234-2668

Ten Eyck Landscape
Architecture, Inc. LA
3807 North 24th Street
Suite 100
Phoenix, AZ 85016
(602) 468-0505

T.K.D. Associates LA
2121 Tahquitz Canyon Way
Suite 1
Palm Springs, CA 92262
(760) 320-8899

James Veltman LA
2801 North Tenaya Way
Las Vegas, NV 89128
(702) 896-2288

WLB Group
2551 Green Valley Parkway
Suite A 425
Henderson, NV 89014
(702) 458-2551

James Zabriskie LD
P.O. Box 2092
Canutillo, TX 79835
(915) 877-2100

J. W. Zunino & Associates
LA
3191 South Jones Boulevard
Las Vegas, NV 89146
(702) 253-9390

BIBLIOGRAPHY

Accent Plants. Desert Butterfly Gardening. Grasses. Ground Covers and Vines. Shrubs. Trees. Wildflowers. Series of pamphlets on desert flora. Tucson: Arizona Native Plant Society, 1990 to 1994.

Arnberger, Leslie P. Flowers of the Southwest Mountains. Tucson: Southwest Parks and Monuments Association, 1982.

Barbour, Michael G., and William Dwight Billings. North American Terrestrial Vegetation. Cambridge, UK: Cambridge University Press, 1988.

Barbour, Michael G., and Jack Major. Terrestrial Vegetation of California. Davis, Calif.: California Native Plant Society: No. 9, 1988.

Beauchamp, R. Mitchel. A Flora of San Diego County, California. National City, Calif.: Sweetwater River Press, 1986.

Beetle, Alan A. Distribution of the Native Grasses of California. Pamphlet published by Redwood City Seed Company. Redwood City, Calif.: 1947.

Behler, John L., and F. Wayne King. National Audubon Society Field Guide to North American Reptiles and Amphibians. New York: Alfred A. Knopf, Inc., 1979.

Brown, David E., ed. Desert Plants: Biotic Communities of the American Southwest–United States and Mexico, Vol. 4, Nos. 1–4. Superior, Ariz.: University of Arizona for the Boyce-Thompson Southwestern Arboretum, 1982.

California Poppy. Fact sheet published by National Garden Bureau. Downers Grove, Ill.: 1992.

Christensen, Jon. "Sin City's Lucky Tortoise." Nature Conservancy (July/August 1992), pp. 8–13.

Connelly, Kevin. Gardener's Guide to California Wildflowers. Sun Valley, Calif.: Theodore Payne Foundation, 1991.

——. Flowerhill: The Silver Lining. Article published by Theodore Payne Foundation. Sun Valley, Calif.: Spring 1992.

Cornett, James W. The Joshua Tree. Monograph published by Palm Springs Desert Museum, Calif., Natural Science Publication 1-91.

David, Tony. "Navigating Flood Control." Tucson Weekly (Apr. 7–13, 1993).

The Desert Tortoise. Pamphlet. Tucson: Arizona-Sonora Desert Museum, 1989.

Dodge. Natt N. Flowers of the Southwest Deserts. Tucson: Southwest Parks and Monuments Association, 1985.

——. 100 Desert Wildflowers in Natural Color. Globe, Ariz.: Southwest Parks and Monuments Association, 1963.

——. 100 Roadside Wildflowers of Southwest Uplands in Natural Color. Globe, Ariz.: Southwest Parks and Monuments Association, 1967.

Duffield, Mary Rose, and Warren D. Jones. Plants for Dry Climates: How to Select, Grow and Enjoy. Tucson: H.P. Books, 1981.

Elmore, Francis H. Shrubs and Trees of the Southwest Uplands. Tucson: Southwest Parks and Monuments Association, 1976.

Exploring Wildflower Country. Study done by Theodore Payne Foundation, Sun Valley, Calif.

Felger, Richard Stephen, and Mary Beck Moser. People of the Desert and Sea. Tucson: University of Arizona Press, 1985.

Firescapes Demonstration Garden. Instruction sheets published by Santa Barbara City Fire Department. Santa Barbara, Calif.: 1990.

Fleming, Theodore H. "Following the Nectar Trail." Bats, the Magazine of Bat Conservation International (Winter 1991), pp. 4–7.

Grow a Native Planting Guide. Booklet published by Santa Barbara Botanic Garden. Santa Barbara, Calif.: 1993.

Guide to Drought-Tolerant Gardening. Booklet published by Alameda County Water District. Fremont, Calif.: 1988.

Hickman, James C., ed. The Jepson Manual: Higher Plants of California. Los Angeles: University of California Press, 1993.

Hoboda, Ted. "Agaves of New Mexico." Native Plant Society Newsletter (May/June 1987).

Holing, Dwight. "California Teaming." Nature Conservancy (March/April 1992), pp. 8–13.

Hooks, R. F., et al. Native Plants for New Mexico Landscapes. Cooperative Extension Service, Circular 513. Las Cruces, N. Mex.: New Mexico State University, August 1994.

Hubbs, Carl L., et al., eds. Torrey Pines State Reserve. Booklet, 3d ed. La Jolla, Calif.: Torrey Pines Association, 1991.

Johnson, Eric A., and David G. Harbison. Landscaping to Save Water in the Desert. Rancho Mirage, Calif.: E&H Products, 1985.

——. Lush and Efficient: A Guide to Coachella Valley Landscaping. Coachella, Calif.: Coachella Valley Water District, 1988.

Johnson, Eric A., and Scott Millard. Beautiful Gardens. Tucson: Ironwood Press, 1991.

——. How to Grow Wildflowers. Tucson: Ironwood Press, 1993.

——. The Low-Water Flower Gardener. Tucson: Ironwood Press, 1993.

Kartesz, John T. A Synonymized Checklist of the Vascular Flora of the United States, Canada, and Greenland, 2d edition, Volume 1 Checklist, 692 pgs.; Volume II Thesaurus, 816 pgs. Published by the Biota of North America Program of North Carolina Botanical Garden. Portland, Oregon: Timber Press, 1994.

Kartesz, J. T., and C. A. Meacham. Digital Floristic Synthesis of North America North of Mexico. Chapel Hill, N.C.: The Biota of North America Program of the North Carolina Botanical Garden, 1999.

Kearney, Thomas H., and Robert H. Peebles. Arizona Flora. Los Angeles: University of California Press, 1960.

Keator, Glenn. Complete Garden Guide to the Native Perennials of California. San Francisco: Chronicle Books, 1990.

Lamb, Samuel H. Woody Plants of the Southwest. Santa Fe, N. Mex.: Suntone Press, 1989.

Landscape Concepts: A Guide to Creating Lush, Water-Efficient Landscapes. Booklet published by City of Palm Desert, Calif.: 1989.

Lawler, Howard. "The Desert Tortoise and Its North American Relatives." Arizona Sonoran Desert Museum Magazine.

Lee, David S., and Mary K. Clark. "Arizona's Night Visitors," *Bats, the Magazine of Bat Conservation International* (Summer 1993), pp. 3–5.

Lenz, Lee W., and John Dourley. *California Native Trees and Shrubs*. Claremont, Calif.: Rancho Santa Ana Botanic Garden, 1981.

Lonard, Robert I., and Frank W. Judd. *Phytogeography of the Woody Flora of the Lower Rio Grande Valley, Texas*. Abstract. Edinburg, Tex.: Dept. of Biology, University of Texas–Pan American: Vol. 45, No. 2, 1993.

Martino, Steve, and Vernon D. Swaback. *Desert Excellence: A Guide to Natural Landscaping*. Phoenix: Bellamah Community Development, 1986.

McKelvey, Susan Delano. *Botanical Exploration of the Trans-Mississippi West 1790–1850*. Corvalis, Oreg.: Oregon State University Press, 1991.

Mielke, Judy. *Native Plants for Southwestern Landscapes*. Austin, Tex.: University of Texas Press, 1993.

Millard, Scott, and Cedric Crocker, ed. *Gardening in Dry Climates*. San Ramon, Calif.: Ortho Books, 1989.

Moore, Michael. *Medicinal Plants of the Desert and Canyon West*. Santa Fe, N. Mex.: Museum of New Mexico Press, 1989.

——. *Medicinal Plants of the Mountain West*. Santa Fe, N. Mex.: Museum of New Mexico Press, 1979.

Munz, Philip A., and David D. Keck. *A California Flora and Supplement*. Los Angeles: University of California Press, 1973.

——. *California Spring Wildflowers*. Los Angeles: University of California Press, 1961.

Native Plant Society of New Mexico. *Proceedings of the Southwest Native Plant Symposium, June 18–19, 1987*. Albuquerque.

Perry, Bob. *Landscape Plants for Western Regions*. Claremont, Calif.: Land Design Publishing, 1992.

——. *Trees and Shrubs for Dry California Landscapes*. Claremont, Calif.: Land Design Publishing, 1989.

Plants of El Camino Real. Catalog and Planting Guide. San Juan Capistrano, Calif.: Tree of Life Wholesale Nursery, 1992–93.

Plants of the Southwest. Seed Catalogs. Santa Fe, N. Mex.

"Plants for a Water-Sensible Future." *Sunset Magazine* (October 1988).

Powell, A. Michael. *Trees and Shrubs of Trans-Pecos Texas*. Alpine, Tex.: Sul Ross State University, 1988.

"Proceedings of the Conference, Landscaping with Wildflowers and Native Plants, March 13–15, 1991." *Wildflower: Journal of the National Wildflower Research Center*. Austin, Tex.: 1991.

Red Rock Canyon National Conservation Area Plants. Pamphlet published by Bureau of Land Management. Las Vegas, Nev.

Roach, Dr. Archibald W. *Outdoor Plants of the Southwest*. Dallas: Taylor Publishing, 1982.

Ropp, Thomas. "Coming Out of Their Shells." *Arizona Republic* (July 29, 1990).

Schmidt, Marjorie G. *Growing California Native Plants*. Los Angeles: University of California Press, 1980.

Schmutz, Ervin M., et al. *Livestock Poisoning Plants of Arizona*. Tucson: University of Arizona Press, 1974.

Simpson, Benny J. *A Field Guide to Texas Trees*. Houston, Tex.: Gulf Publishing, 1988.

Smith, DeWayne. "Study Aims to Put Tortoise in 'Realm of Facts.'" *Phoenix Gazette* (Oct. 4, 1990).

Soil Conservation Society of America, Arizona Chapter. *Landscaping with Native Arizona Plants*. Tucson: University of Arizona Press, 1973.

Stewart, Jon Mark. *Colorado Desert Wildflowers*. Palm Desert, Calif.: Cachuma Press, 1993.

Tanner, Ogden. *Gardening America*. New York City: Viking Studio Books, 1990.

Taylor's Guide to Water-Saving Gardening. Boston: Houghton Mifflin Company, 1990.

Turner, Raymond M., Janice E Bowers, and Tony L. Burgess. *Sonoran Desert Plants: An Ecological Atlas*. Tucson: University of Arizona Press, 1995.

Tuttle, Merlin D. "Bats: The Cactus Connection." *National Geographic* (June 1991), pp. 131–140.

——. "A Decade of Bat Conservation." *Bats, the Magazine of Bat Conservation International* (Spring 1992), pp. 3–10.

——. "Long-Nosed Bats Proposed for Endangered Status." *Bats, the Magazine of Bat Conservation International* (Summer 1998), pp. 3–4.

Warnock, Barton H. *Wildflowers of the Big Bend Country, Texas*. Alpine, Tex.: Sul Ross State University, 1970.

——. *Wildflowers of the Davis Mountains and the Marathon Basin, Texas*. Alpine, Tex.: Sul Ross State University, 1977.

——. *Wildflowers of the Guadalupe Mountains and the Sand Dune Country, Texas*. Alpine, Tex.: Sul Ross State University, 1974.

Wasowski, Sally, with Andy Wasowski. *Native Texas Plants: Landscaping Region by Region*. Houston: Tex.: Gulf Publishing, 1988.

——. *Requiem for a Lawnmower*. Dallas: Taylor Publishing, 1992.

Water, the Power, Promise, and Turmoil of North America's Fresh Water. National Geographic Special Edition, 1993.

Wauer, Roland H. *A Naturalist's Mexico*. College Station, Tex.: Texas A&M University Press, 1992.

Weik, Shirley, and Guy Acuff. "The Creosote Bush." *Plant Press*. Tucson: Arizona Native Plant Society, January 1988.

Welsh, Pat. *Pat Welsh's Southern California Gardening: A Month by Month Guide*. San Francisco, Chronicle Books, 1992.

Weniger, Del. *Cacti of Texas and Neighboring States*. Austin, Tex.: University of Texas Press, 1988.

Western Garden Book. Menlo Park, Calif.: Sunset Books and Sunset Magazine, 1998.

White, John M., and Dr. Wayne Mackay. *El Paso County Suggested Plant List*. El Paso: joint project of Texas Agricultural Extension Service and Texas A&M Research and Extension Center.

Whitford, Walter. "Arroyos: An Endangered Habitat." *Wildflower Magazine* (Spring 1991), pp. 16–18.

——. "Yucca." *Wildflower Magazine* (Autumn 1991), pp. 24–26.

Whiting, Alfred F. *Ethnobotany of the Hopi*. Flagstaff, Ariz.: Northern Arizona Society of Science and Art, June 1939.

Wild, Peter. "Saguaro: Symbol & Linchpin." *Wildflower, North America's Wild Flora Magazine* (Spring 1991), pp. 12–15.

Winegar, David. *Desert Wildflowers: Drylands of North America*. Beavorton, Oreg.: Beautiful America Printing Company, 1982.

ACKNOWLEDGMENTS

Someone once said, "The harder the land, the nicer the people."

Certainly Andy and I found this to be true as we traveled the roads that stretched from El Paso to Los Angeles doing the research and photography for this book. Yes, this is a hard land–dry and rugged and vast. But it is also a beautiful land, often majestically so. It is vibrant and alive. And its people–whether sprung from pioneer stock or relatively recent transplants–proved to be among the most generous and giving we'd ever encountered. Most we met as strangers, but by the time we left we were friends. This book would have been impossible without their help.

Our long thank-you list must begin with the people to whom this book is dedicated: Ron and Maureen Gass, owners of Mountain States Wholesale Nursery in Glendale, Arizona. Initially we had thought to dedicate this book to Ron alone; long before we'd actually met the man, we'd heard numerous "Ron Gass stories." It isn't stretching things at all to tell you that, for many, Ron has acquired legendary proportions. Spend more than five minutes with anyone in this part of the country who is associated with native plants and the inevitable Ron Gass stories come up–tales of his soft-spoken passion in promoting the use and appreciation of natives throughout the Southwest, tales of his big-hearted generosity, tales of his treks into the deserts to discover plants that had never before been used as ornamentals.

One such story, told by Tucson nurseryman Greg Starr, will have to suffice here: Some years back, the two men were in Mexico collecting seed from a *Nolina*–a beargrass that grows like a tree in that country. Greg was standing on top of Ron's shoulders trying to reach the seed stalk. "My hands were getting cut up pretty badly on the razor-edged leaves," he recalls, "and Ron was keeping up a steady line of encouraging chatter, urging caution, and promising to doctor my cuts as soon as I got down. It was only after I was down from his shoulders that I noticed a swarm of very angry bees buzzing around his face. They'd been there the whole time, but he was more concerned about my safety than his own. That, in a nutshell, is Ron Gass to me."

When we finally met Ron, we were surprised to see that he was somewhat shorter than the 12 feet we had by then envisioned. Moreover, it didn't take us long to realize that Maureen is as much a part of the Gass Legend as is her husband. Friends describe them as the ideal match–Ron being the visionary, the man with the mission, while Maureen dots the *I*'s and crosses the *T*'s and generally holds things together. They've been operating this way for 30 years.

Over the years, Andy and I have picked their brains, camped out in their home, and forged a deep friendship.

We cannot leave the Gass nursery without special thanks to the staff, especially Janet Rademacher, who spent many hours phoning ahead for us to set up meetings with many "must-see" contacts.

Major thanks also go to Jeff Bohn at Tree of Life Nursery in San Juan Capistrano and landscape architect Phil Hebets in Cave Creek, Arizona, who, along with Ron Gass, took time from their busy schedules to read the plant entries and make valuable suggestions and corrections, and to Bart O'Brien at Rancho Santa Ana Botanic Garden in Claremont, California, who did all the above *and* double-checked our Latin names and photo IDs.

For this edition, with the help of people like Judy Mielke, Wynn Anderson, Ron Gass, and Mary Irish, we corrected typos and factual errors that had eluded us the first time around. We added photos and changed others, and expanded the preface. We also added a wonderful foreword by Dr. Robert Breunig, the executive director of the Lady Bird Johnson Wildflower Center. Bob's resume includes stints as executive director of both the Desert Botanical Garden in Phoenix, Arizona, and the Santa Barbara Museum of Natural History in southern California, making him exceptionally well qualified to comment on the scope of this book. We're very grateful for all the help these people, and our editor, Anne Knudsen, gave us on this new edition. Our everlasting gratitude also goes to:

In Arizona: Karen and Robert Breunig, Marcus Bollinger, Laura Bowden, Russ Buhrow at Tohono Chul, Carol and Frank Crosswhite at Boyce Thompson Southwestern Arboretum, Gage Davis, Mark Dimmitt, Cliff Douglas, Mary Rose Duffield, Roberta Gibson, John Gray, Guy Greene, Dan James, Warren Jones, Dan MacBeth, Steve Martino, Ann and Ken McQuade, Scott Millard, Kent Newland, George and Kris Pringitore, Pat Schaffer, Greg Starr, John Suarez, Christy Ten Eyck, Charlie White, and Mr. and Mrs. J. R. Wolcott.

In California: Mike Bergan, Diana Bergen, Carol Bornstein, Cheryl and Andy Charles, Ann Christoph, Jeanine DeHart, Tom Doczi, Al Eliel, Eliza Earle and Dennis Bryson at the Theodore Payne Foundation, Ysabel and Roy Fetterman, V. L. T. Gardner, Gail Harrigan, Eric Johnson, Mike MacCaskey, Brian McColgan and Jon Stewart at The Living Desert, Janet Nickerman, Paul Nota, Bob Perry, Jeff Powers, Jana Ruzicka, Mickey Wheatley, Roberta and James Wilson, Walter Wisura, and Lynn Woodberry and Mike Evans and the whole gang at Tree of Life Nursery.

In Nevada: Pam and Jim Blasco, Dr. and Mrs. William Cavin, Jr., Dennis Swartzell, and Dennis and Linda Wood.

In New Mexico: Gary Bill and Steve Rede at Green Thumb Nursery, Lance Harkey, and Russell and Dinah Jentgen.

In Texas: Theresa Cavaretta, Ramona Delaney, Charles Finsley, Terry and Elaine Johnson, Wayne MacKay, Katie McCain, Anai Padilla, John Staten, Harold Stroud, and John White.

Thanks also to George Craft at the American Water Works Association. For additional photography, thanks to Dr. Merlin D. Tuttle and Linda Thompkins-Baldwin at Bat Conservation International, Inc.; Scott Millard at Ironwood Press; and Bart O'Brien at Rancho Santa Ana Botanic Garden.

And a special thank-you to our friends Jess and Gigi Lopez in Los Angeles for their "mi casa es su casa" friendship and hospitality.

We are indebted to our agent, Susan Urstadt, who passed away shortly after the first edition of this book came out. We miss her advice and enthusiasm very much. Thanks also to our current agent, Jeanne Fredericks, who was so helpful in making this new edition a reality, and to the people at Clarkson Potter who had a hand in producing this book the first time out: Lauren Shakely, Diane Frieden, Andrea Connolly Peabbles, Howard Klein, Jane Treuhaft, Lisa Goldenberg, and Bill Peabody.

If we inadvertently left your name out, please know that this in no way reflects upon your contributions but rather on our own frantic efforts to deliver the manuscript by the deadline. To you, also, our heartfelt thanks.

INDEX

Page numbers in **bold italic** refer to illustrations.